UNIVERSITY OF NORTH CAROLINA AT CHAPEL HILL
DEPARTMENT OF ROMANCE LANGUAGES

NORTH CAROLINA STUDIES
IN THE ROMANCE LANGUAGES AND LITERATURES

ESSAYS; TEXTS, TEXTUAL STUDIES AND TRANSLATIONS; SYMPOSIA

Founder: URBAN TIGNER HOLMES

Distributed by:

UNIVERSITY OF NORTH CAROLINA PRESS
CHAPEL HILL
North Carolina 27514
U.S.A.

NORTH CAROLINA STUDIES IN THE
ROMANCE LANGUAGES AND LITERATURES
Symposia
Number 4

MEDIEVAL MANUSCRIPTS AND
TEXTUAL CRITICISM

MEDIEVAL MANUSCRIPTS
AND
TEXTUAL CRITICISM

EDITED BY
CHRISTOPHER KLEINHENZ

CHAPEL HILL

NORTH CAROLINA STUDIES IN THE
ROMANCE LANGUAGES AND LITERATURES
U.N.C. DEPARTMENT OF ROMANCE LANGUAGES
1976

Library of Congress Cataloging in Publication Data

Main entry under title:
Medieval manuscripts and textual criticism.

(North Carolina studies in the Romance languages and literature: Texts, textual studies and translations; no. 4)
Includes bibliographies.
CONTENTS: Diringer, D. The book of the Middle Ages.—Carroll, C. W. Medieval romance paleography.—Stones, A. Secular manuscript illumination in France.—Whitehead, F. and Pickford, C. E. The introduction to the Lai de l'ombre: half a century later. [etc.]
1. Criticism, Textual—Addresses, essays, lectures. 2. Manuscripts—Addresses, essays, lectures.

Library of Congress Cataloging in Publication Data

I. Kleinhenz, Christopher. II. Series.
P47.M4   801'.959   75-29007

ISBN: 9780807891735

DEPÓSITO LEGAL: V. 671 - 1976   I.S.B.N. 84-399-4853-0
ARTES GRÁFICAS SOLER, S. A. — JÁVEA, 28 — VALENCIA (8) — 1976

To my family:

Voi mi date a parlar tutta baldezza.
Voi mi levate sì ch'i' son più ch'io.
Per tanti rivi s'empie d'allegrezza
la mente mia che di sè fa letizia,
perchè può sostener che non si spezza.

DANTE, *Paradiso* XVI

TABLE OF CONTENTS

	Page
PREFACE	13
ACKNOWLEDGEMENTS	15
INTRODUCTION	19
David Diringer. The Book of the Middle Ages	27
Carleton W. Carroll. Medieval Romance Paleography: A Brief Introduction	39
M. Alison Stones. Secular Manuscript Illumination in France	83
Frederick Whitehead and *Cedric E. Pickford.* The Introduction to the *Lai de l'Ombre:* Half a Century Later	103
Cesare Segre. The Problem of Contamination in Prose Texts	117
István Frank. The Art of Editing Lyric Texts	123
Eugène Vinaver. Principles of Textual Emendation (with an Appendix: Lancelot's Two Steps)	139
Arrigo Castellani. Transcription Errors	167
Egidio Rossini. Introduction to the Edition of Medieval Vernacular Documents (XIII and XIV Centuries)	175
George Kane. Conjectural Emendation	211
Aurelio Roncaglia. The Value of Interpretation in Textual Criticism.	227
T. B. W. Reid. On the Text of the *Tristran* of Béroul	245
Christopher Kleinhenz. The Nature of an Edition	273
GLOSSARY	285

LIST OF ILLUSTRATIONS

Page

CARLETON CARROLL: *Medieval Romance Paleography: A Brief Introduction.*

1. Chansonnier provençal *C* (Paris, Bibliothèque Nationale, MS fr. 856), fol. 209ʳa 44
2. Chansonnier provençal *E* (Paris, Bibliothèque Nationale, MS fr. 1749), p. 94a 45
3. Chansonnier provençal *R* (Paris, Bibliothèque Nationale, MS fr. 22543), fol. 37ʳa 46
4. Chansonnier provençal *f* (Paris, Bibliothèque Nationale, MS fr. 12472), fol. 55ᵛ 47
5. Chansonnier français *A* (Arras, Bibliothèque Municipale, MS 657 [formerly 139]), fol 5ʳa 51
6. Chansonnier provençal *S* (Oxford, Bodleian Library, MS Douce 269), p. 14 52
7. Chansonnier provençal *Sg* (Barcelona, Biblioteca Central, MS 146), fol. 20ʳ 53
8. Assisi, Biblioteca Comunale, MS 338, fol. 33ᵛ 54

Between Pages

ALISON STONES: *Secular Manuscript Illumination in France.*

1. Bel-Acueil shows the lover the rose. B.L. Harl. 4425, *Roman de la Rose*, fol. 36 100-101
2. Initial: Galeholt leaves an abbey where he has rested to cure a wound. New York, Pierpont Morgan Library, M. 806, *Lancelot*, fol. 155 100-101
3. Detail: A knight, probably Guillaume de Termonde, kneels before a lady. New Haven, Yale University Library, MS 229, ex-Phillipps 130, *Queste*, fol. 187 100-101
4. Four scenes of combat. B.N.fr. 15104, *La noble chevalerie de Judas Machabée et de ses nobles frères*, fol. 26 ... 100-101

5. Miniature: Philip IV of France, the future Philip V and Charles IV, with their sister Isabella, Louis of Navarre and Charles of Valois. B.N.lat 8504, *Dina et Kalila*, fol 1ᵛ 100-101
6. Miniature: An unknown lady receiving a book from a kneeling man. B.N.fr. 2186, *Roman de la Poire*, fol. 10ᵛ. 100-101
7. Miniature: Mordret and his men besiege the tower of London. B.L. Add. 10294, *Mort Artu*, fol. 81ᵛ 100-101
8. Historiated initial: the siege of Jerusalem. B.N.fr. 9081, Guillaume de Tyr, *Histoire de la guerre sainte*, fol. 77. 100-101
9. The god of love and two lovers. B.N.fr. 2186, *Roman de la Poire*, fol. 1ᵛ 100-101
10. Old Testament scenes: God enthroned, the temptation of Adam and Eve. Oxford, Bodleian Library, MS Douce 381, fol. 123 100-101
11. Miniature: top, Lancelot and Mordret see a white stag surrounded by lions; below, they encounter two knights. New Haven, Yale University Library, MS 229, ex-Phillipps 130, *Lancelot*, fol. 126 100-101
12. Border, Jonah and the whale; ape astride a peacock. B.R. 10607, Psalter of Gui de Dampierre, fol. 177 100-101
13. Miniature: top, Bohort, Gauvain and Lancelot return to Arthur's castle, Guinevere watches their arrival; below, Lancelot speaks to Guinevere, knights stand in the doorways. New Haven, Yale University Library, MS 229, ex-Phillipps 130, *Mort Artu*, fol. 290ᵛ 100-101
14. Miniature: top, king Brangoire assembles men and supplies in the city of Estragoire; below, a combat. B.N.fr. 95, *Merlin*, fol. 205ᵛ 100-101
15. Historiated initial: the Trinity enthroned. B.N.fr. 95, *Estoire*, fol. 1 100-101
16. Beatus initial, Psalm 1. Top, David, enthroned, plays the harp; below, David kills Goliath. B.N.lat. 1076, Psalter, fol. 7 100-101
17. Miniature: the lover sees his reflection in a stream. B.N.fr. 802, *Roman de la Rose*, fol. 12 100-101

EGIDIO ROSSINI: *Introduction to the Edition of Medieval Vernacular Documents (XIII and XIV Centuries)*

1. Verona, Archivio di Stato, *Istituto Esposti*, busta 102, perg. 117 194-195
2. Verona, Archivio di Stato, *Istituto Esposti*, busta 22, perg. 2367 194-195

Between Pages

3. Verona, Archivio di Stato, Carlotti-Trivelli collection, box IV   194-195

4-5. Inscription above East portal of the parish church of Marcellise, Comune di San Martino (Verona)   194-195

I wish to express my gratitude to the Curators of Manuscripts of the Bibliothèque Nationale (Paris), the Bibliothèque Royale (Brussells), the Bibliothèque Municipale (Arras), the British Library (London), the Bodleian Library (Oxford), the Biblioteca Central (Barcelona), the Biblioteca Comunale (Assisi), the Archivio di Stato (Verona), the Yale University Library (New Haven), and the Pierpont Morgan Library (New York) for permission to use illustrations from their collections, as well as to Professor Egidio Rossini for the use of his photograph of the inscription above the East portal of the parish church of Marcellise.

PREFACE

The original idea for this collection of essays was conceived in the course of a graduate seminar on paleography and philology that I was conducting during the academic year 1969-1970. In the intervening years, with much meditation, investigation, consultation, and active preparation on my part, the project gradually evolved to its present form. During the progressive realization of this volume I have incurred many debts. On the one hand, I have benefitted from the large body of critical literature (both theoretical and practical) on the subject. On the other hand, I have been fortunate to have had the opportunity to obtain advice, in some cases first-hand, from specialists in the area, and among these scholars I wish to give special thanks to Professor Eugène Vinaver, who so graciously placed his knowledge of Medieval literature and his wealth of editorial experience at my disposition. Similarly, the numerous insights offered by my students in seminars on textual criticism have contributed in no small way to the formation of this volume. To my several collaborators in this country and abroad I would like to express my sincere appreciation: to those who kindly agreed to the reproduction of previously published material here, and an especially profound sense of gratitude to those who generously prepared original essays on special topics for inclusion in this volume: Professors Alison Stones (University of Minnesota), Carleton Carroll (Oregon State University), Egidio Rossini (Verona, Italy), Cedric E. Pickford (University of Hull), and the late Frederick Whitehead (University of Manchester). Special thanks go to my colleagues and former students at the University of Wisconsin for their translations of the several essays from Italian or French into English: Professors

Arnold Miller, Douglas Kelly, Giancarlo Maiorino (Indiana University), and Anthony Bouchard (Arizona State University). I am especially grateful to the Editorial Board of the North Carolina Studies in the Romance Languages and Literatures for their generous financial assistance toward the publication of this volume, to Jon Vincent Blake for his constant, diligent editorial attention, and to Professors Aldo Scaglione and J. B. Avalle-Arce for their expert guidance and helpful suggestions in the submission and final preparation of the manuscript. Finally, my greatest debt of gratitude goes to my parents, my wife Margaret, and my children Steven and Michael, whose support and encouragement ensured the successful completion of this collection.

C. K.
Madison, Wisconsin
August 14, 1974

ACKNOWLEDGEMENTS

"The *Book* of the Middle Ages," by David Diringer. Abridgment, with the author's approval, of chapter V, "From Leather to Parchment," of *The Hand-Produced Book* (London: Hutchinson's Scientific and Technical Publications, 1953). Copyright 1953 by Hutchinson's Scientific and Technical Publications. Reprinted by permission of the publisher.

"The Introduction to the *Lai de l'Ombre*: Half a Century Later," by Frederick Whitehead and Cedric E. Pickford. Originally written for inclusion in this volume, it has appeared in *Romania*, XCIV (1973), 145-156, with the title, "The Introduction to the *Lai de l'Ombre*: Sixty Years Later." Copyright 1973 by the Société des Amis de la Romania. Reprinted by permission of the Société des Amis de la Romania.

"The Problem of Contamination in Prose Texts," by Cesare Segre. From *Studi e problemi di critica testuale,* a cura di Raffaele Spongano (Bologna: Commissione per i Testi di Lingua, 1961), 63-67. Original title: "Appunti sul problema delle contaminazioni nei testi in prosa." Translated by Christopher Kleinhenz with the approval of the author. Copyright 1961 by the Commissione per i Testi di Lingua. Reprinted by kind permission of Raffaele Spongano, President of the Commissione per i Testi di Lingua.

"The Art of Editing Lyric Texts," by István Frank. From *Recueil de travaux offert à M. Clovis Brunel,* Mémoires et Documents, XII (Paris: Société de l'École des Chartes, 1955), I, 463-475. Original title: "De l'art d'éditer les textes lyriques." Translated by Arnold Miller. Copyright 1955 by the Société de l'École des Chartes. Reprinted by permission of the Société de l'École des Chartes.

"Principles of Textual Emendation (with an Appendix: Lancelot's Two Steps)," by Eugène Vinaver. The first section of this two-part article, "Principles of Textual Emendation," is from *Studies in French Language and Medieval Literature Presented to Professor Mildred K. Pope* (Manchester: Manchester University Press, 1939), 351-369. The second is from the *Mélanges pour Jean Fourquet*, ed. Paul Valentin and Georges Zink (Paris: Klincksieck, 1969), 355-361. Original title: "Les deux pas de Lancelot." Translated by Douglas Kelly with the approval of the author. Copyrights 1939 by the Manchester University Press and 1969 by C. Klincksieck. Reprinted in combined form with the approval and kind permission of the author, the Manchester University Press, and C. Klincksieck.

"Transcription Errors," by Arrigo Castellani. From *Studi e problemi di critica testuale*, a cura di Raffaele Spongano (Bologna: Commissione per i Testi di Lingua, 1961), 35-40. Original title: "Indagine sugli errori di trascrizione." Translated by Anthony Bouchard with the approval of the author. Copyright 1961 by the Commissione per i Testi di Lingua. Reprinted by kind permission of Raffaele Spongano, President of the Commissione per i Testi di Lingua.

"Conjectural Emendation," by George Kane. From *Medieval Literature and Civilization: Studies in Memory of G. N. Garmonsway*, ed. D. A. Pearsall and R. A. Waldron (London: Athlone Press, 1969), 155-169. Copyright 1969 by the Athlone Press, University of London. Reprinted by permission of the Athlone Press, University of London.

"The Value of Interpretation in Textual Criticism," by Aurelio Roncaglia. From *Studi e problemi di critica testuale*, ed. Raffaele Spongano (Bologna: Commissione per i Testi di Lingua, 1961), 45-62. Original title: "Valore e giuoco dell'interpretazione nella critica testuale." Translated by Giancarlo Maiorino with the approval of the author. Copyright 1961 by the Commissione per i Testi di Lingua. Reprinted by kind permission of Raffaele Spongano, President of the Commissione per i Testi di Lingua.

"On the Text of the *Tristran* of Béroul," by T. B. W. Reid. From *Medieval Miscellany Presented to Eugène Vinaver*, ed. F. E. Sutcliffe (Manchester: Manchester University Press, 1965), 263-288. Copyright 1965 by the Manchester University Press. Reprinted by permission of the Manchester University Press.

INTRODUCTION

In recent years literary criticism both in this country and abroad has been revitalized by the work of scholars in the fields of linguistics, semiology, and other more-specialized offshoots such as psycho-linguistics and socio-linguistics. In addition to their phenomenal growth in academic circles, such practical studies have been the catalyst for many lively and often heated debates, directed toward defining in theory the proper application of these various analytical methods to the study of literature. One important result of this trend, in my opinion, has been to reaffirm the primacy of the text in matters of literary criticism. Students and scholars alike have, as it were, rediscovered the language, the very word of the text, and have recognized the need to return to it as the basis for critical commentary. This revival of interest in the fundamentals of the text, in the building blocks of every literary structure, should also serve to focus attention on the essential, but often disparaged role of the editor in the interpretation and, in many cases, the very survival of a work of literature.

In the transmission and preservation of Classical and Medieval literature, the position of the editor is crucial, for these texts have generally come down to us in various manuscripts or in *editio princeps*. Since we lack autograph manuscripts or authorially-approved editions, our interpretation of Homer, Virgil, Dante, Chrétien de Troyes, and, in fact, practically every author from these early periods, is the immediate and direct consequence of the way in which the editor has presented their works. We put our faith in his ability to give us, if not the exact words and thoughts of an author, at least the closest possible approximation of the author's original intention in his work; if he is at fault, then so too are we in our evaluation of the text. Thus, for the reader and critic of Classical and Medieval texts, the role of the editor is tantamount to the creative process of the author, for the duty of the former is to reconstruct, from existing evidence, the intended text of the latter.

Given the importance of the editor to the "life" of a text, it is distressing to note that, even today, many literary critics continue to downgrade his work as too "limited," too "mechanical" or "scientific," or not "scholarly enough." The unfortunate result of this attitude has been the establishment of a sort of academic hierarchy in which the critics have assumed a place superior to the editors, occupying the higher, more important position with regard to the study of literature. Obviously, such a hierarchical structure has no place in academic circles, where critic and editor should work together in harmony and enjoy mutual respect, given the competency that each must demonstrate in his particular field. However, if we were to examine this notion of order more closely and apply it rigidly to the study of literature, we would probably conclude that the editor, all things considered, should occupy the higher position. For, being directly responsible for the text, he is only once-removed from the author and his work and must possess, in addition, a keen critical sense. The critic, then, who is initially dependent willy-nilly on the editor for the foundation of his interpretative edifice, would be twice-removed from the author.

This description of the editor's decisive role in the transmission of Classical and Medieval literature should serve to reinforce my earlier statements on the primacy of the text in matters of literary criticism, a fact that has been increasingly ignored (and alarmingly so!) in recent years. It has been my own unfortunate experience to find on a number of occasions that students and colleagues would prefer to avoid the text in order to pursue "more important" questions, to discuss "literature," as though that topic were something divorced from, or completely extraneous to the text itself. Indeed, discourses of this nature are the proper end of the study of literature; however, they are precisely that: the *end* and not the *beginning* of the literary adventure. The beginning is and always must be the text, and in order to serve both as an end in itself and as a point of departure for broader discussions, the text must be sound in every way.

The establishment of the text is, then, properly speaking, the single most important event in its literary life, after its original creation. Relatively few textual problems are encountered in autograph versions or authorially-approved editions. However, when the work in question is extant in *editio princeps*, in various manuscripts, or both, the task of the editor becomes vital to the interpretation, indeed, in some cases, to the very existence of the work, for it is on him that posterity (not only contemporary critics of literature) necessarily depends for an accurate version of the author's original intention in his creation. In order to ensure the validity of his work, the editor must be knowledgeable in many and diverse disciplines. Besides having read widely in the theory of literature and textual criticism, he should have at his command both an exhaustive knowledge of the language of the text and a profound awareness of the history (literary, social and intellectual) of the age; for these, while allowing him certain insights, would enable him to make crucial decisions regarding the content of the text. Finally, he must be an astute literary critic, capable of making enlightened judgments regarding his text and of relating it to its literary tradition. In short, the editor *par excellence* must be a remarkable and idealistic combination of author and critic. Needless to say, this harmonious mixture is rare. In fact, to describe and find the omniscient editor is, if I may be permitted a Dantean analogy, similar to the description and search for the "illustrious Italian vernacular" *(De Vulgari Eloquentia)* which, as Dante says, may be found in part in every dialect, but which does not reside entirely in one alone. In striving toward his goal, the editor incorporates his expertise in a variety of related disciplines, musters his own critical acumen to meet the challenge, and, thus, attempts to the best of his ability the "reconstruction" or "recreation" of the original work.

The essays in this collection are all devoted to the discussion of textual criticism and the making of a critical edition, in reference to the Medieval Romance vernaculars (French, Italian, Provençal, Spanish, and Portuguese). The points raised in the various articles are, however, universal in their application and, therefore, are not restricted by temporal, geographic, or linguistic confines. The subject matter is drawn primarily from the Romance languages and literatures, although at least one essay does encompass non-literary material as well. It is hoped that the essays presented here, both in reprinted, revised and translated form and as original contributions, will serve two ends: that of introducing the student of literature to the study of Medieval manuscripts and the problems inherent in their edition; and that of providing for student and scholar alike a convenient reference volume of essays that treat the theory and practice of textual criticism and that may serve as a guide to the isolation and resolution of specific textual problems.

The first three essays are concerned with the external features of Medieval manuscripts, and, appropriately, the first of these is a compilation of relevant passages from David Diringer's excellent volume, *The Hand-Produced Book*. Reproduced here are those pages describing the production and composition of manuscripts in the *scriptorium*. It is precisely to the zealous and diligent activity of the monks in the numerous *scriptoria* that we owe the survival of Classical and Medieval texts. However, given the paleographical difficulties and uncertainties of these early handwritten books, it is necessary to obtain at least a rudimentary knowledge and some practical experience in this area before presuming to read, edit, or comment upon such material. Thus, in his essay, Carleton Carroll provides, through a judicious selection of examples from Old French and Provençal codices to serve as a guide to the basic Gothic letter forms and abbreviations, an introduction to Medieval Romance paleography and, in the course of the essay, discusses some of the particular problems such as identification, distribution, and frequency. While the work of the scribe and rubricator represents the essence of the transmitted text, there remains to be discussed another feature, the most external and decorative of the Medieval manuscript: the miniature. Basing her examination on an extensive study of the *Lancelot* manuscripts, Alison Stones traces the principal developments in France from the thirteenth to the sixteenth centuries in terms of texts and patrons, the relationship between secular and religious illumination, and the subsequent French influence on the rest of Europe.

The remainder of the essays in the collection are devoted to articles, both theoretical and practical, that discuss in an informative and/or provocative way the problems inherent in the progressive stages in the making of a critical edition. The goal of the editor is to present a text that conforms to the original intention of the author *(constitutio textus)*. To accomplish this end, he must guide his investigation through two major phases: *recensio* and *examinatio-emendatio*. The first of these is the analysis of all extant manuscript material with the intent to determine which must be considered as "witnesses" to the original tradition. This is the so-called "stemmatic" phase, in which surviving manuscripts with no independent value are discarded *(eliminatio codicum descriptorum)* and the genealogical tree (the "stemma") of manuscripts is drawn up so as to prepare the way for the second stage.

In this collection, three essays are devoted to *recensio*. In their contribution Professors Cedric E. Pickford and Frederick Whitehead re-examine the controversy provoked by Joseph Bédier (Bédier's "paradox") in his edition of the *Lai de l'Ombre*, where he maintained that one may generally assume a single split in any manuscript tradition, so as to form a "two-branch stemma." The related problems of contamination in the text because of "horizontal," and not "vertical" transmission are discussed in theoretical terms by Cesare Segre, who bases the study on his experience in editing Richard de Fournival's *Li Bestiares d'Amours*. István Frank concerns himself with the uncertainties attendant (in the *recensio* process) to the editing of lyrical poetry (specifically Old French and Provençal, with reference to the other Romance vernaculars) and provides, in the course of his discussion, a sort of retrospective commentary on the points raised in the previous two essays with regard to the stemma and contamination.

The second and more complex stage of textual criticism begins with *examinatio*, which is to determine to what degree, from the surviving witness *(codex unicus)* or witnesses to the tradition, the original may be discovered or reconstructed with certainty. If there are doubts regarding the authenticity or logic of a reading or the proper choice of a variant from two (or more) manuscripts of "equal" stemmatical value *(selectio)*, if there exists an obvious corruption or lacuna in the text *(divinatio)*, then the editor is duty bound to attempt to correct it through *emendatio*. The remainder of the essays in this collection are devoted to the elucidation and/or resolution of specific problems encountered at this stage of editing. Appropriately, this section opens with Professor Eugène Vinaver's well-known, but relatively inaccessible study of the various movements in the work of the Medieval scribe, the possible errors that may occur in the process, and the means by which the editor may remedy such corruptions in the text. To complement this article, I have included as a kind of appendix a recent contribution by Professor Vinaver in this area: the note on the enigmatic "two steps" of Lancelot, which elucidates by example the theoretical principles contained in the essay on textual emendation. Along similar lines, but with reference to the editor and not to the scribe, Arrigo Castellani discusses the types of errors possible during transcription and cites representative examples taken from Italian literary and archival sources. Problems of transcription are only one of the several considerations of the essay by Egidio Rossini, who describes the nature of a diplomatic edition and provides an introduction to the paleographical and philological study of non-literary texts in the vernacular, by tracing several documents through the progressive phases of manuscript, diplomatic transcription, and critical edition. The theory set forth by Professor Vinaver in an earlier essay is challenged by Professor George Kane, who, on the basis of his experience in editing *Piers Plowman*, examines the rationale of "conjectural emendation" and outlines the principles by which it may be properly exercised.

While the external limits of textual criticism are fixed, so to speak, during the *recensio* process, the actual establishment of the text is a rather open matter that depends to a large extent on the proper evaluation of internal evidence. Professor Aurelio Roncaglia devotes his essay to an examination of several passages (from Italian, Portuguese, Provençal, and Old French) in order to emphasize the primary importance in textual criticism of *interpretatio*, which is, in his terms, "directed toward the establishment of the text by means of referring to the context, on the assumption of the immanent necessity... of a functional relationship between the rational and irrational elements in both text and context". Along similar lines, T. B. W. Reid in his essay, originally contained in the *festschrift* for Professor Vinaver, presents numerous examples from Béroul's *Tristran* to illustrate the complex and often uncertain tasks facing the editor of texts and the means available to him for their resolution,

My own essay, which concludes the volume, attempts to define, in simple terms and through illustration, the nature and scope of various types of editions and the responsibility of the editor to his reader. Moreover, containing an extensive bibliography, it should serve as a valuable guide for those interested in furthering their practical and theoretical knowledge of textual criticism as it applies to Medieval manuscripts in the Romance vernaculars.

CHRISTOPHER KLEINHENZ
Madison, March, 1974

THE BOOK OF THE MIDDLE AGES

by † *David Diringer*

The hand-written parchment or vellum codex is "the book" *par excellence* of the Middle Ages. Such codices are generally termed "manuscripts" or MSS., from the Latin term *codices* (or *libri*) *manuscripti* "codices (or books) written by hand." From the earliest codices extant, belonging to the third or fourth century C.E., to the invention of the printing press in Europe, *c.* 1450, and the spread of printing in the second half of that century, giving birth to the "modern book," "the book" of the Middle Ages covers a period of well over eleven hundred years.

Side by side with papyrus, parchment was extensively employed for several centuries. This was the prepared skin of animals such as cattle, sheep, goats, and occasionally deer, and preferably from the young of these animals. The finer quality (derived from the calf) was called vellum (in Latin *vitulinum*); it is finer in grain, whiter and smoother than ordinary parchment. The whitest and thinnest kind (made from the skin of an aborted calf) was called *uterine vellum,* and was employed chiefly for elaborate miniatures.

Parchment was, of course, the most beautiful and suitable material for writing or printing upon that has ever been used, its surface being singularly even and offering little or no resistance to the pen, so that every sort of handwriting can be made upon it with equal ease. Although the exact meaning of the words "parchment" and "vellum" is as has just been explained, and although some scholars employ the former for sheepskin and the latter for calfskin, in common but incorrect usage, the two words are synonymous.

The word "parchment" (French, *parchemin;* German, *Pergament;* Italian, *pergamena*) — being a derivation of the Greek *Pergamēnē* and the Latin *Pergamena* (or *charta Pergamena*), i.e. stuff prepared at Pergamum, which was an important city and kingdom in Asia Minor — is strictly associated with a milestone in the history of this writing material. According to Pliny the Elder, 23-79 C.E. (*Natur. Hist.*, xiii, 11f), quoting the earlier Roman writer Varro, King Ptolemy of Egypt — he probably refers to Ptolemy V Epiphanes (*c.* 205 - *c.* 185 B.C.) — jealous of a rival book collector, feared that the library of Eumenes, King of Pergamum — probably, Eumenes II (*c.* 197 - *c.* 159 B.C.) — might come to surpass the library of Alexandria, and he therefore laid an embargo on the export of papyrus from Egypt, in order to retard the literary progress of the rival city. Eumenes, thus debarred from obtaining papyrus rolls, was driven to the invention of parchment. This would imply that parchment was invented about the first decade of the second century B.C. But this account is not considered historical.

Moreover, parchment cannot be considered a true invention. It was rather the result of a slow development, or else an improvement upon an old practice, this being the employment of hides or skins of animals as writing material. Whereas leather is simply tanned, the fabrication of parchment is much more complicated; the skin (of the sheep, lambs, kids, goats, asses, pigs, or cattle, especially calves), washed and divested of its hair or wool, is soaked in a limepit, stretched tight on a frame and scraped clear of the remaining hair on one side and the flesh on the other; it is then wetted with a moist rag, covered with pounded chalk, and rubbed with pumice stone; finally, it is allowed to dry in the frame.

The earliest extant secular works written on vellum codices are on the whole contemporary with the earliest Bible vellum codices. It must, however, be emphasized that the dating of early vellum uncial manuscripts is a precarious task, since few fixed points are available. The task is made still harder by the apparent practice of the scribes of these codices to employ the elegant character of the second century C. E. Thus, the earliest extant Greek uncial codex, the *Iliad* preserved in the Ambrosian Library at Milan, is written in a script which can be dated as early as the second century C. E., but the codex cannot be earlier than the third, and is probably later.

The earliest preserved Latin vellum codices containing secular works probably belong to the fourth century C. E. They are a group of Virgil codices, such as the Vatican, Palatine, and Medicean, and the palimpsest [1] of *De Republica* by Cicero. This date, however, is not agreed upon, and some scholars suggest the fifth century C. E.

The final victory of parchment over papyrus in the sphere of book production is due to the fact that the Christian Church, influenced no doubt by Jewish practice, chose parchment to write their sacred books upon. The Christians, however, soon diverged from the Jews in respect to the form of the "book."

The earliest parchment books, it must be emphasized, were in roll form. Doubtless, gathered sheets of folded parchment were, though rarely, in very early times applied to various literary purposes — for instance, among the Dead Sea Scrolls, a "folded-up" book has been discovered — but the roll seems to have been the most general form for important books.

The Jews have continued until this very day to write ritual copies of the Law on parchment scrolls, whereas Christians favoured the codex, and the Bible in this form was quite common amongst them in the first half of the fourth century.

In addition to its greater convenience for continuous reading, and particularly for reference, the codex form had also the advantages that (1) its size could be increased at will; (2) collections of poems or short treatises, and especially of aphorisms, wisdom, or proverbs, could be more easily transcribed.

---

[1] One of the main advantages of parchment was that writing could be washed or scraped off, so that the parchment could be used again. This practice was due to the scarcity and high cost of writing material. Palimpsests (from Greek *palimpsestos*, "scraped again"; in Latin they were also called *codices rescripti*) were most common between the seventh and ninth centuries — indeed, the most valuable Latin texts are found in the volumes which were re-written in this period; the employment of palimpsests, however, continued even down to the sixteenth century. In the earlier centuries the works of classical writers were obliterated to make room for patristic literature or grammatical works; in the later centuries classical works were written over Biblical manuscripts.

The Christians soon extended its use to their theological literature, and then to literature in general. The parchment or vellum codex, having thus achieved its triumph in the fourth century, remained the chief writing material for books for over a millennium, i.e. until the establishment of paper in general use in the fourteenth century and until the Renaissance.

In the Middle Ages manuscripts were generally on vellum, but sometimes the material, though called vellum, was strictly speaking parchment. Some of the early vellum codices extant, already referred to, particularly those of the fifth and sixth centuries, are made of thin, delicate material, with a smooth and glossy surface. At a later period, as the demand increased, a great amount of inferior material came into the market. In Italy, a highly polished surface seems at most periods to have been in favour, and in the Renaissance period vellum was of extreme whiteness and purity. In England, from the thirteenth to the fifteenth centuries, soft vellum was sometimes used.

One of the many Christian innovations in book production was the great service-book in the churches, such as the missal, the chorale, and the antiphonary. (Many of such works were manufactured in Rome.) So, for instance, an immense volume was laid upon the *lutrin*, or reading-desk, in the middle of the choir and the letters of the words and musical notes, which accompanied them were of such a size, and so black, that they could be read by the canons as they sat in their stalls with as much ease as an inscription on a stone monument. These ponderous volumes, which were seldom removed from the desk, or carried only to the adjoining sacristy, were a part of the furniture, and almost of the fixtures, of the church, and were frequently of great antiquity. Often they were garnished with corners of brass, with bosses, and brass nails, to preserve the bindings from injury in being rubbed on the desk or pulpit, and were protected from dust by massive clasps. Some of the largest of these service-books, but not always the most ancient, were laid upon rollers.

The Christian monasteries were the main book producers of the Middle Ages. With the din of arms around him, it was the monk who, by preserving and, especially, transcribing ancient manuscripts, both Christian and — although in much lesser degree — secular, as well as by recording in writing his observations on contemporary events, was handing down the torch of knowledge to future generations. In the most important abbeys and monasteries a "writing room" or *scriptorium* was assigned to the scribes, who were constantly employed in transcribing, not only service-books for the choir and the church, but also books for the library and the monastery school, and even lay books.

It must be allowed that we know very little for certain about the conditions of book production in medieval times. W. Oakeshott asks: "If a particular twelfth-century book was in a particular monastery in the twelfth century, is that satisfactory evidence that it was produced there, or were books often produced in one monastery for another?" "When did the production of books by commercial scribes, even for monastic use, become usual?" Only partial and tentative answers can be given to these questions. Oakeshott has also pointed out that if an early medieval book carries an inscription, which relates to its production, we do not always know whether the *scriptor* copied the text, designed or completed the decorations, or was responsible for all these things. "We seldom know anything of his status and seldom even his name.... There is nothing to suggest that in the Anglo-Saxon period" — and, for that matter, generally speaking in early medieval times — "the copying of books played anything like the part in monastic life which it was to play later." And "there is nothing positively to show that the decoration of the book, as opposed to the writing of the text, was always done in the monastery," though we often find monks described as painters, and we find artists holding some position in the Church.

The Scriptorium

In some great monasteries the *scriptorium* was a large room, usually over the chapter-house; it was in charge of the *armarius*, whose duty it was to provide, desks, parchment, pens, ink, penknives, awls (to give guiding marks for ruling lines), rulers, metal *stili* (to draw the lines), pumice-stone (to smooth the surface of the parchment), reading frames (to hold the book to be copied), and weights (to keep down the pages of the codices); but even the *armarius* was not allowed to assign work without the abbot's permission. The *scriptorium* was often built in the form of a series of separate little partitions or studies. In some monasteries, especially in early times, the scribes copied in the cloister.

For the support of the *scriptorium*, estates were often granted. That at St. Edmondsbury (Bury St. Edmunds, England) was endowed with two mills. The tithes of a rectory were appropriated to the Cathedral Convent of St. Swithin, at Winchester, in the year 1171. Nigel, in the year 1160, gave the monks of Ely two churches, *ad libros faciendos*.

The *scriptorium*, besides being under the general discipline of the monastery, had special rules of its own. To guard against irreparable loss by fire and for fear of other damage to manuscripts, artificial light was entirely forbidden, so all work had to be done during daylight: the monastic scribe worked about six hours daily. To prevent interruption and distraction, access to the *scriptorium* was denied to all non-scribes who had no leading position in the monastery, and absolute silence was required. Scribes were not allowed even to ask for the books or other things they needed for their work. Thus, a whole system of gesture-communication was introduced: if a scribe wanted to consult a book, he extended his hands and made a movement as of turning over pages; if the book required was a psalter, he made the general sign, and then placed his hands on his head in shape of a crown (alluding to King David); if a pagan book was needed, the general sign was followed by scratching the ear in the manner of a dog. It may, therefore, be assumed that, as a rule, the scribe *copied* his book, and did not write from dictation.

When no *scriptorium* was available, separate little rooms were assigned to book copying; they were situated in such a way that each scribe had to himself a window open to the cloister walk. Only in special cases were private rooms or cells assigned.

In addition to the monks who were secular scribes and illuminators, there were special classes of secular scribes (such as *illuminatores* and *rubricatores*), who were brought to the monasteries when there were no competent men there to do the required job. There were also men, who, though living — but not always — within the monastic precincts, and often adopting the outward dress of the monks, were, in fact, only lay brethren, skilled in various handicrafts or trades. At Osney Abbey (Oxford), for instance, a number of workmen, such as tailors, wax-chandlers, bookbinders and book illuminators, who lived outside the watergate, had their workshops within the abbey precincts; similar arrangements prevailed in other great monasteries.

It is also known that important university towns had scribes and illuminators who worked on a fixed tariff of charges. Particular mention should be made of the guild of binders, scribes and illuminators of the University of Paris.

It has also been suggested that there were numerous travelling groups of artists and urban bookshops, and that between these various systems of book production there was a considerable degree of overlapping.

Copying a Parchment Codex

Since parchment has two distinct sides, care was generally taken in putting together the sheets for the quire to lay them in such a way that hair side faced hair side, and flesh side faced flesh side.

Thus, when the book was opened, the two pages before the reader had the same appearance, either flesh side or hair side. It seems that in the Greek codices, with little exception, the first page of the quire was the flesh side; while in the Latin codices, it was the hair side. A great number of books being left unbound, many scribes usually left blank the first leaf, or at least the *recto* of the first leaf; the blank page or leaf was intended to give some protection against tear and wear.

The arrangement of the leaves of ancient parchment or vellum books was essentially the same as that of modern books. Originally, the books consisted of sheets, each forming two leaves — hence the term folio (from Latin, meaning "sheet"); but normally the parchment book was composed of a series of quires fastened together. A "quarto" volume, called *tetrádion* in Greek, *quaternus* or *quaternio* in Latin, now *cahier* in French and "quire" in English, was formed of four sheets of vellum or parchment (about 10 inches high and 18 inches wide), folded down the middle and placed one inside the other; thus giving eight leaves or sixteen pages. They were fastened, or rather threaded together by the means of a string, thread or fibre, passing down the middle of the crease of the innermost sheet of the quire, and running from the innermost fold right through to the outermost, thus folding the leaves firmly together.

Many variations of form, both smaller and larger than *quarto* are found, and we find also quires of six, ten and twelve leaves. A quire consisting of five sheets (*i.e.* ten leaves or twenty pages) was called *quinternio* ("quinternion").

The quires fastened together to form a book were marked (so that their order might not be lost) and sent to the scribe or copyist to write on.

After the decision as to the style and size of the script to be employed — the largest style being naturally reserved for books to be used for public services — the margins of the pages were determined by holes pricked with a compass or awl *(punctorium)*, and by lines drawn from hole to hole with a hard-pointed instrument or stilus of iron or wood *(ligniculum)* and a ruler *(regula or norma)*; space was left for illuminations. Guide lines for the individual lines of writing were also ruled (the term for "to rule" was *sulcare*) with the stilus, which made a little furrow in the parchment (and, naturally, raised a ridge on the other side). In some early codices ruling was not drawn for every line of writing, but was occasionally spaced, so that some lines of the text lay in the spaces and some stand on the ruled lines.

Ruling with the lead point or plummet came into use in the eleventh century, and in the thirteenth century it became more or less general. In fifteenth-century manuscripts we find also lines ruled with ink. In earlier manuscripts the prickings are often within the width of the text column, and the horizontal lines were not confined within the longitudinal boundaries of the text. In later codices, however, it was the custom to prick off the spaces close to the margin, and to keep the ruled lines within the boundaries of the text, and often the prickings disappeared when the edges were cut off by the binder.

Anciently the text might be written across the face of the page (especially in poetical works), though generally speaking — continuing the arrangements of the papyrus roll — the page was arranged in columns: there were ordinarily two columns, but sometimes — especially in earlier codices or in exact copies of earlier ones — there were three or four.

Indeed, the two great volumes which head the roll of vellum manuscripts of the Greek Bible, the *Codex Vaticanus* and the *Codex Sinaiticus*, having relatively narrow columns, show that they were copied from rolls rather than from codices. Further experience, however, showed the advantage of a wider column. Hence, from the fifth century onwards the arrangement with two columns to the page in the large vellum codices became normal; though occasionally we find such manuscripts with single columns to the page.

Separation of Words — Punctuation

In early codices (with some exceptions, however), as in papyrus rolls, and down to about the ninth century, the text was written continuously without separation of words. When the minuscule writing came into use as the literary hand, separation of words from one another gradually followed, but even then the scribes used to attach short words, for instance prepositions, to the words which immediately followed them, and also to detach a final letter of a word, attaching it to the next following word. In Latin manuscripts, a perfect system of separately written words was established about the eleventh century, whereas in the Greek manuscripts the system was at no time perfectly followed.

The first lines of the main divisions of the text, such as the "book" of the Bible or of the *Iliad*, were often written in red for distinction. The initial letters of sections or chapters, as well as rubrics, titles and colophons, were at first written in the same characters as the text, though the first letter of each page was often made larger than the rest. At a later time different style was used; for instance, in codices written in minuscule the rubrics, titles and colophons might be in capitals or rustic capitals.

In the division of words at the end of the line, the latter generally broke off with a syllable, but there were exceptions: in Greek codices, in the case of compound words, the last consonant of the prefix or of the preposition (and, in some other instances, single consonants, especially the *sigma*) was carried to the next syllable if this began with, or was a vowel; in Latin codices, when two consonants came together, they were generally assigned to their several syllables *(part-em, scrip-sit, misericor-dia)*, but sometimes, under Greek influence, we may find *pa-rtem, scri-psit, miserico-rdia*. This division of words between one line and another is indicated in earlier manuscripts by a dot; the dividing stroke, or hyphen, appears in the eleventh century, and becomes more systematic in the twelfth century, but then it is also repeated at the beginning of the next line. In order to avoid division of a word, and perhaps also to save space, towards the end of the line the letters were often written in smaller characters.

As in papyrus rolls, the paragraphs were at first not distinguished by a blank space, but by a horizontal dividing stroke (in Greek, *parágraphos*), or else a wedge *(diplê)*, which was inserted at the beginning of the new paragraph. At a later stage, the first letter of the new paragraph was made prominent, by making it project slightly into the margin, and by writing it in a larger character.

A regular system of punctuation — consisting of the high point (corresponding to our full stop), the point on the line (corresponding to our semicolon), and the point in a middle position (corresponding to our comma) — is ascribed to Aristophanes of Byzantium (c. 260 B.C.): it was developed in the school of the Alexandrian grammarians. This system of points, or *positurae*, was accepted by the Latin grammarians — the terms being *distinctio finalis, subdistinctio*, and *distinctio media* — but was never employed consistently. In early uncial manuscripts we find the point used as a stop; and a colon, or colon and dash, or a number of points used as a final stop of a paragraph or chapter; in the seventh century we find the high point (= comma), the semicolon (with its modern value), and a combination of points and dashes (= full stop).

In the eighth century C.E., there appears the inverted semicolon (a sort of middle way between our semicolon and comma), the comma, and the interrogation mark. Other marks are found in both Greek and Latin manuscripts, such as the private marks of correctors or readers. There are also critical symbols, such as that known as *diplê* and the asterisk used by Aristarchus in the texts of Homer, or the asterisk and a sign called *obelus* employed by St. Jerome to distinguish certain passages in versions of the Latin Psalter.

The Finish of the Book

When the quire was completed, it was checked by a *corrector*, who compared the written copy with its original; afterwards, it was sent to the rubricator, who added (in red or other colours) the titles, headlines, the initials of chapters and sections, the notes, and so on; and then — if the book was to be illustrated — it was sent to the illuminator. Finally, when all quires were written, corrected, rubricated, and illuminated, the book was sent to the binder.

MEDIEVAL ROMANCE PALEOGRAPHY: A BRIEF INTRODUCTION

by Carleton W. Carroll

Paleography is the science — and one might very well say the art — of deciphering texts. In this introduction to medieval paleography, we shall limit ourselves to a discussion of some of the problems which confront the beginning student of medieval manuscripts, and endeavor to offer some advice to help in resolving these problems. But the scope of the present article must be even further reduced, for during the ten centuries or so normally encompassed by that all-too-vast term "the Middle Ages," numerous styles of writing evolved, and these varied not only with time but also with place. As a result, one cannot speak simply of "French medieval hands" or of "thirteenth-century manuscript writing"; rather, one must specify both place and time before entering into a meaningful discussion, and thus we shall here limit ourselves to an examination of that manuscript writing style generally called Gothic, as it was practised in those parts of western Europe where French, Provençal, and Italian were spoken, and as it has been preserved in literary manuscripts (as opposed to legal documents, which were frequently written in a quite different style) dating from the thirteenth and fourteenth centuries.

The absolute necessity for this narrow limitation comes, of course, from the fact that, before the advent of the printed book, all graphic representation of the spoken word was in the form of hand-written texts. The very name "manuscript" means nothing more, after all, than "hand-written" (Latin *mănu scrīptu(m)*, literally "hand written"). And just as present-day handwriting varies, often markedly, from one individual to another, despite the existence of certain norms — generally accepted ways of making individual letters and of combining them into linked forms to make words — so did medieval hands vary, despite the no less real existence of whatever norms were in effect at any particular place and time. In point of fact, the norms of medieval times must have allowed for far less individual variation than we presently accept, since there was no other form of written communication: if the scribe's hand was not legible, his message simply did not get across. We may draw a parallel with speech: all language is a matter of convention, and is essentially arbitrary. We are able to communicate verbally because of a tacit agreement that each word has one or more accepted meanings and is to be pronounced in a certain way. But precise phonetic studies indicate that a given word, if examined in sufficiently fine detail, is never said exactly the same way twice, even by a given individual. Minute variations, which we may call "idiosyncratic", occur — variations in pitch, intensity, and duration of individual sounds and of sounds in combination. An examination of a given word as pronounced by two or more speakers reveals even greater differences, many of which, of course, can be perceived even by the unaided and untrained ear. Yet these variations still do not go beyond accepted tolerances, and therefore the word is still perceived and understood as being the intended word, and not another. A non-native speaker may, however, pronounce something so different from the norm that it is no longer understood (by a native speaker) as the word in question. The limit of tolerance has then been exceeded, and communication, at least on the level of this one word, has broken down. And so, similarly, in our discussion of Gothic manuscript writing we must restrict ourselves to a presentation of the basic, "normal" form of each letter, and of certain relatively common variations thereupon — for any attempt to present (much less analyse and categorize) the individual, "idiosyncratic" variations would be foolhardy, as the task could be complete only by accounting for every letter of every manuscript.

Before entering into a detailed examination of these basic forms, however, it would be well to consider some underlying problems of paleography, which might be called theoretical problems, as opposed to practical ones. The most basic problem of all, and one which has no simple solution, is that there is no easy way to learn to decipher medieval texts. One cannot be "taught" to do so; it is the sort of ability — or talent — which comes only through practice. As in many other areas, one learns to do by doing. But it is difficult to get started, and the more experienced paleographer can help the novice only to the extent of giving him a number of helpful bits of advice, after which the novice must simply go ahead on his own. As N. Denholm-Young says in his excellent *Handwriting in England and Wales* (Cardiff: University of Wales Press, 1954), "Palaeography cannot be learnt from lectures, from books, nor even wholly by studying facsimiles. Even the best reproductions (collotype plates) give only one point of view. It is essential to go to the manuscripts themselves *and to transcribe them:* for there is a craft in correct transcription not to be learnt from books" (p. 5; italics in the original). A somewhat similar problem occurs when one comes to deciphering a particular manuscript. A knowledge of the language involved is extremely helpful in discovering what the manuscript says, but this knowledge is normally learned from text books, which are inevitably based on generalizations. Any one manuscript, although written in the language one has already mastered in what may be called its "theoretical" form, is likely to differ to a greater or lesser extent from what one has come to consider the "standard" language. And the knowledge of the language of any one manuscript, just as the knowledge of the precise letter-forms through which it is expressed, comes from the study — and the deciphering — of the manuscript itself. There is, it would seem, no escape from this basically circular problem.

Lest the novice paleographer be completely discouraged by the mention of these seemingly insurmountable fundamental difficulties, let us hasten to add that their insurmountable nature is only apparent. With sufficient application, diligence, and perseverance, one can achieve a surprising degree of ease and proficiency in deciphering medieval texts. But very likely one's first contact with a manuscript will involve a considerable amount of shock. One is tempted to throw up one's hands and exclaim that it is impossible to make any sense out of it, that all the letters look alike, and that the medieval scribe seems to have taken a perverse delight in producing what seems to be a beautifully formed but at the same time perfectly unreadable text. Of course these are only first impressions, and they must immediately be dispelled as nonsense. For let us remember what has already been said: the medieval text was meant to be read; we must assume that it was indeed read by medieval people, and therefore surely we "moderns" can learn to do as well. And so we must set out to do so, considering the matter as a challenge, if we like, but not as an impossible task.

* * *

Rather than first examining letter-forms in an abstract and theoretical way, let us at this point examine some photographs of actual medieval manuscripts. The four photographs of Figures 1-4 show one strophe (lines 15-21) of the Old Provençal *canso*, "De la gensor qu'om vey', al mieu semblan," composed by Berenguier de Palazol, a troubadour of the province of Roussillon who probably wrote in the early thirteenth century.[1] The poem is found only in the four manuscripts shown here,[2] and by examining the corresponding lines in the four versions we can simulate on a small scale the type of situation which frequently confronts the editor of medieval material.

Many — indeed most — North American medievalists must, of course, work in large part with microfilms rather than with the manuscripts themselves, a situation which presents both advantages and disadvantages. A well-photographed microfilm can be nearly as easy to decipher as the original manuscript, and occasionally even more so, since a microfilm reader or reader-printer will normally produce a larger projected image than the original from which the microfilm was made. A reel of microfilm is considerably less fragile (to say nothing of being less bulky) than a centuries-old parchment volume, and can be re-photographed if necessary, whereas, of course, a medieval manuscript is irreplace-

---

[1] For further details, see C. W. Carroll, "A Critical Edition of the Poems of Berenguier de Palazol, Troubadour of Roussillon" (unpublished doctoral dissertation, U. of Wisconsin, 1968), introduction and pages 81-88.

[2] Alfred Pillet and Henry Carstens, *Bibliographie der Troubadours* (Halle, 1933), p. 43 (No. 47,5).

able. And microfilms can be made in any quantity, thereby enabling a number of people in widely scattered locations to work on a given text simultaneously, which would be quite impossible if no microfilms existed. On the other hand, however, since there are as yet no microfilms in color (although there is no technical reason why they could not be made), certain markings, which might be perfectly distinguishable in the manuscript because of the different colors of ink used, tend to resemble one another when all is in shades of grey. And, of course, a poorly photographed microfilm, which may be over or under-exposed, out of focus, or otherwise unsatisfactory, is completely useless. Finally, although this may be a purely personal opinion, and is certainly a subjective reaction, there is a great deal of psychological and esthetic satisfaction to be gained from the direct contemplation of a manuscript in which a particular text has survived the ages.

Nevertheless, all of the photographic reproductions accompanying this article were taken from microfilms of the manuscripts, which accounts in part for the considerable variation in the size of the lettering from one Figure to another. But there are at least three factors which lead to this variation. To begin with, the manuscripts themselves are not lettered in a constant size; then the lenses used in the microfilming process may vary, resulting in relatively greater or lesser reduction of the image; finally, the various types of microfilm reader-printers enlarge the microfilm image to varying degrees. Three models currently in use may illustrate this point. The Thermo-Fax Microfilm Reader-Printer "Filmac 100" has three interchangeable lenses, for 9-x, 13-x, and 19-x magnification; the Recordak Motormatic Reader, Model MPG-TL (which becomes a reader-printer when coupled with a Recordak Printer, Model ERG or ERG-1) is equipped with a three-lens turret, providing 14-x, 19-x, and 23-x magnification; the Recordak Magnaprint Reader, Model PE-1A, gives a constant level of magnification, slightly less than that of the 13-x Thermo-Fax lens.

* * *

FIGURE 1

1 Abelha donab belh coꝣs beneſ
2 tan.de bel ſemblan e de gent
3 a culhir. a penas ſai de uos mo
4 mielhs chauzir. ſius uey o no
5 o ſim toꝣn o ſim an.non ai ſa
6 ber ni ſen que mi a on. tan ſuy
7 intratz en uoſtra moꝣ pꝛion. q̊
8 eu non conoſc per on men pueſ
9   cæſſir.

Chansonnier provençal *C* (Paris, Bibliothèque Nationale, ms. fr. 856), fol. 209ʳa, lines 29-37 (from Berenguier de Palazol's "De la gensor qu'om vey', al mieu semblan," lines 15-21). Folio, parchment, XIV c.[3] Note the almost total lack of abbreviations in the text, and the generally clear lettering style. The "cramped" appearance of the left-hand portion of the text results from the difficulty of flattening out the bound manuscript when making the microfilm photograph. (Photo. Bibl. nat. Paris.)

---

[3] The various Provençal *chansonniers* (collections of lyric poetry) are traditionally designated by key letters (as *C* in the present case; a similar system exists for the manuscripts of French *chansonniers*). Details concerning the form, size, and date of this manuscript are taken from Alfred Jeanroy, *Bibliographie sommaire des chansonniers provençaux* (Paris, 1916, reprinted 1966), p. 3. This work will henceforth be cited as "Jeanroy, *Bibliographie sommaire*."

FIGURE 2

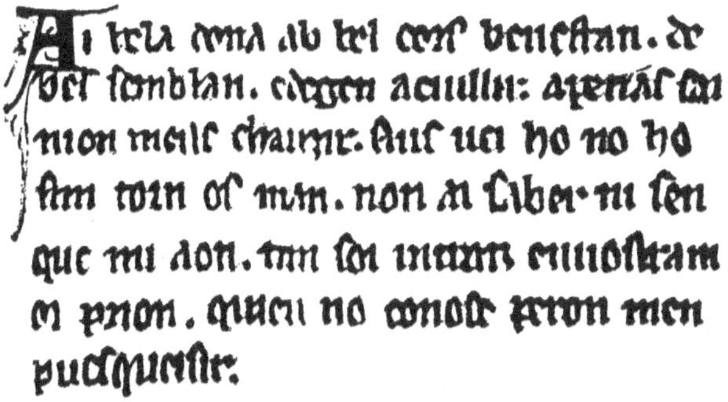

1 Ai bela dona ab bel coʒſ beneſtan.de
2 bel ſemblan. edegen acuillir. apenaſ ſai
3 mon meſlſ chauzir. ſiuſ uei ho no ho
4 ſim toʒn oſ man. non ai ſaber ni ſen
5 que mi aon. tan ſoi intratz enuoſtram
6 oʒ pʒion. quieu no conoſc peron men
7 pueſqueiſir.

Chansonnier provençal E (Paris, Bibliothèque Nationale, ms. fr. 1749), p. 94a, lines 32-38 (same basic text as in Figure 1). Quarto, parchment, XIV c. (Jeanroy, *Bibliographie sommaire*, p. 5). No abbreviations occur in this portion of the manuscript, although abbreviations are used elsewhere. (Photo. Bibl. nat. Paris.)

FIGURE 3

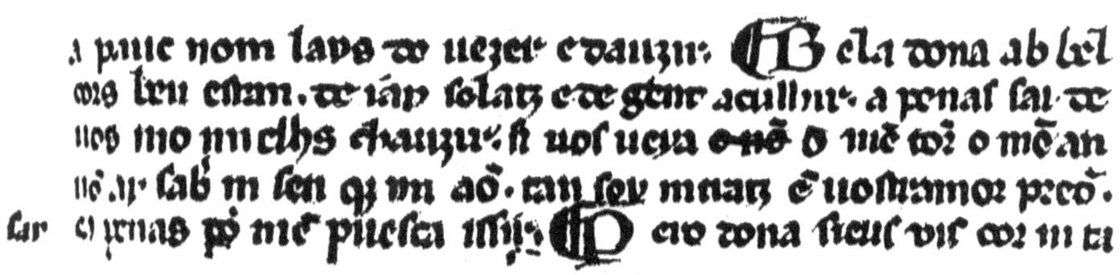

1 a ptuc nom laus to uezer coauzin: ℬ ela dona ab bel
2 cors bru estan. de iap solatz e de gent acullmr. a penas sai de
3 uos mo miclhs chauzur si uos ueia o nō o mē toz o mē an
4 nō ay sab m sen q; mi ao. tan soy mtratz ē uostramoz preō.
5 say cj penas po mē puesca issir: ᴅ co dona sieus vis coz m ti

1   Bela dona ab bel
2 coɀs ben eſtan. de iay ſolatz e de gent aculhir. a penaſ ſai de
3 uos mo mielhs chauzir. ſi uoſ ueya o nō o mē toɀ o mē an
4 nō ay ſab' ni ſen q3 mi aō. tan ſoy intratz ē uoſtramoɀ pɀeō.
5 ſay ca penas pȯ mē pueſca iſſir.

Chansonnier provençal *R* (Paris, Bibliothèque Nationale, ms. fr. 22543), fol. 37ʳa, lines 33-37 (same basic text as in Figures 1 and 2). Large folio, parchment, early XIV c. (Jeanroy, *Bibliographie sommaire*, p. 13). Three instances of scribal error are visible in this fragment: in line 3, a line is drawn to strike out the words *o nō;* in line 5, *ſay* was originally omitted, and has been added in the left-hand margin; the third word in line 5 (after *penas*) has been over-written, and the first letter is now unclear. (Photo. Bibl. nat. Paris.)

FIGURE 4

```
1
2
3
4
```

1 ay bona domnab bel corſ ben eſtan- de bel ſemblant ede gent acui
2 lhir- apenaſ ſay de uoſ mo mielſ chauzir- ſiuſ uey onōoſim torn oſim
3 uan- nō ſai ſaber ni ſen qui mi aon- tant ſoi intratz en uoſtra
4 mor preon- quieu nō conoſc p̣ on men pueſca yſſir-

Chansonnier provençal *f* (Paris, Bibliothèque Nationale, ms. fr. 12472, fol. 55^v, lines 5-8 (same basic text as in Figures 1-3). Small folio, paper, first half XIV c. (Jeanroy, *Bibliographie sommaire*, p. 23). Although this manuscript is very different in style from those of the other Figures, it can still be deciphered by means of reference to the same basic letter-forms. The style is more curvilinear than angular, and gives the impression of having been written in haste, rather than with the painstaking precision evident in the manuscripts of the other Figures. (Photo. Bibl. nat. Paris.)

* * *

As can be seen at a glance, there is a considerable difference in style and form of presentation from one manuscript to another. While those of Figures 1 and 2 resemble one another fairly closely, those of Figures 3 and 4 are quite different from each other and from the other two, particularly insofar as the lettering style of Figure 4 is concerned. It will readily be noted that, although the text represented is a fragment of poetry, the lines of poetry are not separated so that each poetic line coincides with one line of lettering. This now traditional method of arranging poetry on the page was not generally practiced in manuscripts of the type under discussion in this article, although there are a few manuscripts having such an arrangement, and excerpts from two of them are reproduced in Figures 5 and 6.

In order to facilitate a more meaningful comparison, a diplomatic transcription of each fragment is given, in the belief that if the reader undertakes a careful comparison of each diplomatic transcription with the photograph of the manuscript, he will already discover a number of things about the deciphering of Gothic writing. One word of caution must be said, however, concerning this method as an approach to the deciphering of manuscripts. The present author feels, naturally, that these diplomatic transcriptions are accurate, and that they serve to show, as closely as can be done by modern printing methods, precisely what letters and combinations of letters are present in each manuscript fragment. However, many diplomatic transcriptions which have appeared in print are, quite frankly, less trustworthy, in that they simply do not represent with sufficient accuracy the readings of the manuscripts in question. One must therefore exercise extreme caution when using diplomatic transcriptions as an aid to deciphering manuscripts, and it is best to be highly suspicious of the accuracy of any diplomatic edition which one has not personally verified by means of a careful comparison with the manuscript it purports to represent.

Ignoring for the moment the manuscript of Figure 4 (because its lettering style is so different from that of the other three manuscripts) we can make a number of observations which may be confirmed by an examination of other manuscripts. The novice may well find that one of his major problems in identifying individual letters is that of establishing exactly where one letter leaves off and another begins. This problem arises mainly from the scribal technique of fusing adjacent "contrary curves," where one curve is convex to the right, the other to the left. Thus, instead of the combination *be* being written as two separate letters with a small space between, the right convex curve of the *b* is combined with the left convex curve of the *e*, and the two letters are run together, much as is done in modern printing in the ligature œ in such French words as *cœur* and in the ligature æ in such (British) English words as *mediæval* and *æsthetic*. Many possible combinations of this sort exist, involving chiefly the vowels *e* and *o*, and such consonants as *b, c, d,* etc. In the first three lines of Figure 1, the combinations *be, do, de,* and *pe* are linked in this manner. There are numerous other cases of ligature, some of which have found their way into modern printing, in such forms as *ff, fi, fl, ffi,* etc., and some of which have not, since they involve letter-forms no longer current, such as "long *s*", *ſ,* which is normally linked to a following *t* (as in Figure 1, line 7; Figure 2, line 1; Figure 3, line 2; Figure 4, lines 1 and 3).[4] Note also the linked *æ* in the last line of Figure 1, indicating, in this particular case, that the two vowels are to be pronounced together, and count as only one syllable. Not only are letters not individually separated, but words are often run together: a comparison of the first line in the four fragments reveals that Figures 2 and 3 have *dona ab,* but Figure 1 runs the two words together, giving *donab.* (Figure 4 combines the two words in a different way, placing the first *a* above the *n*: *domñab*.) In line 7 of Figure 1, the words *vostra amor* are run together to fit the meter of the poem, but the resulting arrangement looks more like *vostra mor.* We shall have occasion to refer to various other aspects of these fragments subsequently, when discussing problems of detail, such as the forms of individual letters, signs, symbols, etc.

Some additional illustrations from other manuscripts, some of them in other languages besides Old Provençal, will be useful for reference for the remainder of our discussion. A diplomatic transcription of each fragment again accompanies the enlarged microfilm photograph, and the reader is advised to compare the two in each case before reading further. The most useful exercise would no doubt be for the reader to attempt his own transcription, and then to compare his findings with the diplomatic text. But a final word of advice will be appropriate in this connection: "the very possibility of seeing what is actually written often depends on the power of the reader to imagine for himself what ought to have been written, and to check his hypotheses by what

---

[4] The "long *s*" will be discussed in greater detail in the section on individual letter-forms.

he can see: indeed, it is not too much to say that you cannot read a word with certainty unless you know what it is."[5] Of course, this brings us back to the basically circular dilemma mentioned earlier. Nevertheless, if one transcribes not letter-by-letter, but rather in terms of words and thoughts, always keeping the CONTEXT in mind, the risk of incomprehension is greatly lessened.

REMARKS ON INDIVIDUAL LETTER-FORMS

Introduction. Although we call this style of lettering "Gothic," the individual letters are basically the ancestors of those used in present-day printing, and so are generally not too difficult to recognize and identify when examined on an individual basis. (As we have seen, of course, the paleographical problems soon arise when one is confronted with whole texts of such letters linked together into words.) A fairly clear idea of just how manuscript letters were formed can be gleaned from an attentive examination of Figures 5 and 8, in which the greatest degree of magnification has been used. Although the two manuscripts pictured in these Figures are not written in exactly the same style, each of them does nonetheless present a rather standard sort of Gothic writing (insofar as that term can be meaningful), and one can in this way get an idea of what to look for in other manuscripts. It is even possible, in some cases, to discover in what order the various component strokes of the various letters were made, bearing in mind the fact that the pens used produced a line of varying width, depending on how they were held and in which direction the stroke was made.

---

[5] Charles Johnson and Hilary Jenkinson, *English Court Hand A.D. 1066 to 1500, Illustrated Chiefly from the Public Records* (Oxford, 1915, reprinted New York, 1967), xxxvii-xxxviii.

MEDIEVAL ROMANCE PALEOGRAPHY   51

FIGURE 5

1		J	ev⁹ voel moſtrˢ orendroit
2		D	eceſte parole leſens
3		Q	n̊t ·j· hō ſeſt miſ eſ aſſens
4		D	emal faire 7 depourcacier
5		S	iconme cil ki de pecier
6		N	apaoz nepoint dedoutance
7		S	apreſ entrait fozt penitāce
8		7	ſeil granſ mauſ enendure
9		C	eneſt mie par aventure
10		M	aiſ pdı̊t ſelimal lēuienent
11		Qⁱ	pſō meſfait li auienent
12		Q	ant lihom lafolie fait
13		S	il encompere lemeſſait
14		L	ozſ neua paſ dı̊ture aozce
15		7	ildoit mlt̊ ṗⁱier lafozce
16		Qⁱ	ſouffrir lifait boinem̄t
17		S	iqⁱl enuient aſauuem̄t

Chansonnier français A (Arras, Bibliothèque Municipale, ms. 657 [formerly 139]), fol. 5ʳa, lines 1-17 (fragment from Alart de Cambrai's *Moralités aux philosophes*). Small quarto, parchment, latter XIII c.[6] Note the abundance of abbreviations and the arrangement of the lines of poetry in separate lines.

---

[6] Details from Alfred Jeanroy, *Le Chansonnier d'Arras: Reproduction en phototypie* (Paris: Société des Anciens Textes Français, 1875-1925), Introduction, p. 5. Jeanroy says the manuscript "porte le n.º 139 (ancien 657)," but the title page of the manuscript reads "Ms 657 (139)."

FIGURE 6

1	ei enemic ſon caitiu .	S	ei enemic ſon caitiu.
2	t ſei amic ricx 7 ſoꝛſ.	E	t ſei amic ricx 7 ſoꝛſ.
3	ront / oill / naſ / bocha 7 maiſſel	F	ront / oill / naſ / bocha 7 maiſſel
4	lanc peich ab dura mamella .	B	lanc peich ab dura mamella.
5	el taill deſ filz iſrrael .	D	el taill deſ filz iſrrael.
6	t eſ colunba ſeſ fel .	E	t eſ colunba ſeſ fel.
7	er chom ten moẓn 7 penſiu ,	P	er chom ten moẓn 7 penſiu,
8	itant qant eſtau ailloꝛſ .	A	itant qant eſtau ailloꝛſ.
9	uoſ creiſ men gauch 7 dolchoꝛſ .	P	uoſ creiſ men gauch 7 dolchoꝛſ.
10	an del ſeu bel coꝛſ maiſiu .	C	an del ſeu bel coꝛſ maiſiu.
11	aiſſi com de recalliu .	C	aiſſi com de recalliu.
12	rai calt 7 ar freidoꝛſ .	A	rai calt 7 ar freidoꝛſ.
13	t car eſ gaia 7 iſnella .	E	t car eſ gaia 7 iſnella.
14	t de toẓ malſ aipſ pulcella .	E	t de toz malſ aipſ pulcella.
15	m la maiſ per ſaint rafael .	A	m la maiſ per ſaint rafael.
16	e iacob non feẓ rachael .	Q	e iacob non fez rachael.
17	erſ uaiten uerſ mont oliu .	V	erſ uaiten uerſ mont oliu.
18	t dimalaſ trei ſeroꝛſ.	E	t dimalaſ trei ſeroꝛſ.

Chansonnier provençal S (Oxford, Bodleian Library, ms. Douce 269),[7] p. 14, lines 1-18 (from Peire Vidal's "Be·m pac d'ivern e d'estiu," lines 35-52).[8] Oblong octavo, parchment, end XIII c.; Italian hand (Jeanroy, *Bibliographie sommaire*, p. 14). Note the arrangement of the lines of poetry in separate lines and the almost complete lack of abbreviations.

---

[7] Reproduced here with the kind permission of the Bodleian Library, Oxford.

[8] Cf. *Les Poésies de Peire Vidal*, ed. Joseph Anglade, 2d ed. (Paris, 1923, reprinted 1965), pp. 48-49.

FIGURE 7

Pistola.

1   A   pzes lo uers comença.del comte la lissos.el pistola qⁱ gença
2   ab humils ditz ecars q̄n cezueri ses tença.tramet als fracs
3   juglars e doctozs de pzoença.p cuy fenten razos.caz passat
4   son ·v· an lay no fo men auzi.fait ne dit benestan nel bo |
5   princep no ui.
6   Frayzes sauetz pesança ne t'men pyllozs.caz leu ue malenaça duzs
7   e guiatz affars.aiatz el coz mebzança q̄ deus sofri pesazs.caix can re ses
8   dubtança ne ses maltrait no fos.q̄l t'ra p senblan tra mal laygua tresi.
9   lairs el focs qⁱ resplan mantas ues com lauci.

Chansonnier provençal *Sg* (Barcelona, Biblioteca Central, ms. 146), fol. 20ʳ, lines 5-14 (from Cerverí de Gerona's *pistola* (letter), "Apres lo vers comença," lines 1-24).[9] Quarto, parchment, XIV c.; of Catalan origin (Jeanroy, *Bibliographie sommaire*, p. 14). Note the abundant use of abbreviations.

---

[9] Cf. *Obras completas del trovador Cerverí de Girona*, ed. Martín de Riquer (Barcelona, 1947), pp. 47-48.

FIGURE 8

1 Laudato sie misignore cu tucte le tue cria
2 ture. spetialmte messor lo frē sole. loqua
3 le iorno ¬ allumini noi p loi. Et ellu e bella
4 e radiante cū grande splendore. de te altissi
5 mo porta significatōe. Laudato si misignore
6 p sora luna e le stelle. in celu l ai formate
7 clarite ¬ priose ¬ belle. Laudato si misigñe
8 p frē uēto ¬ p aere ¬ nubilo ¬ sereno ¬ onne
9 tēpo. p loquale ale tue creature dai sustē
10 tamēto. Laudato si misignore p sor aqua. la
11 quale e multo utile ¬ humile ¬ priosa ¬ casta.
12 Laudato si misignore p frē focu. p loquale
13 enn allumini la nocte. e dello e bello ¬ iocūdo
14 ¬ robustoso ¬ forte. Laudato si misignore p
15 sora nr̄a matre t̄ra. laquale ne sustenta

Assisi, Biblioteca Comunale, ms. 338, fol. 33ᵛ, lines 1-15 (from San Francesco d'Assisi's "Cantico delle creature," lines 5-21). Parchment, 320 × 230 mm., XIV c.[10] Note the abundant use of abbreviations. (For diplomatic transcription, see following page.)

---

[10] Details from Giuseppe Mazzatinti, *Inventari dei manoscritti delle biblioteche d'Italia* (Forlì, 1896), IV, 75. In addition to a description of the manuscript and its contents, this work gives a diplomatic edition of the "Cantico delle creature" (IV, 76-77), but with expanded abbreviations, without indicating which words were abbreviated in the original.

Diplomatic transcription for Figure 8.

```
 1  -laudato ſie miſignoʒe cū tucte le tue crea
 2  ture. ſpetialm̄te meſſoʒ lo fr̄e ſole. loqua
 3  le ioʒno 7 allumini noi p loi. Et ellu ebellu
 4  eradiante cū grande ſplendore. De te altiſſi
 5  mo poʒta ſignificatōe. -laudato ſi miſignore
 6  p ſora luna ele ſtelle. in celu lai foʒmate
 7  clarite 7 p̄tioſe 7 belle. -laudato ſi miſigr̊e
 8  p fr̄e ūeto 7 p aere 7 nubilo 7 ſereno 7 onne
 9  tēpo. p loquale ale tue creature dai ſuſten
10  tam̄to. -laudato ſi miſignore p ſoʒ aqua·la
11  quale emulto utile 7 hūile 7 p̄tioſa 7 caſta.
12  -laudato ſi miſignore p fr̄e focu. p loquale
13  ennallumini la nocte. edello ebello 7 iocūdo
14  7 robuſtoſo 7 foʒte. -Laudato ſi miſignore p
15  ſora nr̄a matre t̄ra. laquale ne ſuſtenta
```

* * *

It must be said at the outset that the following remarks concerning individual letter-forms apply to minuscule (also called "small" or, in printing terminology, "lower-case") letters only, and not to majuscule ("capital" or "upper-case") letters, in which the greatest imaginable variation in form is to be found. A representative catalogue of majuscule forms would have to be very large in order to be meaningful at all, for they frequently formed an integral part of the decoration and embellishment of the page, including, in extreme cases, the illuminated capitals.[11] Fortunately, however, there is usually a fair amount of consistency within a given manuscript, and it is frequently possible to guess the identity of a decorative capital from the context of the remainder of the word, in those cases where the letter itself is not recognizable. In this study, under the discussion of each letter, we shall limit ourselves to giving an indication of the

---

[11] A good source of letter-forms for non-decorated majuscules is the "table" of such manuscripts as Chansonnier provençal C (used for our Figure 1), where examples of virtually all the letters of the alphabet may be found.

capital letters found in the Figures, with a few comments on those particular forms.

a

In many forms of Gothic writing, minuscule *a* is not very different from the lower-case *a* found in most type styles in modern printing. It is composed of two strokes, the "head" and "back" in one stroke, with the "head" clearly curved to the left, the bottom of the down-stroke usually presenting a serif to the right, and a *c*-shaped loop to the left of the vertical "back" stroke (Figures 1, 5, and 8 offer numerous clear examples, as in 1:1 *belha, donab;* 5:2 *parole;* 8:1 *crea*).[12] This *c*-shaped loop sometimes seems to be detached from the vertical "back," and this can lead to confusion, since the left side of the loop may actually touch and seem to be part of the preceding letter (8:9 *dai*). The proportions of the *a* in Figures 2 and 6 are rather different from the usual; in the latter case there is little if any space between the "head" and the *c*-shaped loop. In Figure 4 we find a different form of *a*, composed of a loop and a vertical stroke which does not form a "head" at the top, thus: *a*. This style, which has been called "headless *a*" (Johnson and Jenkinson, *English Court Hand*, I, 2-3), is perhaps less common than that mentioned first, but is by no means rare. Figure 7 mixes the two styles, as in 7:1 *començ$_a$, l^a, piſtol^a, genç$_a$*. Examples of A: 1:1; 2:1;' 6:8, 12, 15; 7:1 (the latter is a fairly ornate, though non-representational, illuminated initial).

b

Minuscule *b* is usually easy to recognize in most Gothic manuscripts, although the fusing of the right-hand side of the bow with the left-hand side of a following *e, o*, or similarly shaped letter frequently occurs (1:1 *belh*) and may be a source of confusion. The letter is composed of a tall down-stroke which

---

[12] References to the Figures will regularly be given in this way, the number preceding the colon referring to the Figure, the number following the colon referring to a line of the Figure. Thus, 8:9 is to be read as "Figure 8, line 9." When two or more lines of one Figure are referred to together, the line-numbers will be separated by commas, thus: 5:7, 10, 12.

curves to the right at the bottom and a clockwise curved stroke begun at or near the straight portion of the down-stroke and connected to the end-point of the first stroke to form a bow. A clear example occurs in 1:1 *(donab)*. There may be a serif to the left at the top of the down-stroke; those of Figure 1 generally have a slight serif, those of Figure 3 clearly do not, as in 3:1 *(ab, bel)*. The bow of the letter is frequently open, i. e., the closing stroke was not begun at a point touching the vertical stroke. In some cases the vertical stroke is hardly taller than the top of the bow (1:1 *belha*). Note the slightly notched top of the vertical stroke in 5:16. Examples of *B:* 3:1; 6:4.

c

Minuscule *c* is basically an open curve, more or less angular in the different manuscripts shown (5:4 *pourcacier*). When followed by a letter such as *e* or *o*, there is usually no space left between the two, which can be confusing (1:1 *cors;* 7:3 *cuy*). The top of the *c* may be somewhat exaggerated, and carried well beyond the lower part of the curve (4:1 *cor/*). In some manuscripts confusion between *c* and *t* is possible, depending on the relative angularity of the *c*. The two can usually be distinguished, however, under sufficient magnification (8:1 *tucte,* 5 /*ignificatōe,* 13 *nocte*). See the section on *t* for other references. Depending on the language of the particular manuscript, *ç* may also be found (particularly in Provençal texts). The precise form of the cedilla may vary considerably, and may be more or less visible. In 7:3 *pɀoença* and 7:7 *mēbɀança* the *ç* is clearer than elsewhere in Figure 7 (see diplomatic transcription for other instances). Examples of *C:* 5:9; 6:10, 11.

d

Rather than a "straight-backed" *d* as in modern printing, Gothic manuscripts normally present an angled shaft, the upper part of which extends as far left as the left edge of the loop below (and sometimes beyond: 3:1 *dona*). The angle of the upper part of the shaft varies widely, from approximately horizontal (1:1 *donab*) to a relatively steep slope (5:1 *orendroit;* 7:1 *del*), and may be slightly recurved, the extremity approaching the vertical (4:1 *de;* 5:4 *de*) or even going beyond it (4:1 *domñab*). The curved sides of the loop of the *d* are frequently fused with the curves of adjoining letters, particularly in the case of a following *e* or *o* (5:4 *de,* 6 *doutance*). A straight-shafted *d* occasionally occurs, as in 8:13 *edello,* but this form is rare. (It will be noticed that the usual form of *d* in Figure 8 is that described first, as in *laudato,* 8:1 et passim, and *iocūdo,* 8:13.) Examples of *D:* 5:2, 4; 6:5; 8:4 (simply a slightly larger letter, with the same form as the minuscule *d*—cf. *grande* and *∫plendore* in the same line).

e

Figure 5 (5:1 *Je, voel*) gives a clear picture of the basic form of *e* current in Gothic manuscripts. It is formed of two basic strokes: a curved line much like that of *c,* to the top of which is joined an oblique line in two segments, the first a broad stroke downward to the right and then a second, narrow stroke, downward to the left, which rejoins the first stroke. The bottom of the first stroke usually curves to the right and diminishes into a very fine upward-slanting line. The final narrow stroke (sloping downward to the left) is sometimes so fine that it is not visible in microfilm photographs (2:1 *bela, bel*), and *e* may thus be easily confused with *c* (cf. 2:1 *coz∫*). In Figure 4 there is frequently no trace of this final stroke (4:1 *bene∫tan,* 2 *de*), and the second stroke sometimes appears separated from the first (4:3 *∫aber*). In some manuscripts this third stroke seems to have been made from left to right, since it constitutes a tie or continuation-stroke joining *e* to the following letter (6:1 *enemic,* 5 *Del, de∫;* 8:2 *me∫∫oz* et passim). It will be noticed that this trailing stroke occurs even in word-final position (6:11 *de,* 14 *de;* 8:1 *mi∫ignoze, tucte le tue,* et passim). Examples of *E:* 6:2, 6, 13, 14, 18; 8:3.

f

The basic difficulty concerning minuscule *f* lies in its similarity to the "long *s*" (∫) used in manuscripts of the types we have been discussing. A close examination of Figures 5 and 8, however, will readily show that the resemblance is quite superficial, and that the two can easily be distinguished after a bit of practice.[13] For the most part, *f* in these manuscripts is readily recognizable, as in 5:4 *faire*, 5:7 *fort*, and 5:12 *folie, fait*. Basically one finds a letter composed of three strokes (vertical staff, top, and crossbar); such variation as does occur appears in the curvature and length of the top and in the relative development of serifs. Thus in 5:7 *(foʐt)* the serif to the right at the bottom of the *f* is quite visible, whereas elsewhere in Figure 5 the serif is much smaller (5:4 *faire*, 12 *fait*), and in Figure 7 (7:2 *frācs*, 4 *fo)* there is none at all. The crossbar of the *f* frequently constitutes a tie to the following letter, as in all the examples mentioned thus far and in 6:5 *filz*, 6:6 *fel*, 8:2 *fr̄e*, 8:6 *foʐmate*, etc. In the case of *ff*, the two letters are normally united by a single crossbar, and the top of the first touches that of the second near the top of the vertical stroke (7:7 *affars*). Examples of *F:* 6:3; 7:6.

g

Even within the rather limited corpus of the illustrations used here, considerable variation may be found in the forms of *g*—so much so, in fact, that it is difficult to single out examples which may be said to be "typical." Perhaps that of 2:2 *(gen)* and that of 3:2 *(gent)* come closest, with a slightly exaggerated form appearing in 4:1 *(gent)*. All are variations on a basic model consisting of a closed loop somewhat smaller than that of an *o*, to which is added a curved tail and, generally, a horizontal stroke connecting the loop to the following letter at about the level of the top of such "small" letters as *a, e, n, o, r,* etc. Another version is seen in Figure 8 *(grande,* 8:4, *miſignoʐe* 8:1 et passim), where the horizontal tie-stroke connecting the loop of the *g* with the next letter is rather longer than in the other manuscripts illustrated. But the precise forms of the different strokes may vary considerably without leading to confusion with other letters, as may be seen in the various Figures. Thus, instead of a rounded loop we sometimes find (1:2 *gent;* 7:1 *gença)* something resembling a flat-topped *c* closed off by a recurving down-stroke forming the tail. Figure 6 (6:9 *gauch,* 13 *gaia)* presents a more straight-backed

---

[13] For further discussion of this problem, see the section devoted to *s* and *ſ*.

variety of this type of g. Quite an unusual form occurs in 5:8 *(granſ)*, where the g somewhat resembles a *b* with a "top" added to the down-stroke. (This letter is quite distinct from the *b* in 5:16, however.) Elsewhere in the manuscript a more usual g is used. No examples of G occur in the Figures.

h

Minuscule *h* usually presents rather little difficulty. It is composed of two strokes, a down-stroke and a curved limb, which usually touches the down-stroke at its mid-point and descends clearly below the base-line (the line on which the letters seem to rest). The curved line may terminate at a point directly below the down-strokes, as in 1:1 *(belha, belh)*, or may even be re-curved, as in the more "flamboyant" style of Figure 4 (4:2 *chauzir*). Some variations shown by other manuscripts are represented in 2:3 *(ho)*, where a more angular second stroke is used, and in 8:11 *(hūile)*, where the vertical stroke hardly extends above the top of the following *u*. In 7:2 *(humils)* the curved stroke does not extend below the base line, and the resulting letter somewhat resembles a *b* (cf. preceding word *ab*). The down-stroke may have a serif at one or at both extremities (1:3 *aculhir*, 4 *chauzir*), or the top may be notched (5:3 *hō*, 12 *hom*). No examples of H occur in the Figures.

i

The same basic stroke is used for *i* as is used in combination in *m*, *n*, and *u*, and much confusion can result from this, in certain manuscripts at least. Fortunately, however, the medieval scribes were generally aware of this potential source of confusion, and many of them — at least the more careful ones — took pains to distinguish *i* from these other letters, particularly when it directly preceded or followed one of them.[14] This distinction was accomplished by means of a fine line slanting upward to the right from a point above the body of the letter — the forerunner of the dot used in printing and writing today. Examples of this may be seen in 1:3 *aculhir* and 1:5 *ſim;* 4:2 *chauzir*,

---

[14] For a discussion of words involving problems of this sort, see the section following the discussion of abbreviations, pp. 73-75.

/iu/; 5:1 *orendroit* (the line above *i* is very clear throughout Figure 5); and 6:1 *caitiu*. In looking elsewhere in these same Figures, however, one will note that these slanting lines are often difficult to see. This is frequently due to the microfilming process, in which some detail is lost; these lines are sometimes so fine as to be nearly invisible even when the manuscript is examined at first hand. In other manuscripts (our Figures 2, 3, 7, and 8) there seems to be no trace of such lines. It will be noted that these lines are often partially or even wholly above the following letter rather than above the *i*. This is not normally a problem, however, due to the distinctive form of the slanting lines, which is clearly different from that of the basically horizontal bars (written with a much heavier stroke) indicating the omission of a nasal consonant (cf. 5:10 *lēuienent*). The body of the *i* is usually not a straight vertical line, but is rather slightly curved (5:3 *mi/* et passim), since it was formed with a single stroke, including serifs both top (left) and bottom (right). Sometimes a slightly longer form of the letter, resembling a *j*, is used in final position in some manuscripts (7:5 *ui*, 9 *lauci*). No examples of *I* occur in the Figures.

j

In the bulk of medieval manuscripts of this period, *j* is not used as a separate letter distinct from *i*. Its presence in a given manuscript depends on the particular language of the scribe. The manuscript of Figure 5 is the only one, of those used here, in which *j* occurs (5:3 ·*j*·), and there it is used not in a word but rather as a numeral, replacing the indefinite article *uns*. It will be noted that, in this example, the same type of fine line is used above the *j* as is used above *i* elsewhere in the same manuscript. In other manuscripts, the tail of the letter does not always form a closed curve, rejoining the shaft as it does here. A notch may be seen in the top of the letter, as in the down-stroke of the following *h* and in those of other letters in this manuscript having a similar stroke, namely *b*, *k*, and *l*. Example of *J*: 5:1.

k

Like *j*, *k* does not occur in most Romance-language manuscripts of this time, although it occurs more frequently in French than in Italian and Provençal. The only example in the accompanying Figures is in 5:5 *(ki)*, and there is little to be said about the letter besides pointing out this one example: it is unlikely that *k* would be confused with any other letter, and it should be readily recognizable when it does occur. As in the case of other letters in this manuscript having a similar vertical stroke *(b, h, j, l)*, the top of the down-stroke is notched. It will be noted that this manuscript uses the abbreviation Q^i whenever the same word *(qui* and *ki* being alternate spellings) occurs at the beginning of a line (5:11, 16). No examples of *K* occur in the Figures.

l

There is very little that needs to be said concerning *l;* it is one of the simplest letter-forms in the Gothic repertory, and one finds very little variation on the basic form: a single tall down-stroke. Almost any example would do, but 1:2 *(ſemblan)* and 5:2 *(leſens)* are particularly clear. What little variation is to be found occurs in the serifs at the top (left) and bottom (right) of the vertical stroke. They may completely disappear, as in 4:1 *(ſemblant)*, or be quite long, especially at the top, as in 3:1 *(Bela, bel)*. In some words *l* is made with a notched top in the manuscript of Figure 5, as in 5:2 *(parole)* and 5:12 *(li)*, but this is by no means uniform throughout the text. Examples of *L:* 5:14 (where it is virtually indistinguishable in form from minuscule *l*) and 8:14.

m *and* n

These two letters, *m* and *n*, may be treated together, since they are composed of exactly the same sort of short, basically vertical strokes, commonly called minims (Johnson and Jenkinson, *English Court Hand*, I, 30-31). As was mentioned in our discussion of *i*, considerable confusion frequently arises from the similarity of strokes used in the four letters consisting of minims, *i, m, n,* and *u* (see footnote 14). A close examination of the more carefully lettered, more standard (one might even say more "classical") manuscripts, such as those of Figures 1 and 5, reveals that the three minims of *m* and the two of *n* are not rigorously identical (1:1 *beneſ*, 2 *ſemblan;* 5:1 *moſtr^s, orendroit*). The leftmost minim is frequently a straighter stroke, whereas the rightmost minim shows more curvature. All of the Figures show basically the same sort of letter-forms for *m* and *n,* with the exception of Figure 4, where these letters seem to have been formed without lifting the pen, much as is done in present-day cursive writing (4:1 *ſemblant,* 2 *mo mielſ*). Example of *M:* 5:10; example of *N:* 5:6 (quite an unusual form).

o

Minuscule *o* is formed of two curving strokes, the first moving downward and then to the right, forming the left side and bottom of the letter, and the second moving to the right and then downward, and completing the closure of the loop. The two strokes may be more angular than smoothly curved, but basically there is rather little variation in form. Figure 1:1 *(dona, cozs)* and Figure 5:1 *(voel, moſtrˢ, orendroit)* show basic (but rather slight) variations on the standard letter-form. Figure 4 again presents a divergent form resembling cursive writing (4:1 *bona, domñ̄*): there is somewhat less visible variation in the thickness of the different parts of the letter, and it seems to have been made with a single counterclockwise stroke, terminated in some cases in a small loop on top of the large one and a tie-stroke leading to the next letter (4:2 *onō,* 3 *aon).* No examples of *O* occur in the Figures.

p

Minuscule *p* is usually readily recognized when used as a simple letter. In addition, however, it serves as the basic figure for a considerable number of abbreviations, in which *p* is the only letter, and to which various additions have been made. (See the discussion of abbreviations, following the presentation of individual letters.) The letter consists of a down-stroke descending below the base-line, a more-or-less horizontal cross through the down-stroke from left to right, which forms the bottom of the loop, and a clockwise curve from at or near the top of the down-stroke down and around to meet the horizontal cross stroke. The loop of the *p* is thus frequently slightly open at the top (5:2 *parole,* 9 *par).* As with most letters involving a convex curve, the right-hand side of the loop is frequently run together with the left-hand side of a following *e* or *o* (5:7 *penitāce,* 6 *point).* The lower end of the down-stroke frequently has a hook to the right; this is particularly visible in Figure 5 (5:2 *parole*, 7 *penitāce*, 9 *par*, etc.). The down-stroke descends a bit lower in Figure 4 than in the other manuscripts illustrated, and the open top is quite visible (4:2 *apenaſ*, 4 *preon*). Examples of *P*: 6:7, 9.

q

As in the case of *p*, *q* frequently serves as the basic figure for abbreviations (q. v.). The simple letter *q* is usually composed of two or three strokes: a counter-clockwise *c*-shaped curve, which may then be closed to make the loop of the *q* either by means of a more-or-less flat top and a descending vertical stroke, or by means of a clockwise curve which is prolonged into the down-stroke. The former, three-stroke *q* is more angular in appearance (1:6 *que*; 2:5 *que*; 5:17 *q^{i}l*; 6:8 *qant*; 7:1 *q^i*) than is the two-stroke *q* (3:4 *q3*; 4:3 *qui*; 8:2 *loqua*). The tail of the *q* is frequently hooked to the right, as in 5:17, or else slightly bent to the right, as in 6:8. The length of the tail can vary considerably, sometimes barely extending below the base line, as is usually the case in Figure 8 (8:2 *loqua*, 9 *loquale*, 10 *aqua*, etc.), and sometimes extending quite far, as in Figure 4 (4:3 *qui*, 4 *quieu*). Examples of *Q*: 5:3, 11, 12, 16; 6:16.

r and ʒ

Two distinct forms are used for minuscule *r* in the manuscripts under consideration and in most others of the same general period and type. The "standard" form, rather closely resembling a lower-case printed *r*, is formed of a minim much like those used for *i*, *m*, *n*, and *u*, and a very short oblique stroke placed to the right of the minim, near the top. This stroke is in many cases so short that it is no longer than it is broad; it seems logical to assume, however, that it was made from upper left to lower right (1:4 *chauzir* — note the very nearly identical strokes used for the minims of *i* and *r*). The second stroke of the *r* can be longer, as in Figure 5, where in some cases it shows a double curvature rather like that of a tilde (5:4 *faire*), particularly in final position (5:4 *pourcacier*, 5 *pecier*, 15 *p^{i}ſier*). There is frequently a space between the minim and the second stroke, as in 3:2 (*aculhir*),

3:3 *(chauzir)*, and throughout Figure 4 (4:2 *chauzir*, 4 *yſſir*), where the second stroke is nearly horizontal and, in most cases, quite long. The letter of 1:9 *(cæſſir)* seems to be a "standard" *r* with an extra (decorative) stroke added apparently because of its place at the end of a strophe (one finds similar embellishments at the ends of other strophes in the same poem). No examples of *R* occur in the Figures.

Concerning the "secondary" form of *r*, Johnson and Jenkinson's remarks, although describing English court hands, are applicable to Romance-language manuscripts as well. This form of *r* is "derived from the ligature of *OR*," and "is at first only used after *o*." Its form "is more or less like an Arabic 2; but in rapid writing the curve of the head and the sharp angle at the base tend to be effaced, so that some late examples are reduced to a mere zig-zag line" (*English Court Hand*, I, 40-41). Among the accompanying Figures, this type of *r* most resembles an Arabic 2 in Figure 2 (2:1 *cozſ*, etc.) and Figure 8 (8:10 *ſoz*, 14 *fozte*, etc.). In Figure 6 the base of the "2" slopes upward to the right, forming a sharper angle with the "head" of the letter (6:2 *ſozſ*, etc.). Elsewhere the letter is more of a "mere zig-zag line" (1:1 *cozs*; 3:3 *toz̄*; 5:7 *fozt*; 7:3 *doctozs*), the last stroke of which may be extended in final position, as in 5:6 *(paoz)*.

The distribution of this type of *r* varies widely from one manuscript to another and even considerably within one manuscript. In most of the manuscripts which have come to the attention of the present writer, the "2-form" *r* is most widely used after *o*, and never occurs as the first letter of a word. Many manuscripts frequently present this form after *p*, *b*, and *d* as well, but it is not uncommon to find examples of both types of *r* used after the same letter within the text of a single short poem. Thus, in Figure 8, *misignore* is written with "2-form" *r* in line 1, but with a "standard" *r* in lines 5, 10, 12, and 14. In 8:10 we find *ſoz*, but *ſora* in lines 6 and 15. Among the present Figures, the greatest variation in usage appears in Figure 7, where "2-form" *r* occurs not only after *o* but also after *p* (7:1 *Apzes*), *b* (7:7 *mēbzança*), *a* (7:3 *caz*, 7:6 *caz*, 7:7 *peſazs*), *e* (7:2 *cezueri*), *u* (7:6 *duzs*), and *y* (7:6 *Frayzes*). Note that in 7:2 *(cezueri)* we find *ez* and *er* in the same word. The manuscript of Figure 4 does not use the "2-form" *r* at all.

ſ *and* s

In many manuscripts of the type under consideration, two types of minuscule *s* occur. By far the more widespread is the "long *s*", ſ, usually formed with two strokes: a straight down-stroke ending in a slight serif or foot to the right, either on or slightly below the base line, and a curved "head" running from left to right across the top of the down-stroke and usually curving downward somewhat at its right-hand extremity. The second stroke was often begun so as to leave a slight projection to the left of the down-stroke, which was kept in the form of a serif in printed books for as long as ſ was still preserved as a separate form (until at least the early nineteenth century). This slight projection, and, of course, the absence of a cross-bar, usually makes it quite an easy matter to distinguish ſ from *f*. Figure 5 includes a number of clear illustrations of ſ (5:8 *ſeil, granſ, mauſ*), including ſ and *f* juxtaposed (5:11 *meſfait*, 13 *meſfait*, 16 *ſouſfrir*). In this last example, it will be noted that the first ſ has a clear serif to the left of the down-stroke, but that such a projection is clearly missing from the second ſ. The precise form of ſ may vary in other ways: those of Figure 8 do not generally have a serif or foot at the base (8:1 *miſignoze*, 2 *ſole*, etc.), whereas those of Figure 4 have quite a long tail, extending well below the base line (4:1 *corſ*, 2 *ſiuſ*, etc.). The ſ of Figure 4 does not usually have a visible projection to the left of the down-stroke. The second stroke or head of the ſ is sometimes rather elongated into a stroke resembling a tilde, particularly in final position as in 5:3 *(miſ)* and 5:7 *(apreſ)*. The head of the ſ frequently touches a following tall letter, particularly *t*, in which case *ſt* regularly takes the form of a ligature (1:7 *uoſtra;* 5:1 *moſtr^s*, 2 *ceſte*, etc.), but also *f* (5:11 *meſfait*, 16 *ſouffrir*) and a second ſ (1:9 *cæſſir;* 5:3 *aſſens;* 7:1 *liſſos*). Long *s* is only a minuscule form; see the end of this section for examples of S.

In the manuscripts illustrated, and in others of the same type, ſ is far more prevalent than *s*. In Figures 1-8 there are something over two hundred occurrences of some form of the letter *s*, only thirty-five of which are the short *s*. The rules for distribution of the two letter-forms are generaly quite regular. Briefly stated, minuscule *s* is used only in final position, never initially or medially. Some manuscripts, of course, do not use *s* at all, and so even in final position one finds ʃ. This is the case of our Figures 2, 4, 6, and 8.

Minuscule *s*, derived from capital S, seems to have been formed in three parts, the middle part of the letter first and then the top and bottom (1:1 *cozs*, 3 *uos*; 5:2 ʃ*ens*, 3 *a*ʃʃ*ens*, etc.). The *s* of Figure 7 is a less compact form, composed of an oblique down-stroke ending in a long thin "tail", and a very short top (7:1 *uers*, 2 *als*, etc.). Another type of *s*, not illustrated by our Figures, occurs in some manuscripts: it is similar in form to that of Figure 7, but is positioned above the base line, so that the tail descends only to about the level of the top of such letters as *e, o*, and *u*. Examples of S: 5:5, 7, 13, 17; 6:1.

t

Minuscule *t* has, for the most part, evolved rather little in form from Gothic writing to present-day printing. The letter was regularly formed in two strokes, a down-stroke ending in a foot to the right, on the level of the base line, and a horizontal cross-bar (1:2 *gent*, 5 *tozn*; 5:1 *orendroit*; 8:1 *tucte, tue*). Generally the cross-bar is very near the top of the down-stroke, and extends very little to the left of it; the cross-bar is at the level of the tops of such short letters as *a, e, o*, and *u*, and frequently serves as a connecting stroke, linking *t* to the following letter (6:1 *caitiu*, 7 *ten*; 2:4 *tozn*; 8:1 *tucte*). As mentioned in the preceding article, *t* is regularly joined to a preceding ʃ. A ligature between *t* and a following *z* (usually in final position) is also quite a regular phenomenon (3:2 ʃ*olatz*, 4 *intratz*; 4:3 *intratz*; 7:2 *ditz*), although the manuscript of Figure 1 does not make this ligature (1:7 *intratz*). The foot of the *t* may be more or less developed; the manuscript of Figure 4 again constitutes an exceptional case, for the down-stroke is recurved and prolonged to rejoin the cross-bar (4:1 *e*ʃ*tan*, ʃ*emblant, gent*). The cross-bar generally tends to be longer when *t* occurs in final position (5:7 *entrait*,

11 *auienent,* 12 *fait,* etc.); this is particularly true of the manuscript of Figure 4 (4:3 *tant*). No examples of *T* occur in the Figures.

u *and* v

In the manuscripts under examination, and in others of the same general type, *u* is the prevalent form, and a distinct form of *v* is rather rare. The precise sound value to give to the letter *u* in these manuscripts must thus depend on what is known of the subsequent development of each word in which it occurs. As was mentioned earlier, confusion between *u* and *n* (and between *m* and the combinations *in, ni, iu, ui,* etc.) is highly likely in certain manuscripts; in others, the distinction is clearly made, the minims being joined at the top for *n* (and *m*), and at the bottom for *u*. Examples of *u*: 1:3 *uos,* 4 *chauzir;* 3:3 *uo/, ueya;* 5:4 *pourcacier;* 6:1 *caitiu;* 7:1 *uers;* 8:1 *tucte, tue.* (For further discussion of *i, m, n,* and *u,* and the problem of confusion in reading them, see the section on that subject following the discussion of abbreviations.) No examples of *U* appear in the Figures.

As distinct from *u, v* simply does not occur in many manuscripts. Of those illustrated in our Figures, the clearest examples may be seen in Figure 5 (5:1 v^9 *voel,* 9 *aventure*). The letter is composed of two strokes, the left side usually begining clearly above the top of the small letters *(a, e, o,* etc.) and being somewhat curved, the right side consisting of a single clockwise stroke, rather sharply curved, so that it is frequently fused with a counter-clockwise curved stroke in the next letter (as in 5:1 *voel*). This does not always occur, however: the two curves of *v* and *e* in *aventure* (5:9) are kept clearly separate. Another use of *v* is as a numeral, replacing the word *cinc, cinq,* etc., an example of which may be seen in 7:4. Note the presence of the dot on either side of the letter. This seems to have been standard usage to indicate that a letter was being used as a numeral (cf. 5:3 ·*j*· and the discussion under *j; x, l,* and *c* as numerals can be found in other manuscripts). Example of *V:* 6:17 (note the use of *u* for *v* in two other words in the same line, *uaiten uer/*).

w

Like *k*, *w* does not occur in most Romance-language manuscripts of the type under discussion; there are no examples of either *w* or *W* in the accompanying Figures. See Appendix I.

x

Only two examples of *x* appear in the Figures (6:2 *ricx;* 7:7 *caix*);[15] the letter occurs rather infrequently, and primarily in Old Provençal. It is sometimes replaced by *cs*. The letter is formed of two diagonal strokes, the one from upper left to lower right usually considerably broader than the other, and also shorter; the upper-right-to-lower-left stroke is generally rather fine, and frequently extends clearly below the base line, as can be seen in 6:2. It would seem unusual to find examples of *X*. None occur in the figures, but two which have come to the author's attention may be mentioned as a curiosity. They appear in the "table" of *Chansonnier provençal C* (the manuscript from which Figure 1 is taken), in the titles of two poems by Guiraut Riquer de Narbona, "Xpiſtias uey perilhar" and "Xpiſtian ſon per ihezuchriſt nomnat",[16] where the letters *Xp* have the value of the Greek letters χρ, usually transliterated by *Chr*.[17]

y

The use of *y* varies considerably from one manuscript to another, in that it is not always used as a letter distinct from *i*. It does not occur in our Figures 2, 5, 6, and 8. The form of the letter varies rather little, for the most part, among the manu-

---

[15] This latter example is unfortunately unclear, apparently because of a blot in the manuscript.

[16] The titles appear on fols. 12ᵛ and 13ʳ, respectively; the texts appear on fols. 298ᵛb-299ʳa and 307ʳa-b, respectively. In the latter poem, the form *Xpiſtz* also occurs.

[17] Etymologically related forms using *xp* also occur numerous times in the Oxford manuscript of the *Chanson de Roland*: *xpienſ* (= *chrestiens*), *xpiene* (= *chrestiene*), *xpientet* (= *chrestientet*), etc. (*La Chanson de Roland: Reproduction phototypique du manuscrit ... d'Oxford*, éditée ... par le Comte Alexandre de Laborde [Paris, 1932 and 1933].) See for example fols. 1ᵛ (line 38 of the poem), 2ʳ (line 85), 2ᵛ (line 102), 8ᵛ (line 431), etc.

scripts which do use it, however. A fairly standard form of minuscule *y* may be seen in Figure 1 (1:4 *uey*, 6 *ʃuy*). The letter consists of an oblique stroke running at a slight angle from the vertical, from upper left to lower right, and a second, curved stroke, beginning nearly parallel to the first, then curving to cross the first stroke at its foot, and terminating in a slender tail extending well below the base line. The general angularity of the letter may vary: in Figure 7 the second stroke is formed in two parts, a short, broad stroke and then a long slender one forming the tail of the letter (7:4 *lay*, 6 *Frayzes*). The letter *y* in Figure 4 has a long, recurving tail, and is marked with the same sort of line as is used above the letter *i* (4:2 *uey*, 4 *yʃʃir*). In Figure 3 the tail of the *y* is not visible, although this may be the fault of the microfilm photography (3:2 *iay*, 3 *ueya*). No examples of Y occur in the Figures.

z

This is a relatively uncommon letter, found chiefly in Provençal texts (it does not appear in our Figures 5 and 8), and there most often in the verbal ending *tz*. As mentioned in the discussion of *t*, the two letters are usually linked in this case, the cross-bar of the *t* extending to form the top of the *z* (3:2 *ʃolatz*, 4 *intratz*; 7:2 *ditz*). A few examples may be seen of *z* in a non-final position: *chauzir* in Figures 1-4 (1:4; 2:3; 3:3; 4:2) and *razos* (7:3); there are also a few cases of final *z* without *t* (6:5 *filz*, 14 *toz*, 16 *fez*). The basic form of the letter is something resembling the numeral 3, with, in many cases, a straight top (either horizontal or sloping downward to the right), a second straight line sloping downward to the left, and a third, clockwise curving segment forming the tail, descending below the base line. This is the form found in Figures 1, 2, 6, and 7, while that of Figures 3 and 4 is more curvilinear, particularly when *z* is not joined to a preceding *t*. In Figures 4 and 6, the line downward to the left from the right-hand end of the top of the letter extends well beyond the upper end of the third ("tail") stroke. No examples of Z occur in the Figures, since *z* occurs only rarely in initial position.

ABBREVIATIONS AND OTHER SIGNS

As in the case of individual letter-forms, an immense variation occurs from one manuscript to another — and, less commonly, within a single manuscript — in both form and use of abbreviations. Even within one manuscript, a given word will sometimes be abbreviated and at other times spelled out in full, without there being any immediately discernible reason for the variation. A number of the most common abbreviations are illustrated in the accompanying Figures, and we shall limit our discussion to these. Other forms encountered can frequently be deduced from context; otherwise one may have recourse to the dictionaries of abbreviations and other works listed in the bibliography.

Probably the most widespread abbreviation is the more or less horizontal line or bar above (or slightly off-center to the right of) a vowel, or, less frequently, another letter, indicating an omitted m or n (3:3 $n\bar{o}$, $m\bar{e}$, $to\bar{z}$, $m\bar{e}$, etc.). A similar bar over the letter q usually indicates the omitted letters ue (7:2 $\bar{q}n$, 7 $\bar{q}$, 8 $\bar{q}l$). The use of this type of bar is more complex in Figure 8, where we find /petialm̄te = spetialmENte (l. 2),[18] ff̃e =frATe (11. 2, 8, 12), /ignificatōe = significatIONe (l. 5), p̄tio/e = pREtiose (l. 7; cf. p̄tio/a, l. 11), /u/tentam̄to = sustentamENto (l. 10), nr̄a = nosTra (l. 15) and tr̃a = tERra (l. 15; cf. t'ra = tERra in 7:8).

As was mentioned in discussing p and q, these letters frequently serve as the basis for abbreviations. Among those involving p, the commonest is probably ℘, a p with a cross-bar through the down-stroke, below the base line, the abbreviation for pER, pAR, or pOR, depending on the language of the manuscript (4:4; 5:10, 11; 7:3, 8; 8:3, 6, 8, 9, 10, 12, 14). This extra stroke may be more than a simple horizontal bar, as in the somewhat exaggerated case of 5:11. A horizontal bar above the p may indicate pRE, as in 8:7 and 8:11 (pREtiose, pREtiosa). Similarly, ⁻p usually represents pRO.

In addition to $\bar{q}$ = qUE, already mentioned, one frequently finds q^i = qUI (1:7; 5:17; 7:1, 9) and, with a capital letter as

---

[18] $\bar{m}$ = mEN in adverbial endings also occurs in 5:16 and 5:17.

well, Q^i (5:11, 16). A less common abbreviation is q followed by a figure rather like a *3*, meaning qᴜᴇ, as in 3:4. The manuscript used for Figure 3 uses both *q3* and $\bar{q}$ for *que*. The various abbreviations based on q frequently involve more than one word; thus $\bar{q}n$ (7:2) = qᴜᴇ·ɴ and $\bar{q}l$ = qᴜᴇ·l (7:8; abbreviations as expanded in Martín de Riquer's edition of the text illustrated), and $q^i eu$ (1:7-8) = qᴜ'ɪeu.

Superior letters. One sometimes finds letters placed above the normal line of writing, looking as though they had been added as an afterthought. These superior letters are frequently smaller than the corresponding forms used in the normal position. They also take a different form, sometimes unrecognizable as the same letter, and in many cases they indicate the omission of some other letter or letters in addition to the superior letter. Thus, *a* above Qnt (5:3) = Qᴜᴀnt; *o* stands for omitted *ro* in 5:10 and 5:14 (dʀoit, dʀoiture) and for *no* in 8:7 (misigɴore). The superior *i* used with q, mentioned earlier, really belongs under this heading, since an omitted *u* is implied. In 5:15 a superior *i* indicates the omission of *ri:* pʀɪsier. An example of a superior letter whose form no longer resembles the original letter is found in 3:4 and 5:1, where the final *er* is indicated by a superior letter more reminiscent of *s*, being merely an angular zig-zag line. Other such cases are the curved stroke resembling a backward *c* above the line in 7:6, which Martín de Riquer expands as tᴜʀmen, and the short line atop the *t* of *mlt́* in 5:15: which could be expanded either to *mult* or *molt*.

Non-alphabetical abbreviations. The most common of these is undoubtedly the symbol for "and" *(et* or *e,* depending on the language of the manuscript). This symbol generally resembles an Arabic 7, as in Figures 6 and 8 (6:2, 3, etc.; 8:3, 7, etc.). The oblique down-stroke may be somewhat curved, bringing the foot around to the right. In Figure 5 this symbol has a fully developed base, and a horizontal cross-bar is added through the oblique stroke (5:4). This manuscript also presents the rather unusual use of a "majuscule" form of this symbol (5:8, 15), drawn larger and a bit more elaborately, and set apart from the following minuscule letters, just as is done with the capital letters in the other lines. The only other clear example, in our Figures, of a non-alphabetical sign occurs in 5:1, a symbol resembling a somewhat angular Arabic 9 placed a little above the line. This abbreviation is normally expanded as *us* or *os*, depending on the language of the manuscript (thus v^9 = *v*os), and one frequently finds it in pl^9 = *pl*us. Virtually the same symbol, placed lower with the loop of the 9 resting on the base line, stands for *con, com, cun,* or *cum* (again, depending on the language of the manuscript), as in *9me* = con*me*.

Punctuation. There is generally very little punctuation of any sort in the manuscripts of the type under discussion. Most commonly one finds a sort of square dot, formed with a single short broad stroke, separating successive poetic lines (or, in prose, clauses or sentences). This use is fairly regular in the manuscript of Figure 1, and somewhat less so in the other manuscripts in which poetry is arranged in run-on lines (a horizontal dash is used for this purpose in Figure 4; both dot and dash are used in several places in Figure 8). When the poetic lines are separated, as in Figures 5 and 6, the need for such markers is less — although the scribe of the manuscript of Figure 6 placed a dot at the end of every line. A rather unusual usage is found in 6:3, where a fine oblique line, sloping upward to the right, has been placed after each of the first three words. These are elements in a series, and the oblique lines thus serve the same purpose as commas in present-day usage. Something similar occurs in 8:10, where a short oblique stroke is used to separate two clauses. When a word is split between two lines, the first part of it being at the right-hand margin, a fine oblique line, sloping upward to the right, may sometimes be seen. These lines, performing the function of hyphens in later usage, are frequently so light that they are not visible on microfilm photographs.

PROBLEMS INVOLVING *i, m, n,* AND *u*

In the discussion of these letters, we have mentioned the problem which frequently arises in distinguishing *n* from *u, in* or *iu* from *m,* etc. A few examples, with comments, taken from each of the Figures, should shed further light on the methods used by the medieval scribes in distinguishing these letters, and on the problems they present for the paleographer.[19]

Figure 1. The scribe of this manuscript was quite careful to make *n* and *u* differently (1:4 *uey, no,* 7 *en uo/tra*), and a fine line is often used to distinguish *i* from the other letters composed of minims (1:5 */im* [twice]). Confusion is possible, however, in */ius* (1:4) and *ni* (1:6) - the latter could easily be read as *iu* — but *mi* (1:6) is less ambiguous.

Figure 2. Minim-letters are not very well distinguished in this manuscript. In *acuillir* (2:2) the minims of *u* and *i* look like three identical, equally-spaced vertical strokes, and the same is true of */ius* (2:3). The distinction is a bit clearer in */im* and *ni* (2:4), but in general a good deal of conjecture — based, of course, on context — is needed in dealing with this manuscript (cf. *intratz* and *enuo/tram,* 2:5).

Figure 3. The same may be said of this manuscript, although the style is somewhat different from that of Figure 2. Such sequences of minims as one finds in *mielhs* (3:3), *ni, mi,* and *intratz* (3:4) are not really very clearly distinguished.

---

[19] An amusing example of these problems is related by B. L. Ullman in *Ancient Writing and Its Influence* (1932; rpt. Cambridge, Mass., 1969), pp. 132-133: "At its best Gothic is beautiful but hard to read; at its worst it is extremely ugly and illegible. In the various types letter confusions of various sorts developed. Most notable was the confusion brought about by the angularity of *i, u, m, n*. Strokes and dots for *i,* hooks for *u* helped to remedy this defect. How well this weakness was realized is indicated by an anecdote composed in the thirteenth or fourteenth century for the purpose of illustrating the difficulties of the script. The story tells of a letter sent to the senate at Rome by actors of small stature expressing their unwillingness to give up their function of distributing to the actors the wine obtained from certain vineyards near the walls:

> mimi numinum niuium minimi munium nimium uini muniminum imminui uiui minimum uolunt.

'The very short mimes of the gods of snow do not at all wish that during their lifetime the very great burden [*munium* is *neuter singular*] of (distributing) the wine of the walls to be lightened.' When this is written in Gothic characters without dots for the *i*'s and with *v* written as *u,* it makes a first-class riddle."

Figure 4. We have often had occasion to note the unusual writing style of this manuscript, generally much more cursive than the angular writing found in the other manuscripts illustrated. The letters *m, n,* and *u* all seem to have been made with a single zig-zag stroke, but there is a slight difference between *n* and *u:* compare these letters in *uan, nō, ſen, qui,* and *tant* (4:3). The letter *i* is clearly distinct because of the "slash" line regularly placed above it, as in *ni, qui, mi,* and *intratz* (4:3).

Figure 5. This manuscript is, for the most part, carefully lettered, and there are rather few cases of confusion between one and another of the minim-letters. A "slash" above *i* is visible in most cases (5:5 *pecier,* 7 *entrait),* but even when it is not (5:6 *point)* there is little problem. *N* and *u* are generally quite distinct, as in *granſ mauſ enendure* (5:8), but in other combinations such as *conme* (5:5) or *ſouſfrir* and *boinem̃t* (5:16), they are somewhat less so. The present author found only one really puzzling reading in this portion of the manuscript: the last word in line 17, which seems to be *aſauuem̃t,* but which may in fact be something else.

Figure 6. Adjacent minim-letters are very clearly separated in this manuscript, so that there is virtually no confusion among the letters in question. See *enemic* (6:1), *amic* (6:2), *colunba* (6:6), *ſaint* (6:15), and the rhyme-words in *-iu* in lines 1, 7, 10, 11 and 17.

Figure 7. Generally the minim-letters are quite distinct, with the minims clearly joined at the top for *m* and *n* and at the bottom for *u: uers, començа, comte, gença* (7:1). Even when they occur in combination there is little doubt as to which letters are used: *humils* (7:2), *guiatz* (7:7).

Figure 8. The minim-letters are generally quite clear in this manuscript, as in the combination *mi* in the numerous instances of *misignore* (8:1, 5, etc.). Elsewere, *n* is clearly closed at the top, and *u* is closed at the bottom. Compare the two letters in *ſuſten* (8:9). Even such long series of minims as occur in *allumini* (8:3) and *ennallumini* (8:13) can be deciphered with a minimum of difficulty, despite the absence of distinguishing "slashes" over the letter *i.*

APPENDIX 1

w

Three works containing photocopies of manuscripts in which *w* is used have come to the author's attention; the inquisitive reader may wish to seek them out. They are *La Chancun de Willame*, edited by George Dunn (London, 1903),[20] *La Vie d'Edouard le Confesseur*, edited by Östen Södergård (Uppsala, 1948),[21] and the facsimile edition of the Oxford manuscript of the *Chanson de Roland* (Bodleian, Digby 23), published by Alexandre de Laborde (Paris, 1932 and 1933).[22] All of these works are in the Anglo-Norman dialect; it seems that the letter *w* was more generally used by Anglo-Norman scribes than by those working in other Romance-language areas. In the first of the works cited (the illustration, from a 13th-century manuscript, faces lines 1-25 of the text), examples occur of both *w* (in *Lowis*, col. a, line 6) and *W* (*Willame*, col. a, lines 7 and 15; col. b, lines 17, 23 and 25). In all six cases, the letter is made in the same way, rather like two *v*'s interlocked. The left side of each is a broad downward stroke, slanting from upper-left to lower-right, and rather straighter than the left side of the letter *v* as it occurs in our Figure 5 (and considerably straighter than that of the initial *V* in *Viuien* in the same illustration — col. a, line 12; col. b, lines 10 and 12 — or of *v*, as in *nevov*, col. a, line 12). The second

---

[20] George Dunn's name does not appear in this edition; cf. *La Chançun de Willame*, ed. Nancy V. Iseley (Chapel Hill, 1961), p. ix. For further details concerning the manuscript, see pp. xiii-xiv of the Iseley edition; the use of *w* is discussed briefly on p. xxi.

[21] For details concerning the manuscripts illustrated, see pp. 46-48 of Södergård's edition.

[22] For further details concerning the manuscript, see Charles Samaran's "Etude paléographique du manuscrit d'Öxford," pp. 9-58 of Laborde's facsimile edition.

downward stroke is parallel to and somewhat longer than the first, and in most cases the two are linked by a common serif at the top. Each of the two *v*'s that make up the *w* or *W* is then completed by a clockwise stroke, rather angular in shape; the first of these seems to cut through the rightmost of the two broad downward strokes, so that the end result looks something like this: ᛰ. The illustrations in *La Vie d'Edouard le Confesseur* (following page viii) are from two manuscripts, one from the early 14th century and the other from the 12th or 13th, and present slight variations on the letters described above. The first of these contains the name *edward* twice (col. a, line 18; col. b, line 13), and here the *w* seems to have been made in three strokes, the first two much like slightly slanted minims and the third a simple curved clockwise stroke, like that forming the right-hand side of the letter *o* or *v* as described earlier. The illustration from the second manuscript contains the name *Westmustier* (col. a, line 37), in which the *W* is basically like those found in the manuscript of the *Willame*, as described above. (This illustration also contains the king's name twice, but it is spelled *eduuard* each time, using two "standard" Gothic *u*'s in succession — col. a, line 17; col. b, line 20.) The letter *w* occurs in a number of places in the 12th-century manuscript of the *Chanson de Roland*, in such words as *ewe(s)*, *wigres*, and in the proper name *Willalme*. In all the cases examined by the author, the letter has basically the same form as is found in the manuscript of the *Willame*, the main difference being that the left side of each *v* is much more curved, even to the point of resembling an elongated *S*. (See for example fol. 33^v, line 1831 of the poem.) In his paleographical study of the manuscript, Charles Samaran lists "les traits essentiels par lesquels l'écriture du *Roland* s'apparente à celle des autres manuscrits anglo-normands du xiie siècle", including "[le] développement parfois exagéré des *a*, des *w* et des *z*" (pp. 19-20).

BIBLIOGRAPHY

I do not claim that the following bibliography is exhaustive; the bibliographies of some of the works listed, such as those by Johnson-Jenkinson and Prou, list many additional titles. Besides the works referred to in the body of this article, there are a number of others of potential value for the paleographer — novice or experienced — and a list of facsimile editions of manuscripts. Numerous works on Latin paleography contain useful information for the paleographer working with medieval Romance texts, and are consequently included. It must be said that the two dictionaries of abbreviations (Cappelli, Chassant) are only infrequently helpful for work involving manuscripts of the type we have been concerned with here, although each presents a large variety of generally useful illustrations of each letter-form at the head of the section of abbreviations beginning with that letter. Works reproducing, either in whole or in part, single manuscripts, are listed under the heading "Facsimile Editions." Many of the works listed in the first section, below, contain facsimiles taken from a wide variety of manuscripts.

GENERAL WORKS AND COLLECTIONS OF FACSIMILES

Anderson, Donald M. *The Art of Written Forms: The Theory and Practice of Calligraphy*. New York: Holt, Rinehart and Winston, 1969.
Archivio paleografico italiano. Roma: Pompeo Sansaini [etc.], 1882-to date.
Bassi, Stelio. *Monumenta Italiæ Graphica*. Cremona: Società Editoriale "Cremona Nuova," 1956-1957.
Bibliothèque de l'Ecole des Chartes. Paris: Impr. de Decourchant [imprint varies on later volumes], 1839/40-to date.
Blunt, Wilfrid. *Sweet Roman Hand: Five Hundred Years of Italic Cursive Script*. London: James Barrie, 1952.
Boyle, Leonard E. "The Emergence of Gothic Handwriting." *Journal of Typographic Research*, 4 (1970), 307-316.
Cappelli, Adriano. *Dizionario di abbreviature latine ed italiane....* 6th ed. Milano: Ulrico Hoepli, 1960.
Carroll, Carleton W. "A Critical Edition of the Poems of Berenguier de Palazol, Troubadour of Roussillon." Diss. Wisconsin, 1968.
Cerverí de Girona. *Obras completas del trovador Cerverí de Girona*, ed. Martín de Riquer. Barcelona: Instituto Español de Estudios Mediterráneos, 1947.

Chancun de Willame, La, ed. George Dunn (without his name). Two hundred copies in limited edition. London: Chiswick Press, 1903.

Chançun de Willame, La, ed. Nancy V. Iseley, with an etymological glossary by Guérard Piffard. Chapel Hill: University of North Carolina Press, 1961. (Studies in the Romance Languages and Literatures, No. 35.)

Chassant, L.-Alph. [= Alphonse Antoine Louis]. *Dictionnaire des abréviations latines et françaises....* 4th ed. Paris: Auguste Aubry, 1876.

———. *Paléographie des chartes et des manuscrits du XIe au XVIIe siècle.* 8th ed. Paris: Auguste Aubry, 1885.

Clark, Albert Curtis. *The Descent of Manuscripts.* Oxford: The Clarendon Press, 1918.

Colloque International de Paléographie Latine (Paris, 28-30 avril 1953). *Nomenclature des écritures livresques du IXe au XVIe siècle.* Paris: Centre National de la Recherche Scientifique, 1954.

Delisle, Léopold Victor. *Album paléographique[,] ou recueil de documents importants relatifs à l'histoire et à la littérature nationales....* Paris: Maison Quantin, 1887.

Denholm-Young, Noël. *Handwriting in England and Wales.* Cardiff: University of Wales Press, 1954.

Ecole des Chartes (Paris). *Recueil de fac-similés à l'usage de l'Ecole des Chartes.* Paris: Alphonse Picard, 1880.

Fairbank, Alfred. *A Book of Scripts.* Revised and enlarged edition. Baltimore: Penguin Books, 1968.

——— and Berthold Wolpe. *Renaissance Handwriting: an Anthology of Italic Scripts.* London: Faber and Faber, 1960.

Jeanroy, Alfred. *Bibliographie sommaire des chansonniers français du moyen âge (manuscrits et éditions).* Paris: Honoré Champion, 1918. (Classiques Français du Moyen Age, No. 18.)

———. *Bibliographie sommaire des chansonniers provençaux (manuscrits et éditions).* Paris: Honoré Champion, 1916; rpt. 1966. (Classiques Français du Moyen Age, No. 16.)

Johnson, Charles, and Hilary Jenkinson. *English Court Hand A.D. 1066 to 1500....* Oxford: Oxford University Press, 1915; rpt. New York: Frederick Ungar, 1967.

Kirchner, Joachim. *Scriptura gothica libraria....* Monachii et Vindobonae: Rudolf Oldenbourg, 1966.

———. *Scriptura latina libraria....* Monachii: Rudolf Oldenbourg, 1955.

Leroquais, Abbé V. *Les Bréviaires manuscrits des bibliothèques publiques de France.* Paris, 1934.

———. *Les Pontificaux manuscrits des bibliothèques publiques de France.* Paris, 1937.

López de Toro, José. *Abreviaturas hispánicas.* Madrid, 1957.

Lowe, Elias Avery. "Handwriting." *The Legacy of the Middle Ages*, ed. C. G. Crump and E. F. Jacob, pages 197-226. Oxford: The Clarendon Press, 1926.

———. *Palaeographical Papers, 1907-1965*, ed. Ludwig Bieler. 2 vols. Oxford: The Clarendon Press, 1972.

Mazzatinti, Giuseppe, et al. *Inventari dei manoscritti delle biblioteche d'Italia.* 88 vols. Forlì: Luigi Bordandini [imprint varies on later volumes], 1892-1972.

Monaci, Ernesto. *Esempi di scrittura latina dal sec. I di Cristo al XVIII*.... Roma: B. Lux, 1898.

———. *Fac-simili di antichi manoscritti per uso delle scuole di filologia neolatina*. Roma: Martelli Tipografo, 1881-1887.

———. *Facsimili di documenti per la storia delle lingue e delle letterature romanze*. Roma: Domenico Anderson, 1910.

Osley, A. S., ed. *Calligraphy and Palaeography: Essays Presented to Alfred Fairbank on His 70th Birthday*. London: Faber and Faber, 1965; New York: October House, 1966.

Peire Vidal. *Les Poésies de Peire Vidal*, ed. Joseph Anglade. 2nd ed. Paris: Honoré Champion, 1923; rpt. 1965. (Classiques Français du Moyen Age, No. 11.)

Pelzer, Auguste. *Abréviations latines médiévales[:] Supplément au Dizionario di abbreviature latine ed italiane[,] de Adriano Cappelli*. 2nd ed. Louvain: Publications Universitaires; Paris: Béatrice-Nauwelaerts, 1966.

Pillet, Alfred, and Henry Carstens. *Bibliographie der Troubadours*. Halle: Max Niemeyer, 1933.

Prou, Maurice. *Manuel de paléographie latine et française du VI° au XVII° siècle*.... 2nd ed. Paris: Alphonse Picard, 1892.

———. *Manuel de paléographie latine et française*. 4th ed. Paris: Auguste Picard, 1924.

———. *Manuel de paléographie[:] Recueil de fac-similés d'écritures du V° au XVII° siècle (manuscrits latins, français et provençaux)*.... Paris: Alphonse Picard, 1904.

———. *Nouveau Recueil de fac-similés d'écritures du XII° au XVII° siècle (manuscrits latins et français)*.... Paris: Alphonse Picard, 1896.

Reynolds, Leighton Durham, and Nigel Guy Wilson. *Scribes and Scholars: A Guide to the Transmission of Greek and Latin Literature*. London: Oxford University Press, 1968.

Romanò, Angelo. *Il Codice degli Abbozzi (Vat. Lat. 3196) di Francesco Petrarca*. Roma: Giovanni Bardi, 1955.

Schiaparelli, Luigi. *Avviamento allo studio delle abbreviature latine nel medioevo*. Firenze: Leo S. Olschki, 1926.

Scriptorium, revue internationale des études relatives aux manuscrits; international review of manuscript studies. Anvers: Standaard Boekhandel; Bruxelles: Editions Erasme [imprint varies on later volumes], 1946/47- to date.

Steffens, Franz. *Lateinische Paläographie*. 2nd ed. Berlin und Leipzig: Walter de Gruyter, 1929; rpt. 1964.

Thomson, Samuel Harrison. *Latin Bookhands of the Later Middle Ages, 1100-1500*. Cambridge: Cambridge University Press, 1969.

Ullman, Berthold Louis. *Ancient Writing and its Influence*. New York: Longmans, Green & Co., 1932; rpt. New York: Cooper Square Publishers, 1963; rpt. Cambridge, Mass.: M.I.T. Press, 1969.

Vie d'Edouard le Confesseur, La, ed. Östen Södergård. Uppsala: Almqvist & Wiksells Boktryckeri AB, 1948.

FACSIMILE EDITIONS

Altona (Hamburg), Christianeum, Bibliothek. *Dante's Divina Commedia, Codex Altonensis.* 2 vols. Hrsg. Hans Haupt (et al.). Berlin: Gebr. Mann Verlag, 1965.
Annonay: see Serrières-sur-Rhone (Ardèche).
Arras, Bibliothèque Municipale, Ms. 657, formerly 139 (chansonnier français A). *Le Chansonnier d'Arras,* reproduction en phototypie; introduction par Alfred Jeanroy. Paris: Société des Anciens Textes Français, 1925.
El Escorial. Biblioteca del Monasterio de San Lorenzo, cód. h-I-15. *Lapidario del Rey D. Alfonso X,* códice original. [Prólogo de José Fernández-Montaña, reproducción fotocromolitográfica de Antonio Selfa. Informe a la Academia de la Historia por los Académicos de número A. Fernández-Guerra y P. de Madrazo.] Madrid: [Impr. de la Iberia, á cargo de J. Blasco], 1881.
El Escorial, Real Biblioteca, cód. j.T.6 fol. *Das spanische Schachzabelbuch des Königs Alfons des Weisen vom Jahre 1283,* ... vollständige Nachbildung der Handschrift in 194 Lichtdrucktafeln / *El Tratado de ajedrez ordenado por mandado del Rey D. Alonso el Sabio, en el año 1283,* ... reproducción completa en 194 láminas fototípicas. [Introduction by John G. White.] Leipzig: Karl W. Hiersemann, 1913.
Hamburg: see Altona.
Milan, Biblioteca Trivulziana, Cod. 1080. *Il Codice Trivulziano 1080 della Divina Commedia* riprodotto ... sotto gli auspici della sezione milanese della Società Dantesca Italiana ... con cenni storici e descrittivi di Luigi Rocca. Milano: Ulrico Hoepli, 1921.
Oxford, Bodleian Library, Ms. Digby 23. *La Chanson de Roland,* reproduction phototypique..., éditée... par le Comte Alexandre de Laborde...; étude paléographique de M. Charles Samaran. Paris: présentée aux membres du Roxburghe Club de Londres, 1932 (limited edition, 120 copies); Paris: Société des Anciens Textes Français, 1933.
Paris, Bibliothèque de l'Arsenal, Ms. 5198 (chansonnier français K). *Le Chansonnier de l'Arsenal (trouvères du XIIe-XIIIe siècle),* .... transcription du texte musical ... par Pierre Aubry, introduction et notices par Alfred Jeanroy. Paris: Paul Geuthner, 1909-1914[?]. [The copy examined (in 4 vols.) contained only 64 pages of transcription, covering the first 184 pages (out of 384) of the Ms. It is not known whether the transcription of the remainder of the Ms. was ever published.]
Paris, Bibliothèque Nationale, Ms. esp. nº 37. *Cancionero de Baena,* reproduced in facsimile from the unique manuscript in the Bibliothèque Nationale; forward by Henry R. Lang. New York: Hispanic Society of America, 1926; rpt. 1971.
Paris, Bibliothèque Nationale, Ms. fr. 403. *L'Apocalypse en français au XIIIe siècle,* reproduction phototypique, publiée par MM. L. Delisle et P. Meyer. 2 vols. Paris: Firmin-Didot, 1900-1901. (Société des Anciens Textes Français.)
Paris, Bibliothèque Nationale, Ms. fr. 837. *Fabliaux, dits et contes en vers du XIIIe siècle,* facsimilé ... publié sous les auspices de l'Institut de France (Fondation Debrousse) par Henri Omont.... Paris: E. Leroux, 1932.

Paris, Bibliothèque Nationale, Ms. fr. 844. *Le Manuscrit du roi*, reproduction phototypique..., analyse et description raisonnées du manuscrit restauré, par Jean Beck... et madame Louise Beck. 2 vols. Philadelphia: University of Pennsylvania Press, and London: Oxford University Press, 1938.

Paris, Bibliothèque Nationale, Ms. fr. 846. *Le Chansonnier Cangé*, reproduction phototypique..., description et tables, transcription des chansons, notes et commentaires par Jean Beck. 2 vols. Philadelphia: University of Pennsylvania Press, and Paris: H. Champion, 1927.

Paris, Bibliothèque Nationale, Ms. fr. 19093. *Villard de Honnecourt, kritische Gesamtausgabe des Bauhüttenbuches*..., [hrsg.] Hans R. Hahnloser. Wien: Anton Schroll, 1935. *The Sketchbook of Villard de Honnecourt*, ed. Theodore Bowie. Bloomington, Indiana, and London: Indiana University Press, undated [copyright 1959]. [Earlier editions: Lassus/Darcel (Paris, 1858; London, 1859); Omont (Paris, 1906; later editions 1926, 1931).]

Paris, Bibliothèque Nationale, Ms. fr. 20050 (chansonnier français U). *Le Chansonnier français de Saint-Germain-des-Prés*, reproduction phototypique avec transcription par P. Meyer et G. Raynaud. Paris: Firmin-Didot, 1892. (Société des Anciens Textes Français.) [The transcription mentioned in the subtitle was to constitute a second volume; it appears that it was never published.]

Serrières-sur-Rhône (Ardèche), fragments conservés dans les archives de Mᵉ Léon Boissonnet, notaire. Chrestien de Troyes, *Le Manuscrit d'Annonay*, édité par Albert Pauphilet. Paris: E. Droz, 1934.

Vatican City, Biblioteca Apostolica Vaticana, Cod. Barberiniano latino 4086. *Il Convivio di Dante Alighieri*, riprodotto in fototipia... per cura della Biblioteca Vaticana con introduzione di Federico [= Friedrich] Schneider. Città del Vaticano: Biblioteca Apostolica Vaticana, 1932.

Vatican City, Biblioteca Apostolina Vaticana, Cod. Vaticano Lat. 3196. *Il Codice Vaticano Lat. 3196 Autografo del Petrarca*, [con introduzione di Manfredi Porena]. Città del Vaticano: edizione speciale per la Biblioteca Apostolica Vaticana, 1941.

Vatican City, Biblioteca Apostolica Vaticana, Cod. Vaticano 4803. *Cancioneiro Português da Biblioteca Vaticana*, reprodução facsimilada. Lisboa: Centro de Estudos Filológicos, Instituto de Alta Cultura, 1973.

Venice, Biblioteca San Marco, francese IV, fol. 69^r-88^r. *Les Textes de la Chanson de Roland*, II: *La Version de Venise IV*, ed. Raoul Mortier; étude paléographique de Robert Barroux. Paris: Editions de la Geste Francor, 1941.

SECULAR MANUSCRIPT ILLUMINATION IN FRANCE

by M. Alison Stones

The flowering of French medieval literature may be said to begin around 1100 with the composition of the *Chanson de Roland*. This epic theme and those that emerge later in the century, whether classical, like the trilogy *Thèbes*, *Troie* and *Énéas*, or Arthurian like the *Tristan* of Thomas and Béroul or the works of Chrétien written in the third quarter of the century, constitute a core of material whose popularity continues throughout the Middle Ages, not only in France but in the rest of western Europe. By the thirteenth century the prose versions of these earlier verse texts continue an established tradition which is enriched with new themes both in verse and prose through the fourteenth and fifteenth centuries.

There is evidence from the twelfth century and before, that literary themes provided inspiration for artists.[1] The illumination

---

Abbreviations
B.L.   London, British Library
B.N.fr.   Paris, Bibliothèque Nationale, fonds français
B.N.lat.   Paris, Bibliothèque Nationale, fonds latin
B.Ars.   Paris, Bibliothèque de l'Arsenal
Vienna Ö.N.B.   Vienna, Österreichische Nationalbibliothek

[1] In western Europe one of the earliest examples is the Franks Casket (British Museum), late seventh century, which contains some scenes from norse mythology; one of the earliest Arthurian examples is the lintel of Modena cathedral north door, which contains scenes based on a text that is now lost. See R. S. and L. H. Loomis, *Arthurian Legends in Medieval Art*, New York, 1938, figs. 4-8. The lintel is to be dated in the early twelfth

of French literary manuscripts, however, does not begin until shortly before the middle of the thirteenth century, with the emergence of the lay craftsman. It flourishes between the thirteenth and sixteenth centuries, when illumination gives place on the one hand to panel painting, murals and tapestries, and on the other to the printed book with its mass-produced illustrations. The purpose of this essay is to present an outline of the main developments that take place during that period in terms of texts and patrons, in the layout and style of the miniatures and their relation to liturgical illumination, and the influence of French secular illustration on production elsewhere in Europe. *Literary fashion and secular illumination.*

The sequence of secular illumination in France, as elsewhere, is governed to a large extent by literary fashions. The MSS that survive are only a fraction of what the total output must originally have been, but they nevertheless give some idea of the relative popularity of the texts they contain. Some of these texts were popular only for a limited period of time, falling out of favour as new compositions took their place; others seem to have withstood changes in literary taste, remaining in demand from the time of their composition to the end of our period and beyond.

Among the latter are the *Roland* and the *Tristan* mentioned above, although in both cases it is the later variants on the earliest versions that were more widely read and illustrated, just as the prose *Lancelot*, composed in the early thirteenth century, has survived in far more MSS than have the texts of Chrétien. The prose *Tristan* and the prose *Lancelot* were two of the most popular texts of all, if one may judge on the basis of the numbers of MSS still extant. [2] They also contain two of the longest cycles of miniatures; the complete *Lancelot* cycle, including *Estoire, Merlin, Lancelot, Queste,* and *Mort Artu,* was often contained in a single volume of over 400 pages of large folio, with a cycle of over

---

century. Themes from *Roland* also appear in the twelfth century in sculpture, at Cremona cathedral, for example; see R. Lejeune and J. Stiennon, *La Légende de Roland dans l'art du moyen âge,* Brussels, 1966, and D. J. A. Ross, "The Iconography of Roland," *Medium Aevum,* 1968, pp. 46-65.

[2] The MSS of prose texts are listed in B. Woledge, *Bibliographie des romans et nouvelles en prose française antérieurs à 1500,* Geneva, 1954.

200 miniatures, and the *Tristan* cycle is almost as lengthy.[3] The *Alexander* romance, its various French versions deriving from the classical texts,[4] and the *Roman de la Rose* by Guillaume de Lorris and Jean de Meung,[5] were also most prolifically reproduced.

Little is known of the circumstances under which these works were composed, who were the original patrons of the poets, and indeed who the poets themselves were, for even when their names are known, there is little further information about their lives. Information is also lacking as to the original patrons of most of the extant MSS of these texts. Jean, Duke of Berry, owned a *Lancelot*, B.N.fr. 117-20, and a *Roman de la Rose*, B.N.fr. 380; both were made for him between about 1380 and 1400; they contain his name and appear in his inventories.[6] One may cite earlier cases of documentary evidence for the ownership of MSS, like the inventory of Jean d'Avesnes, count of Hainaut (d. 1304), at the head of which appears "uns grans roumans a rouges couvertures ki parolle de Nasciien, de Mellin et de Lancelot du Lach." Robert de Béthune, count of Flanders (d. 1322) also owned a *Lancelot*, which appears in his inventory, while among the books confiscated by Robert of Artois from Mahaut in 1316 there are three *Tristan* MSS. There is also evidence that ecclesiastics owned secular books; the will of Guillaume d'Avesnes, bishop of Cambrai (d. 1296) and brother of Jean d'Avesnes, count of Hainaut, requests that his "livre de gestes" be given to the monks of the monastery of Saint-Sépulchre, Cambrai, since one of them had had it made for him.[7] The wording of the will is not precise enough for one

---

[3] For example, the Bonn Lancelot, Bonn, University Library, MS 526, which contains all five branches of the cycle, is 477 pages long and contains over 230 miniatures, while the Vienna *Tristan*, Ö.N.B. 2542 has 500 ff. and 198 miniatures and historiated initials.

[4] See D. J. A. Ross, *Alexander Historiatus*, London, 1963.

[5] See E. Langlois, *Les Manuscrits du Roman de la Rose*, description et classement, Paris/Lille, 1910; A. Kuhn, *Die Illustration des Rosenromans*, Freiburg/Breisgau, 1911; J. V. Fleming, *The Roman de la Rose, A Study in Allegory and Iconography*, Princeton, 1969. The earliest MS of the *Roman de la Rose* is B.N.fr. 1559, c. 1300.

[6] M. Meiss, *French Painting in the Time of Jean de Berry*, vol. 1, *The Patronage of the Duke*, London/New York, 1967, pp. 312, 313.

[7] These documents and many more are published by C. Dehaisnes, *Documents et extraits divers concernant l'histoire de l'art dans la Flandre, l'Artois et le Hainaut avant le XVe siècle*, Lille, 1886. For further information

to tell whether the book had actually been made at the monastery, but it would seem unlikely as the available information indicates that at this date both scribes and illuminators were predominantly laymen. [8]

There is no proof that any of the MSS of Guillaume or Jean d'Avesnes, Robert de Béthune, or Robert or Mahaut of Artois are among those extant today. The library of Jean de Berry on the other hand is not only exceptional in itself, but also later in date, and consequently better preserved and better documented. Many of the most splendid secular MSS contain no precise clues that identify their original owner: such are the Harley *Rose* B.L.Harl. 4425 (c. 1500) [fig. 1], the Bodleian Alexander, Oxford, Bodleian, Bod. 264 (1338-44), and the Pierpont Morgan *Lancelot*, New York, Pierpont Morgan Library 805-6 (c. 1300-20) [fig. 2]. Where there are clues, they are often of doubtful interpretation. Shields of arms sometimes appear in the margins, but these may be later additions, [9] or purely decorative, disobeying fundamental rules of heraldry by employing metal on metal or colour on colour, [10] or they may simply be unidentifiable. [11]

---

on Mahaut of Artois see J. M. Richard, *Une petite-nièce de Saint-Louis, Mahaut, comtesse d'Artois et de Bourgogne*, Paris, 1887.

[8] There is more information on this for Paris than for the provinces. The main source of information is the tax rolls, which generally refer to the taxpayers by name and by profession. Scribes and illuminators are mentioned from the middle of the thirteenth century, see R. Branner, "Manuscript Makers in Mid-Thirteenth Century Paris," *Art Bulletin*, 1966. See also H. Géraud, *Paris sous Philippe le Bel, d'après des documents originaux, et notamment d'après un MS contenant le rôle de la taille imposée sur les habitants de Paris en 1292*, Paris, 1837; J.-A. Buchon, *Le Livre de la taille de Paris en l'an mil trois cent treize*, Paris, 1827; K. Michaelsson, *Le Livre de la taille de Paris*, Acta Universitatis Gothoburgensis, LXIV, 1958, 4; LXVII, 1961, 3.

There appear to be no documents for Cambrai itself.

[9] B.M.Roy.20.D.iv, *Lancelot*, was owned by Humphrey of Bohun, Duke of Gloucester, in the late fourteenth century. The book was made in Flanders c. 1310-20. Humphrey added his coat of arms and had some of the miniatures, including the opening one, overpainted. See M. Rickert, *Painting in Britain in the Middle Ages*, Harmondsworth, 1966, for Humphrey's library.

[10] B.M.Roy.14.E.iii, *Lancelot*, has on its opening page some arms that are later additions and others that have colour on colour.

[11] The basis for identifying shields used in this way is the contemporary rolls of arms, of which the most important for France are 'Wijnbergen',

The Yale *Lancelot,* Yale University Library 229, ex-Phillipps Collection 130, is one of the few major MSS whose owner may perhaps be traced on the basis of the heraldry. A marginal knight appears on the opening page of the *Queste* section of the text [fig. 3], with a horse whose housing contains the arms or a lion sable, a bend gules. The representation is small in scale, and inconspicuously placed on an inner page, but the arms are identifiable from Wijnbergen [12] as those of Guillaume de Termonde, second son of Gui de Dampierre, count of Flanders. Guillaume was born in 1248 or 49 and died in 1312; there is no precise date for the MS, but c. 1280-90 would seem reasonable on the basis of the style.

The documentary evidence for the books owned by the counts of Flanders is scant, and there is no inventory of the possessions of Guillaume. His name does come to mind again in connection with books of the second main category, those that enjoyed limited popularity and exist in only very few copies. Most of these MSS are presentation copies, intended for the patron who commissioned not only the manufacture of the MS but also the composition of the text itself. Guillaume's name is connected with MS B.N.fr. 15104, *La noble chevalerie du Judas Machabée et de ses nobles frères* [fig. 4]. The text was composed in 1285 for "mon seigneur Guillaume, de Flandre." [13] There are no arms or other marks of ownership on the MS, and there is no absolute proof that B.N.fr. 15104 is in fact the original MS, but the fact that this is the only MS containing this version of the text would support the suggestion. It is true that the style of the illumination is rather different from that of the Yale *Lancelot,* but a date of 1285 seems convincing for it, and there is no reason to suppose that Guillaume might not have acquired MSS from different sources, illuminated in different styles, just as Mahaut of Artois did in the early years of the fourteenth century. [14]

'Berry', 'Navarre', and 'Gelre'. The oldest is Wijnbergen, the date of which is between 1265 and 70. See P. Adam-Even and L. Jéquier, "L'Armorial Wijnbergen," *Archives Héraldiques Suisses,* 1951-4.

[12] *Ibid.,* p. 72, no. 1235.

[13] Edited by J. R. Smeets, Assen, 1955. The patron is mentioned in the text, lines 7944-65.

[14] She purchased books locally at Hesdin, also in Arras, and from two booksellers in Paris. See Dehaisnes and Richard, *op. cit.*

The relationship between the commissioning of a work of literature and the presentation manuscript are rather more explicit in Parisian products of the years around 1300. This was an important moment for activity under the patronage of the French royal court. The works of the poets Girart d'Amiens and Adenet le Roi figure large among the texts illustrated at the court workshops. It was probably for Marguerite, daughter of Philip IV and Marie de Brabant that Girart composed *Méliacen*. She is included in a royal portrait miniature on the opening page of the text of the earliest MS, B.N.fr. 1633, and she and the other figures may be identified on the basis of the heraldic garments they are wearing.[15] The MS can be dated between 1285, since Philip IV is included, crowned, and 1291, date of the death of Jeanne de Châtillon, and it is almost certainly the presentation copy intended for the patroness, Marguerite.

A similar royal gathering is to be found in the opening miniature of B.Ars. 3142, a compendium of poetry featuring largely the writings of Adenet le Roi. This time the poet himself, wearing a crown as his nickname suggests, is represented amidst the royal group that includes Marie of France, wife of Philip III (married 1275), Blanche of France, widow of Ferdinand de la Cerda (died 1320), and Mahaut of Artois. It has been suggested that the MS was dedicated to Mahaut,[16] but there is no evidence for this other than her inclusion in the miniature; it could have been intended for Marie.

There is no element of uncertainty about the recipient of B.N.lat. 8504. It is a Latin translation of *Dina et Kalila*, from the Spanish, made in 1313 for Philip IV. On the opening page is a royal group with the king seated in the center, and an inscription beneath the miniature names the patron and gives the date of the translation. This is undoubtedly the presentation copy given to the king[17] [fig. 5].

The *Dina et Kalila* MS stands isolated; the texts of Girart and Adenet, on the other hand did enjoy a certain popularity in the

---

[15] G. Graf Vitzthum, *Die Pariser Miniaturmalerei*, Leipzig, 1907, pl. III, pp. 24-32.
[16] *Ibid.*, p. 56, pl. X.
[17] *Ibid.*, p. 170 ff.

years around 1300. One of the latest MSS contains both texts: B.R.IV 319. Stylistically it is similar to B.N.fr. 22495, written in 1337, and probably produced in Paris.

From earlier in the thirteenth century there are a few isolated MSS that most probably were presentation copies, though the identity of the patron is obscure. One outstanding example is the lavishly illuminated *Roman de la Poire*, B.N.fr. 2186 [fig. 6], made perhaps for the lady represented on f. 10v, who receives a book from a kneeling male figure. Both wear garments with the same heraldic device, which has so far eluded identification.[18] This is a particularly sumptuous MS containing a cycle of full-page miniatures [fig. 9], which is very unusual in French secular illumination, and this also suggests that some important person was to be the recipient. It is also the only surviving illustrated copy of this text.

A special case of isolation is met with in the books associated with René, duke of Anjou and king of Sicily. Two texts are involved, both composed by René himself. One is the *Livre du cœur d'amour épris*, Vienna Ö.N.B. 2595, and the other the *Livre des tournois*. Several copies of the latter are extant, all dating, as does the *Cœur* MS, from c. 1460-65. Two original MSS of the *Tournois* text are extant: B.N.fr. 2695-6, illuminated by the same hand as that of *Cœur*. Indeed it has been suggested that René himself was responsible for the execution of the miniatures as well as the composition of the texts, and this constitutes a unique case of the patron fulfilling the additional roles of both author and artist.[19]

Secular book production in relation to liturgical MSS.

Developments in both the layout and the style of secular illustrations are closely related to those of liturgical or devotional books, and in many cases there is evidence that both were produced by the same workshops and artists. While this is generally the rule, many of the outstanding and sumptuous literary

---

[18] The arms are France charged with a cross or lozengy gules.
[19] See O. Pächt, *René d'Anjou et les Van Eyck*, Cahiers de l'Association internationale des études françaises, 1956; O. Smital and E. Winkler, *Le Livre du Cuer d'Amours espris*, Vienna, 1927; Pognon, Verve vol. IV, no. 16.

MSS have no parallel in liturgical books, while the opposite is also true, and there are splendid liturgical books illuminated by artists who appear not to have participated in secular MS illustration.

No secular MS is comparable, for instance, with the elaborate cycle of full-page miniatures illustrating scenes from the Old Testament in the Pierpont Morgan Library, MS 638, dating from the middle of the thirteenth century, [20] although certain moduli from this are taken up again much later in secular illustration. [21] Similarly there is no secular MS illuminated by the hand of Honoré as it appears in the frontispiece to the Breviary of Philippe le Bel, B.N.lat. 1023, f. 7v. or in the *Somme le Roi* B.L.Add. 54180, [22] although the Girart and Adenet MSS referred to above were undoubtedly produced in the circle of Honoré's influence. No secular MS illuminated by the hand of Pucelle has come to light, [23] while the secular MSS made later in the fourteenth century for Jean de Berry and around 1400 are rarely the work of the well-known illustrators of his noted devotional books, such as Jacquemart, the Boucicaut Master, and the Limburg brothers. [24]

Cases of outstanding secular MSS without parallel in liturgical books are less frequent, but the Bodleian Alexander, MS 264, [25] and the René MSS find no exact counterparts, and the same is true of the Harley *Rose*, B.L.Harl. 4425 [fig. 1].

Close connections between secular and liturgical MSS do exist from the beginnings of secular illumination in France, shortly before the middle of the thirteenth century. The earliest MS of

---

[20] Facsimile edited by J. Plummer, London, 1969.

[21] For instance, the motif of the falling knight in B.L.Add. 10294, f. 81v [fig. 7], may be compared with f. 9 of the Picture-Bible.

[22] Honoré's name is in the Paris tax rolls of 1292, 1296, 1297, 1299, 1300, and the Breviary was paid for in 1296. The quality of the works attributed to him varies considerably and it is probable that he was head of a shop and worked with assistants. See E. G. Millar, *The Parisian Miniaturist Honoré*, London, 1959, and D. H. Turner, "The Development of Maître Honoré," *British Museum Quarterly*, XXXIII, 1-2, pp. 53-64.

[23] See K. Morand, *Jean Pucelle*, Oxford, 1962.

[24] Meiss, *op. cit.* and vol. 2, *The Boucicaut Master*, London 1968. Two of Jean de Berry's Boccaccio MSS are attributed to the Boucicaut Master; his *Rose*, B.N.fr. 380 is attributed to the circle of Jacquemart, while his *Lancelot* B.N.fr. 117-20 is attributed to the Master of the *Cleres Femmes*.

[25] Facsimile edited by M. R. James, Oxford, 1933.

the crusading epic, *Histoire de la guerre sainte,* by Guillaume de Tyr [26] [fig. 8], is very similar stylistically to the Toledo MS of the Bible moralisée, whose frontispiece with its portrait of Saint Louis is now in the Pierpont Morgan Library, MS M. 240. It is likely that both were made for Saint Louis before his departure to the Holy Land in 1248, and it is probable that the Guillaume de Tyr MS was made for Saint Louis himself, although it contains no specific marks of ownership.

The style and layout of the *Roman de la Poire,* B.N.fr. 2186 [fig. 9] may be closely paralleled in the fragments containing scenes from the Old Testament, Oxford, Bodleian Library, Douce 381 [fig. 10], and in the Psalter Douce 50. Later in the thirteenth century the Yale *Lancelot* [fig. 11], probably made for Guillaume de Termonde, may be related to liturgical books. This time the relationship is rather more complex than in the case of *Poire* because two hands are involved in the illumination. One may be related to the illustration in the Psalter made for Gui de Dampierre, father of Guillaume, B.R. 10607 [27] [fig. 12], while the other [fig. 13] reappears in B.N.fr. 95, [28] *Estoire, Merlin* [fig. 14-15], *Sept Sages, Pénitence Adam,* and a group of liturgical MSS that include B.N.lat. 1076 [fig. 16], Psalter, and Marseille 111, Book of Hours. [29] Since the work of the two hands is interspersed throughout the Yale MS, it is likely that they are to be considered as two artists of different training employed in the same workshop. Where this workshop was located is uncertain; the only clue is

---

[26] A thorough study of the Guillaume de Tyr MSS has been made by J. Folda, *The Illustrations of William of Tyre's History of Outremer,* thesis, Johns Hopkins University, Baltimore, 1968.

[27] This MS is very problematical, see L. M. J. Delaissé, *Miniatures médiévales,* Brussels, 1959, no. 9, p. 50, pl. 149v-50.

[28] Loomis, *op. cit.,* p. 95, suggests that B.N.fr. 95 and the Yale *Lancelot* were intended as two of a three-volume set of the complete prose Lancelot cycle. (The first part of the *Lancelot* proper, now missing, would be the third volume.) Although the illumination is in part very close indeed, fr. 95 also includes two non-Arthurian texts, *Sept Sages* and *Pénitence Adam,* while none of the other complete *Lancelot* compendia have any other texts. It is probable that this workshop made several *Lancelots,* some complete, others containing only part of the cycle. See Woledge, *op. cit.,* for a list of which MSS contain which parts of the cycle.

[29] See J. Billioud, "Très anciennes heures de Therouanne," *Trésors des Bibliothèques de France,* 1935, no. 5, pp. 165-85, pl. LXI-IV.

provided by the liturgical use of the Book of Hours and by the calendar of the Psalter, both of which indicate the diocese of Therouanne. This included parts of Flanders.

There is perhaps a sharper division between liturgical and secular books in the fourteenth and fifteenth centuries than in the earlier period, and the examples that do show work by the same illuminators in both types of books are frequently among the less well-known products of the period. Jean de Berry's *Lancelot*, B.N.fr. 117-20, while not the work of his most noted illuminators, is related to the Bible, B.Ars. 5058, [30] and the *Lancelot* B.N.fr. 96 [31] finds a close stylistic parallel with the Book of Hours, Chantilly lat. 13621. [32] Similarly the name of Jean Colombe, who completed the Très Riches Heures left unfinished at the death of the brothers Limburg in 1416, has been linked with the illustrator of the *Estoire* B.R. 9246. [33]

As far as the layout of the illumination is concerned, the main difference between liturgical and secular books is in the use of the full-page miniature. This was employed far more frequently in liturgical than in secular books. It is the regular choice for the Crucifixion miniature standard in Missals, and for the cycle of the Life and Passion of Christ that are frequent in the illustration of Psalters and Books of Hours [fig. 10].

Cycles of full-page miniatures are rare in French secular illustration, and this is particularly interesting in relation to German secular manuscripts. [34] There are some isolated examples in the thirteenth century in France, notably the *Roman de la Poire*, B.N.fr. 2186 and the *Roman de Troie*, B.N.fr. 1610. [35] The former contains either a single scene or two scenes contained within roundels or quatrefoils, while the latter has scenes arranged in two or three registers. The Bodleian *Alexander* has several

---

[30] Loomis, *op. cit.*, p. 106.
[31] *Ibid.*, p. 108.
[32] J. Meurgey, *Les principaux manuscrits à Chantilly*, Paris, 1930, pp. 102-3, pl. LXVI.
[33] Loomis, *op. cit.*, p. 111.
[34] See below, p. 97.
[35] This was written in 1264. See F. Saxl, *Lectures*, London, 1957, "The Troy Romance in French and Italian Art," pp. 125-38, pl. 74 a, b; 75 a, b; 78 a; 79 a.

full-page miniatures subdivided to include various scenes; the *Tournois* manuscript of René has the exceptional arrangement of full-page miniature over two pages, a verso and the following recto, containing a single scene.

The nearest approximation to the full-page miniature in most secular books is found on the opening page, which is usually treated differently from the rest of the decoration of the book. In the fifteenth century the opening page usually contains a miniature taking up three quarters of the page, with a single scene or divided into several scenes, with the first few lines of the text at the bottom. The rest of the illumination of the book generally takes the form of small miniatures in one column of the text.

The idea of emphasizing the opening page is already present at the beginning of the thirteenth century; some of the earliest secular MSS contain only one miniature at the beginning of the text. By the middle of the thirteenth century when cycles of secular illumination have developed it is usual to find some distinction in the opening illustration. Either it is larger in scale than the rest, or it is different in type; for instance it may be a historiated initial [fig. 15] if the rest of the illustration consists of miniatures, or vice-versa. By 1300 it is the established practice to mark the opening page by a series of miniatures, two or four, three or six, depending on whether the text is written in two or three columns. An alternative is a single miniature divided into compartments, and this is the arrangement that leads on to the fifteenth-century practice of including a large miniature with a single scene or a composite one.

Decorative borders are employed from the last quarter of the thirteenth century as part of the opening page layout. This represents the adaptation, on a much reduced scale, of an element that forms an important part of northern French and Flemish liturgical illustration from the late 1260s to the middle of the fourteenth century. The main element in the border is a leaf stalk which emanates from the initial at the top of the page and runs down the left-hand side of the page and into the bottom margin. An integral part of such borders is the inclusion not only of leaves, but also of hybrids, grotesques, apes, and human figures playing games, hunting, and indulging in a wide variety of activities. Paradoxically, this kind of marginal decoration plays a major part in the illustration of the small-scale Psalters and Books of Hours that were the popular aid to private devotion in the period 1280-1340. Marginal decoration of this sort, usually totally unrelated to the text on the page, appears on most pages of these small-scale books. In the MSS containing secular texts, by contrast, such decoration is almost always (the Yale *Lancelot* and the Bodleian *Alexander* are exceptions) confined to the opening page only, or for the opening page of each new text in a volume. The far greater size of the pages in the secular books as well as their great length probably explain why border decoration fills only a minor rôle.

In the thirteenth and early fourteenth centuries the scheme for the cyclical pictures scattered in the body of the text may be either miniatures or historiated initials. Both are to be found in Bible illustration, where they mark the beginning of each of the books of the Bible, and historiated initials are used to mark the main divisions in the text of Psalters.[36] After the second quarter of the fourteenth century the historiated initial becomes obsolete. The reason is doubtless inherent in the form, which allows little scope for the battle scenes, banquets and the like, which make up the standard repertoire of secular illumination.

From the last third of the thirteenth century the miniature may take a variety of forms. Mention has already been made of the composite miniatures of opening pages. There are two main possibilities for the miniatures of the main illustrative cycle. Either they may be small, square or rectangular in one text column, usually representing a single scene; very occasionally (the Yale *Lancelot* and B.N.fr. 95) [figs. 11, 13, 14] they may be divided into two registers, an idea probably derivative from Psalter illustration in which such division is frequent in full-page miniatures. The alternative is long rectangular miniatures extending horizontally over the whole of the written space, generally two or three columns of the text. The earliest MS in which these long rectangular miniatures appear is B.Ars. 3139, *Chevalier au cygne*, written in 1268. The arrangement is taken up in the well-

---

[36] G. Haseloff, *Die Psalterillustration*, Kiel, 1938, provides an analysis of the subject-matter of the historiated initials.

known *Lancelot* B.N.fr. 342,[37] written in 1274, the Pierpont Morgan *Lancelot* [fig. 2], and occasionally in the fifteenth century, for instance in B.N.fr. 117-20, the duke of Berry's *Lancelot*. This layout appears to be without parallel in liturgical illumination. One of its main advantages is that it enables scenes of continued action to be represented, showing one scene following directly on another, or the continued actions of one episode.

The stylistic developments that one can observe in secular MS painting between the thirteenth and sixteenth centuries parallel those in liturgical illumination, and indeed, in the later part of the period, those in the other two-dimensional media like panel-painting and tapestry. The introduction of marginal illustration in both liturgical and secular books in the 1260s bears witness to a growing interest in levels of reality (or of fantasy) beyond those of the picture-plane of the main miniature. This is just one aspect of the growing awareness of space and pictorial depth and the ability to render them in two-dimensional media that is one of the most important developments in this period. It is accompanied by the increasing interest shown in natural forms used in border illustration around 1300 and later employed within the miniatures themselves, where gold and diaper 'sky' backgrounds are replaced by natural colours, landscapes are better adapted to the scale of the figures in them, and architecture is rendered in convincing perspective.

Techniques and Transmission

The number of scenes included in the longest secular cycles is so vast that there is necessarily some degree of repetition. The stock repertoire consists to a large extent of general scenes that can be used regardless of specific context, such as scenes of joust battle and tournament, banquets, encounters with hermits, conversations between knights and ladies, kings receiving letters, characters in bed, and so on. Some such scenes may be equally applicable to religious subjects: royal banquets with a king in the center and a servant on the nearside of the table fits the standard iconography for the Last Supper with Christ in the center and

---

[37] Loomis, *op. cit.*, pl. 213-6.

Judas on the near side of the table; battle scenes may be purely secular, or they may illustrate the books of Kings or Macchabees from the Bible; and there are many more such examples. In the same way 'moduli' — figures in certain positions, or parts of scenes rather than the scene in its entirety — may be reused from scene to scene, manuscript to manuscript, and from secular book to liturgical as well as vice-versa.

It is clear from an analysis of the cycles of MSS containing any one text that the position of the illustrations in the text and the content of the illustrations were not invented afresh for each manuscript. They tend to remain fairly standard, and it is possible to work out recensions for the iconographical cycles in much the same way as it may be done with texts. [38] Artists relied both on visual models and on written instructions. The visual models could be derived either from another MS of the same text with the same illustrative cycle, or from a model-book containing representations of stock scenes. [39] They could be transferred directly to the space they were intended to occupy in the MS in preparation, or they could be sketched roughly in the margin first, to act as guides. Such a system as this presupposes a large workshop in which various individuals were involved in the production of the book. The marginal sketches probably were intended to be rubbed out or removed by trimming, but a few have been preserved [40] [fig. 17]. The written instructions were doubtless also intended to be removed once the miniatures were completed. They are usually generalized in type, not mentioning the characters in question by name, but they often include precise information about such things as the tinctures and devices to be represented on shields [fig. 2]. It is possible too that in some MSS where there are rubrics, or captions above the miniatures

---

[38] For Psalters see Haseloff, *op. cit.* A corpus of Bible illustration in the 12th and 13th centuries is being prepared by Professor P. Brieger at the University of Toronto. For *Alexander* see Ross, *op. cit.*, and for Guillaume de Tyr, see Folda, *op. cit.* For the *Queste* and *Mort Artu* sections of the *Lancelot*, see M. A. Stones, *The Illustration of the French prose Lancelot*, thesis, University of London, 1970.

[39] See R. W. Scheller, *A Survey of Medieval Model Books*, Haarlem, 1963.

[40] Little has been written on these sketches, see, however, D. J. A. Ross, "Methods of Book-Production in a Fourteenth Century Miscellany," *Scriptorium*, VI, 1952, pp. 63-75.

Bel-Acueil shows the lover the rose. B. L. Harl. 4425, *Roman de la Rose*, fol. 36. [Reproduced by permission of the British Library Board.]

Initial: Galeholt leaves an abbey where he has rested to cure a wound.
New York, Pierpont Morgan Library, M. 806, *Lancelot*, fol. 155

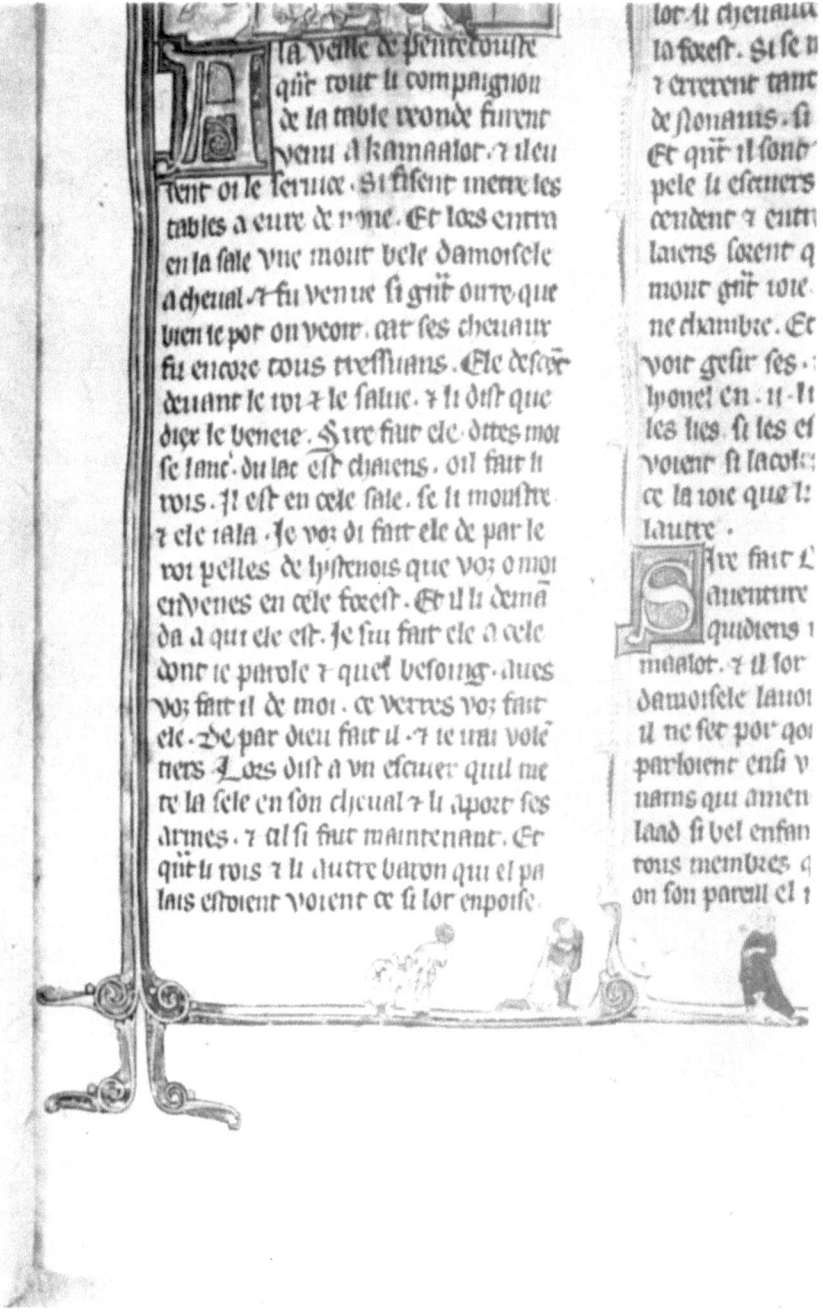

Detail: A knight, probably Guillaume de Termonde, kneels before a lady. New Haven, The Beinecke Rare Book and Manuscript Library, Yale University, MS 229, ex-Phillipps 130, *Queste,* fol. 187

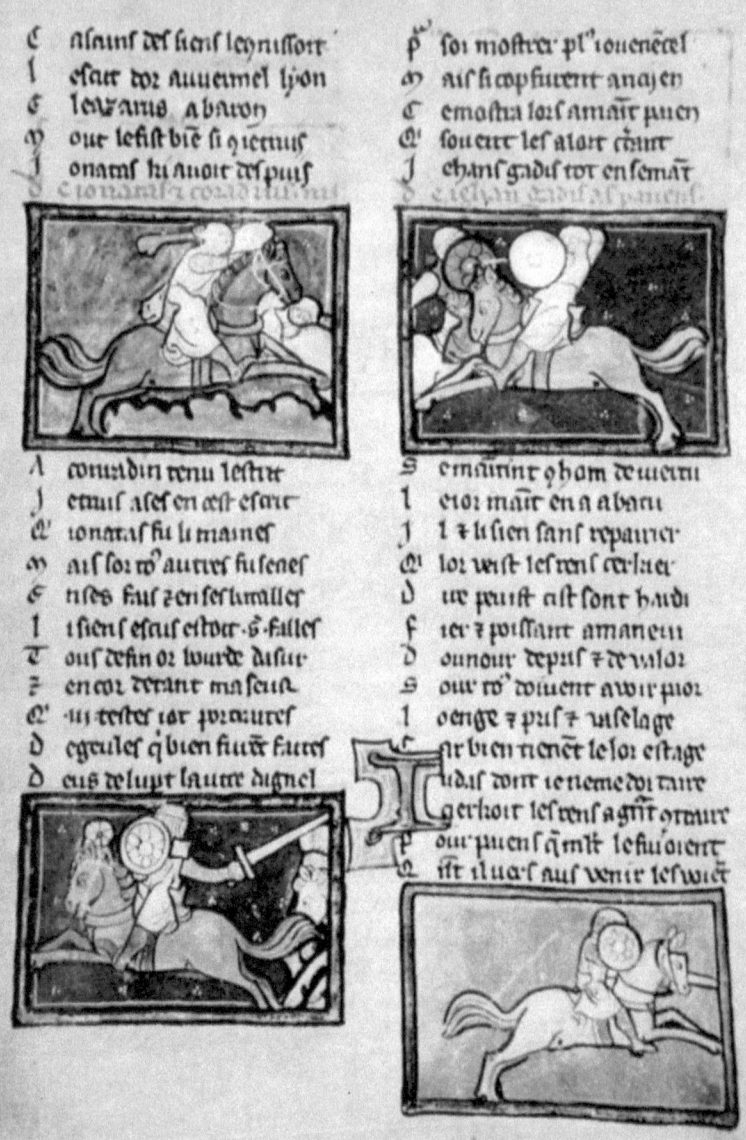

Four scenes of combat. Paris, Bibliothèque Nationale fr. 15104, *La noble chevalerie de Judas Machabée et de ses nobles frères*, fol. 26. (Photo. Bibl. nat. Paris.)

Miniature: Philip IV of France, the future Philip V and Charles IV, with their sister Isabella, Louis of Navarre and Charles of Valois. Paris, Bibliothèque Nationale lat. 8504, *Dina et Kalila*, fol. 1ᵛ. (Photo. Bibl. nat. Paris.)

Miniature: An unknown lady receiving a book from a kneeling man. Paris, Bibliothèque Nationale fr. 2186, *Roman de la Poire*, fol. 10ᵛ.
(Photo. Bibl. nat. Paris.)

Miniature: Mordret and his men besiege the tower of London. B.L. Add. 10294, *Mort Artu*, fol. 81ᵛ. [Reproduced by permission of the British Library Board.]

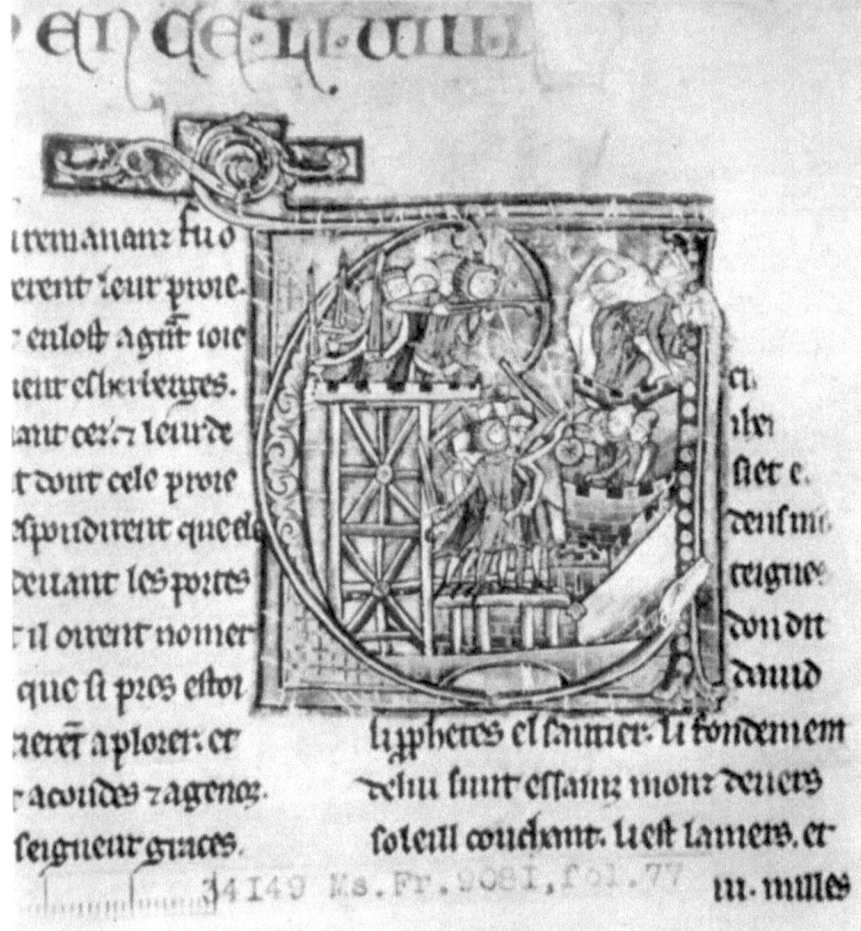

Historiated Initial: the siege of Jerusalem. Paris, Bibliothèque Nationale fr. 9081, Guillaume de Tyr, *Histoire de la guerre sainte*, fol. 77.
(Photo. Bibl. nat. Paris.)

The god of love and two lovers. Paris, Bibliothèque Nationale fr. 2186, *Roman de la Poire*, fol. 1ᵛ. (Photo. Bibl. nat. Paris.)

Old Testament scenes: God enthroned, the temptation of Adam and Eve.
Oxford, Bodleian Library, MS Douce 381, fol. 123

Miniature: top, Lancelot and Mordret see a white stag surrounded by lions; below, they encounter two knights. New Haven, The Beinecke Rare Book and Manuscript Library, Yale University, MS 229, ex-Phillipps 130, *Lancelot*, fol. 126

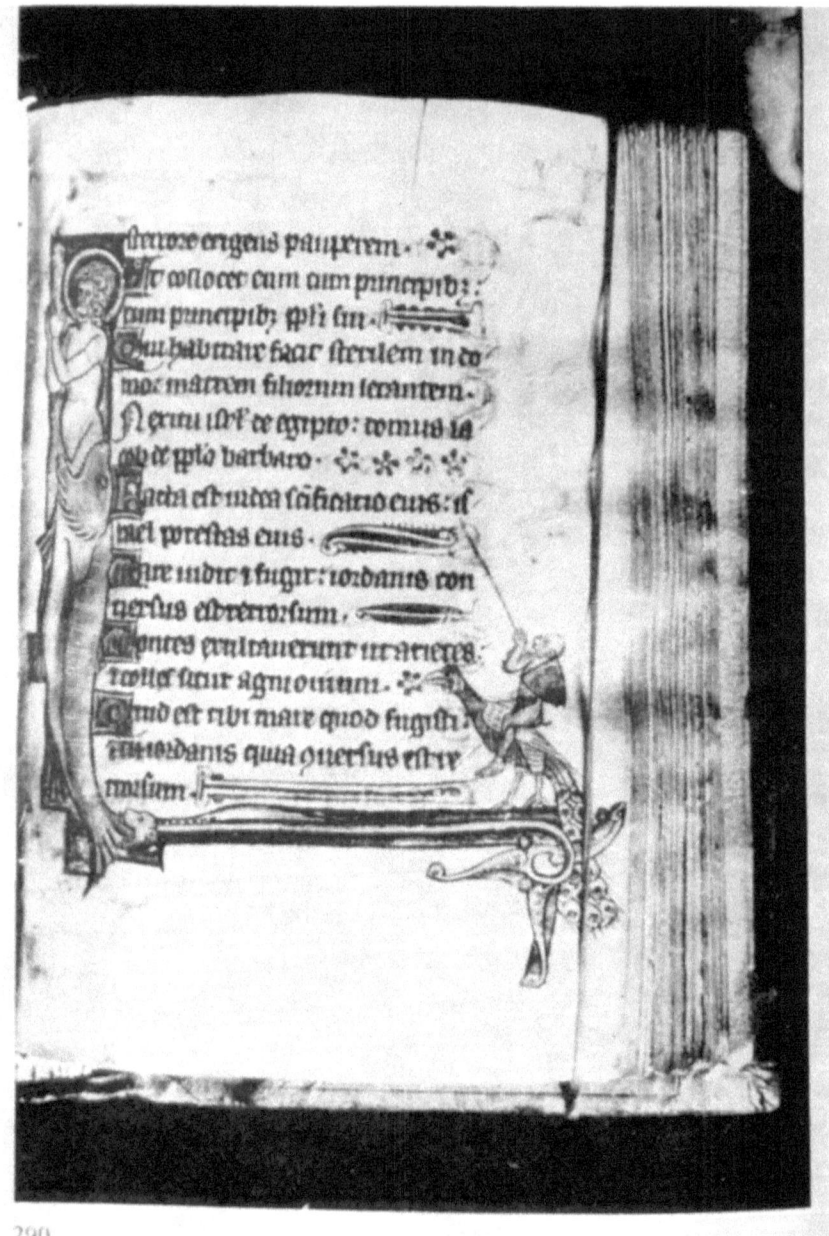

Border: Jonah and the whale; ape astride a peacock. B. R. 10607, Psalter of Gui de Dampierre, fol. 177ʳ. [Copyright Bibliothèque Royale Albert 1ᵉʳ, Bruxelles.]

Miniature: top, Bohort, Gauvain and Lancelot return to Arthur's castle, Guinevere watches their arrival; below, Lancelot speaks to Guinevere, knights stand in the doorways. New Haven, The Beinecke Rare Book and Manuscript Library, Yale University, MS 229, ex-Phillipps 130, *Mort Artu*, fol. 290ᵛ

Miniature: top, king Brangoire assembles men and supplies in the city of Estragoire; below, a combat. Paris, Bibliothèque Nationale fr. 95, *Merlin*, fol. 205ᵛ. (Photo. Bibl. nat. Paris.)

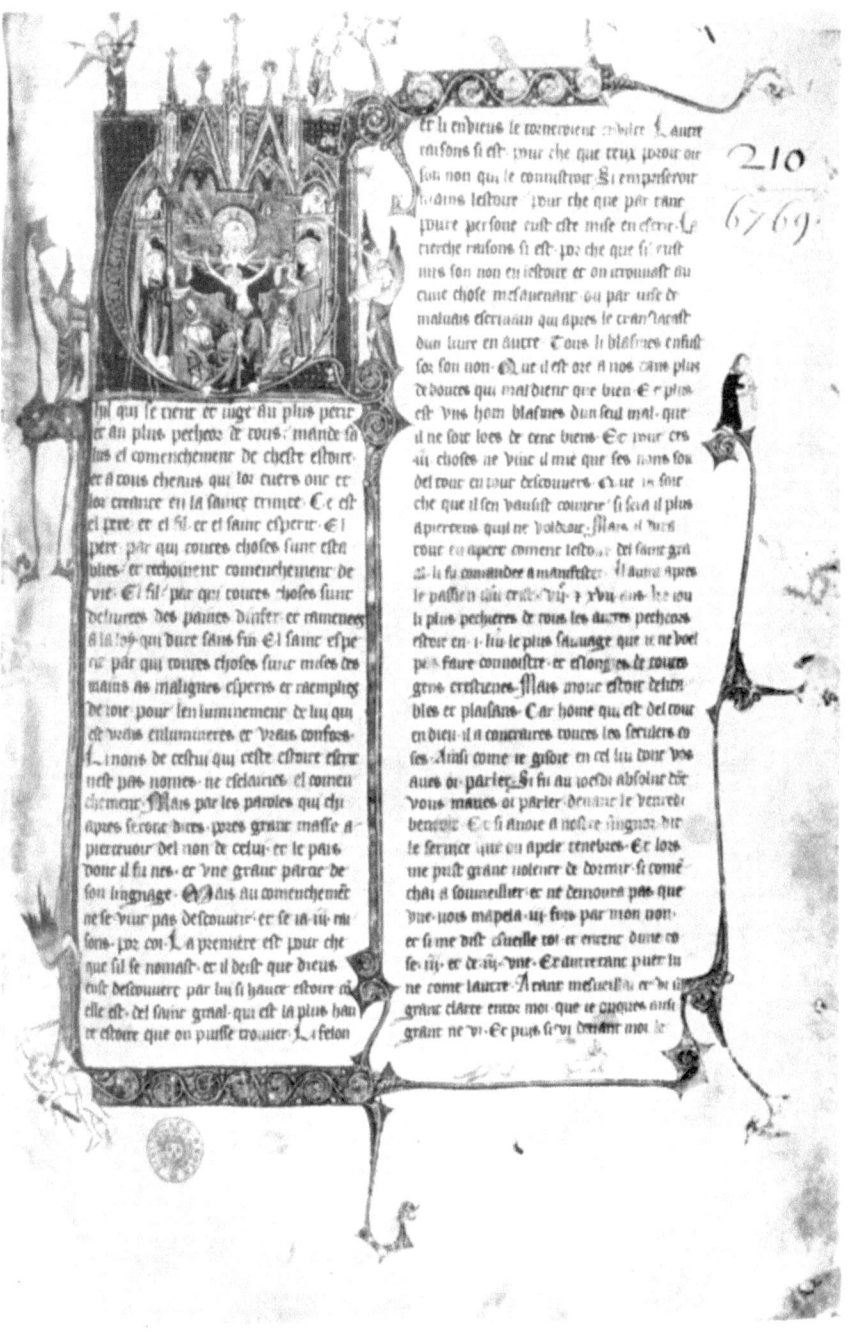

Historiated initial: the Trinity enthroned. Paris, Bibliothèque Nationale fr. 95, *Estoire*, fol. 1. (Photo. Bibl. nat. Paris.)

Beatus initial, Psalm 1: top, David, enthroned, plays the harp; below, David Kills Goliath. Paris, Bibliothèque Nationale lat. 1076, Psalter, fol. 17. (Photo. Bibl. nat. Paris.)

Miniature: the lover sees his reflection in a stream. Paris, Bibliothèque Nationale fr. 802, *Roman de la Rose*, fol. 12. (Photo. Bibl. nat. Paris.)

explaining their content, that these may have been used also as guides to the illuminators. [41]

Secular manuscript illustration outside France

The beginnings of secular illumination are better documented in Germany than they are in France. Many of the earliest examples are MSS containing texts that are based on French works, like the *Ruolantesliet*, Heidelberg University Library Pal.Germ. 112, dated between 1180 and 1195. [42] Its decorative scheme consists of line-drawings interspersed with text, a form rare in France, though found in England and Italy. Almost as rare in French secular illumination is the full-page layout, which is standard in much of German work, notably in Heinrich von Veldecke's *Eneit*, Berlin, Mgf 282, [43] dating from c. 1220, and Wolfram's *Parzival*, Munich cgm 19, of c. 1250. [44] There is no parallel for such a scheme in French illumination of this date, since both *Poire* and the *Troie* B.N.fr. 1610 are both at least a decade later than 1250. Whether one may assume lost French prototypes for the MSS with full-page decoration, to parallel the French source of the texts, is uncertain. What has been convincingly suggested, however, is that the *Ruolantesliet* may depend in part at least on a lost French *Chanson de Roland* MS, perhaps of English manufacture. [45]

In Italy secular manuscript illumination is dominated by Dante's *Divine Comedy*, of which detailed study has recently been made. [46] What is interesting from the point of view of French texts is that many MSS were written in French by Italian scribes and illustrated in Italy. The most popular texts were the

---

[41] See C. E. Pickford, *L'Évolution du roman arthurien en prose*, Paris, 1959, *Deuxième partie, la technique*, pp. 129-75, and F. Wormald, "A Medieval Description of Two Illuminated Psalters," *Scriptorium*, VI, 1952, pp. 18-25.

[42] See Lejeune and Stiennon, *op. cit.*, chapter XIV, pp. 111-138, pl. 84-90, 92, 94-124.

[43] Saxl, *op. cit.*, pl. 73.

[44] Loomis, *op. cit.*, pl. 355-358.

[45] Ross, *Iconography*, pp. 55-59.

[46] P. Brieger, M. Meiss, C. S. Singleton, *Illuminated Manuscripts of Dante's Divine Comedy*, Princeton, 1969.

prose *Lancelot* and *Tristan, Roland* and Guillaume de Tyr's *Histoire de la guerre sainte*.[47]

The best known MSS from the Iberian peninsula are the songbooks, notably the *Cantigas* of Alfonso X, but it seems that a few French MSS may have been illuminated in Spain, among which is B.N.fr. 750, a *Tristan* written in France but probably illuminated in Spain.[48] An interesting situation arises where the Crusading Kingdom of Jerusalem is concerned. Manuscripts were written and illuminated there by the Acre scriptorium on the one hand, and there is also evidence that a French illuminator went there and illuminated books, two of which are Guillaume de Tyr MSS,[49] a third a *Lancelot*, Tours 951.

England seems to have produced very little secular illumination in the Middle Ages by comparison with Italy and Germany. There is no great tradition of Chaucer illustration to correspond to that of Dante in Italy. In fact none of the MSS containing Chaucer's texts have narrative cycles to illustrate them, and even the most splendid, the Ellesmere MS of the *Canterbury Tales*, now in the Huntington Library, San Marino, California, has only small marginal pictures showing each of the pilgrims next to the opening lines of his tale. The portraits of Chaucer in manuscripts of his and Hoccleve's work add a new dimension to secular illustration[50] which makes the lack of illustration of the texts themselves the more surprising. Against such paucity of illustrated English texts, one may set the few illustrated French texts made in England. Matthew Paris' workshop seems to have given rise around the middle of the thirteenth century to a small group of secular manuscripts illustrated in line drawing like the *Chanson d'Aspremont*, B. M. Landsdowne 782, and the *Roman de toute chevalerie* by Thomas of Kent, Cambridge, Trinity, 0.9.34.[51]

---

[47] Loomis, *op. cit.*, pl. 305-337.
[48] *Ibid.*, pl. 210-212.
[49] H. Buchthal, *Miniature Painting in the Latin Kingdom of Jerusalem*, Oxford, 1957, and Folda, *op. cit.*, Part I. Folda names the French illuminator the 'Master of the Knights Hospitaller.'
[50] Rickert, *op. cit.*, pp. 185-6. Cf. also the portrait of Adenet in B.Ars. 3142, p. 88 above.
[51] D. J. A. Ross, "A thirteenth century Anglo-Norman workshop illustrating secular literary manuscripts?," *Mélanges Lejeune*, Liège, 1968, pp. 689-94.

In general, then, French manuscripts did play a part in the development of secular illumination outside France, while in France itself the exceptionally large number of them produced from the thirteenth century onwards bears witness to the degree of public interest of which they were the object in the late middle ages. The different libraries of Europe and the United States, in which they are now located, testify also to the tastes of the bibliophiles of the succeeding centuries, and it is fitting that so much recent scholarship has turned its attention to their illumination.

SELECT BIBLIOGRAPHY

The items listed here are primarily concerned with French illumination and with texts written in the vernacular. No attempt is made to cover fully the illumination of Latin texts or works of history, biography, or travel. Brief reference is made to the secular illumination of England, Germany, Italy, and Spain.

I. *General works on secular art*

Pickering, F. P. *Literature and Art in the Middle Ages*, London, 1970.

Ross, D. J. A. *Alexander Historiatus*, Warburg Institute Surveys, I, London, 1963.

——. *Illustrated Medieval Alexander-Books in Germany and the Netherlands*, London, 1971.

Loomis, R. S. and L. H. *Arthurian Legends in Medieval Art*, New York, 1938.

McGrath, R. L. *The Romance of the Maccabees in Medieval Art and Literature*, Ph.D. thesis, Princeton, 1963.

Lejeune, R. and Stiennon, J. *La Légende de Roland dans l'art du moyen âge*, Brussels, 1966.

Scherer, M. R. *The Legends of Troy in Art and Literature*, New York and London, 1964.

Buchthal, H. *Historia Troiana*, Studies of the Warburg Institute, 32, London, 1971.

Folda, J. *The Illustration of William of Tyre's History of Outremer*, Ph.D. thesis, Johns Hopkins, 1968.

II. French secular illumination

Bossuat, R.: *Manuel bibliographique de la littérature française du moyen âge,* Melun, 1951; Suppléments, 1954-60, 1955-61.

Woledge, B.: *Bibliographie des romans et nouvelles en prose français antérieurs à 1500,* Genève, 1954.

Woledge, B. and Clive, P.: *Répertoire des plus anciens textes en prose français, depuis 842 jusqu'aux premières années du 13e siècle,* Paris/Genève, 1964.

Alexandre, le roman de: ed. James, M. R. Oxford, 1933 (facsimile) (see also I above).

Anjou, René de: ed. Smital, O. and Winkler, E. *Herzog René von Anjou, Livre du cuer d'amours espris,* Vienna, 1927.

———. *Le Mortifiement de vaine plaisance* ... New York, 1926.

———. *Traité de la forme et devis d'un tournois,* ed. Pognon, Verve vol. IV, no. 16, 1946.

———. ed. Quatrebarbes, Theodore, comte de *Œuvres complètes du roi René,* Angers, 1843-6.

Boccacio: Martin, H. M. R. *Le Boccace de Jean sans Peur, Des Cas des nobles hommes et femmes,* Brussels, 1911.
 Meiss, M. *The First Fully Illustrated Decameron,* in *Essays in the History of Art Presented to Rudolf Wittkower,* London, 1967.

Bus, Gervais du: *Le Roman de Fauvel,* ed. Aubry, P. Paris, 1907 (facsimile).

Chansonniers: Jeanroy, A. *Bibliographie sommaire des chansonniers provençaux,* Paris, 1916.
 Ibid. *Le Chansonnier d'Arras,* Paris, 1925.
 Rokseth, Y. *Polyphonies du treizième siècle, Le MS H 196 de la Faculté de Médecine de Montpellier,* 4 vols. Paris, 1935-9.

Chevalerie Vivien, ed. Weeks, R. University of Missouri Studies, Literary and Linguistic Series, I, 1909 (facsimile).

Fauvain, L'Histoire de: ed. A. Langfors, Paris, 1914 (reproduction en phototypie).

Franc, Martin le: ed. Bayot, A. de *L'Estrif de Fortune et de Vertu,* étude du MS 9510 de la Bibliothèque Royale de Bruxelles, Brussels, 1928.

Garin le Loherain: *La Chanson de Geste de Garin le Loherain mise en prose par Philippe de Vigneulles, de Metz* (reproduction des miniatures d'après le MS ... appartenant à M. le comte d'Hunolstein, Paris, 1901.

Lancelot: Stones, M. A. *The Illustrations of the French prose Lancelot,* Ph.D. thesis, London, 1970.

Livre des deduis du roi Modus et de la reine Ratio: Nordenfalk, C. A. J., *Kung praktiks och drottning teoris jaktbok,* Stockholm, 1955.

Lorris, G. de, and Meung, J. de: *Le Roman de la Rose:* Fleming, J. V. *The Roman de la Rose, A Study in Allegory and Iconography,* Princeton, 1969.

Lorris, G. de, Kuhn, A. *Die Illustration des Rosenromans*, Leipzig, 1912.

Ovid: Durrieu, P. and Vasselot, J.-J. Marquet de *Les MSS à miniatures des Héroïdes d'Ovide*, Paris, 1894.

Phebus, Gaston, *Livre de la chasse*, ed. Couderc, C. Paris, 1909.

Pisan, Christine de: Schäfer, L. *Die Illustrationen zu den HSS der Christine de Pisan, Marburger Jahrbuch für Kunstwissenschaft*, 1937, pp. 119-208.

Terence: Martin, H. M. R. *Le Térence des ducs*, Paris, 1907.

III. *Secular Illumination outside France*

England: Varty, K. *Reynard the Fox, A Study of the Fox in Medieval English Art*, Leicester, 1967.

Germany: Frühmorgen-Voss, H. Mittelhochdeutsche weltliche Literatur und ihre Illustration, in Deutsche Vierteljahrschrift für Literaturwissenschaft und Geistesgeschichte, 43, 1969, pp. 23-75 (references to the many facsimiles).

Italy: Brieger, P. Meiss, M., and Singleton, C. *Illuminated MSS of the Divine Comedy* 2 vols. Princeton, 1969.

Spain: Lovillo-Guerro, J. Las Cantigas, *Estudio Arqueológico de sus Miniaturas*, Madrid, 1949.

    White, J. G. *Das spanische Schachzabelbuch des Königs Alfons des Weisen*, Leipzig, 1913.

IV. *General works on French illumination*

Avril, F. *La Librairie de Charles V*, Paris, 1968 (Bibliothèque Nationale, Paris exhibition).

Buchthal, H. *Miniature Painting in the Latin Kingdom of Jerusalem*, Oxford, 1957.

Delaissé, L. M. J. *La Miniature flamande, le mécénat de Philippe le Bon*, (Bibliothèque Royale, Brussels, exhibition), Brussels, 1959.

Doutrepont, *La Littérature française à la cour de Bourgogne*, Paris, 1909.

Deuchler, F. *Looking at Bonne of Luxemburg's Prayerbook, Bulletin of the Metropolitan Museum*, xxix, 1971, pp. 267-278.

Haseloff, G. *Die Psalterillustration im dreizehnten Jahrhundert*, Kiel, 1938.

Meiss, M. *French Painting in the Time of Jean de Berry*, I, *The Patronage of the Duke*, London/New York, 1967, II, *The Boucicaut Master*, London/New York, 1968.

Morand, K. *Jean Pucelle*, Oxford, 1962.

Millar, E. G. *The Parisian Miniaturist Honoré*, London, 1958.

Pickford, C. E. *L'Evolution du roman arthurien en prose*, Paris, 1958.

Porcher, J. *MSS à peintures du treizième au seizième siècles*, Paris, 1955 (Bibliothèque Nationale, Paris, exhibition).

Vitzthum, G. von *Die Pariser Miniaturmalerei*, Leipzig, 1907.

Wormald, F. *Bible Illustration in Medieval Manuscripts*, in *Cambridge History of the Bible*, ed. Lampe, G. W. H., Cambridge, 1969, pp. 309-337.

V. *Printed sources relevant to French illumination*

Adam-Even, P. and Jéquier, L. *L'Armorial Wijnbergen, Archives héraldiques suisses* 1951-4, pp. 1-80.

Baron, F. *Enlumineurs, peintres et sculpteurs parisiens des treizième et quatorzième siècles, Bulletin archéologique des travaux historiques et scientifiques, nouvelle série, fasc.* 4, 1968, pp. 37-121, Paris, 1969.

Bouton, V. *Gelre's Wapenboek*, Paris, 1881.

Branner, R. *Manuscript Makers in Mid-thirteenth Century Paris, Art Bulletin,* 1966, pp. 65-67.

Buchon, J.-A. *Chronique métrique de Godefroy de Paris, suivie de la taille de Paris en 1313*, Paris, 1827.

Dehaisnes, C. *Documents et extraits divers concernant l'histoire de l'art dans la Flandre, l'Artois et le Hainaut avant le quinzième siècle*, Lille, 1886.

Delalain, P. *Etude sur le libraire parisien du treizième au quinzième siècle*, Paris, 1891.

Géraud, H. *Paris sous Philippe le bel, d'après des documents originaux et d'après un MS contenant le rôle de la taille imposée sur les habitants de Paris en 1292*, Paris, 1837.

Guiffrey, J. *Inventaires de Jean duc de Berry (1401-1416)*, Paris, 1894-1896.

Michäelsson, K. *Le livre de la taille de Paris*, Acta Universitatis Gothoburgensis, LXIV, 1958, 4; LXVII, 1961, 3.

Praet, L. van. *Recherches sur Louis de Bruges*, Paris, 1881.

Prost, B. *Inventaires mobiliers et extraits des comptes des ducs de Bourgogne de la maison de Valois (1363-1477)*, Paris, 1902-1913.

Richard, J.-M. *Une petite-nièce de Saint-Louis, Mahaut, comtesse d'Artois et de Bourgogne, (1302-1329)*, Paris, 1887.

VI. *Techniques of illumination*

Branner, R. *The Manerius Signatures*. Art Bulletin, 1968, p. 183.

Porcher, J. Jean Lebègue, *Les Histoires que l'on peut raisonnablement faire sur les livres de Salluste*, Paris, 1962.

Ross, D. J. A. *Methods of Book-Production in a Fourteenth-Century French Miscellany, Scriptorium* VI, 1952, pp. 63-75.

———. *A Late Twelfth-Century Artist's Pattern-Sheet, Journal of the Warburg and Courtauld Institutes*, XXV, 1962, pp. 119-128.

Scheller, R. *A Survey of Medieval Model Books*, Haarlem, 1963.

Wormald, F. *A Medieval Description of Two Illuminated Psalters, Scriptorium*, VI, 1952, pp. 18-25.

THE INTRODUCTION TO THE *LAI DE L'OMBRE:* HALF A CENTURY LATER

by † Frederick Whitehead and Cedric E. Pickford

Dissatisfaction with traditional methods of stemmatology (Lachmannian methods) and with critical editions of texts founded on these found expression as long ago as 1913, in J. Bédier's introduction to his edition of the *Lai de l'Ombre* for the Société des Anciens Textes français. The appearance of this edition marked the death-knell of the old style critical edition as far as the medieval French field was concerned. The attitude of extreme negativism towards textual emendation, and the motto "preserve and justify wherever possible the reading of the manuscript" that inspired Bédier's work from this time onwards strongly influenced a whole generation of textual critics, especially in England, and at a time when A. E. Housman was denouncing an earlier generation of classical scholars who had approached the editing of Greek and Latin texts with the same conservatism that Bédier was now advocating. Bédier's conservatism found its most intense expression in the articles on the text of the *Chanson de Roland* that appeared in *Romania* shortly before the outbreak of the Second World War, a cataclysm which *felix opportunitas mortis*, he mercifully escaped. Much has happened in the intervening thirty years in the sphere of textual criticism and bibliography which may give to the issues arising out of the introduction to the *Lai de l'Ombre* a curiously old-fashioned air: on the other hand, we can see more clearly now than in 1939 what the real issues are.

The impact of the *Lai de l'Ombre* was sensational in the field of stemmatology. The Lachmannian method of classifying manuscripts seemed to rest on impeccable logical bases. Bédier however drew attention to the fact that the traditional methods of stemmatology almost always seemed to result in a two-branch stemma and that this dichotomy seemed in most cases to run through the whole tradition, not merely as regards the main families but within the families themselves.[1] We shall discuss later Bédier's own explanation of what seemed to him a very untoward phenomenon, and it is by no means so radical as at first sight appears.

Nevertheless, the discredit that the argument from the 'two-branch stemma' casts on traditional methods of stemmatology arises from its appeal to uninstructed common-sense: a method which produces the same result time after time must, it would seem, be radically vicious. More than one critic has nevertheless doubted the appeal to uninstructed common-sense in this instance; and indeed things that appear obvious to common-sense are frequently far from being so.

W. W. Greg did not regard the two-branch stemma as in any way remarkable, but asserted, without giving proof, that it is the expected consequence of decimation.[2] More recently, J. Fourquet tried to prove the converse proposition, namely that a two-branch stemma represents the way in which a manuscript tradition normally grows.[3] According to Fourquet, if we represent a growing manuscript tradition by a series of points (a, b, c, d, ... n) on a straight line whose origin is X, X being the author's

---

[1] Bédier's count of dichotomous and multitomous stemmata has been re-examined by A. Castellani, who shows that the preponderance of dichotomous stemmata is not so overwhelming as Bédier thought. One curious fact is that when one considers the stemmata proposed by editors of lyric poetry, those that are not dichotomous are almost all due to one editor, Stronski, in his editions of Elias de Barjols (Toulouse 1906) and of Folquet de Marseille, (Cracow, 1910). A count of stemmata throws perhaps more light on the ways of critics and editors than it does on manuscript traditions!

[2] W. W. Greg, "Recent Theories of Textual Criticism" *Modern Philology*, XXVIII, 1930-1, p. 403, and more recently in a letter to C. E. Pickford dated 18 January 1952.

[3] "Le paradoxe de Bédier" in *Mélanges 1945 II. Etudes Littéraires*, Strasbourg and Paris (1946) pp. 1-16.

THE INTRODUCTION TO THE "LAI DE L'OMBRE" 105

autograph MS. and a, b, &c. productive manuscripts, then a new family arises because a line of productive manuscripts diverges from the main stem at one of the points *a, b,* &c. It is obviously a rare event for two lines of productive manuscripts to diverge from the main stem at the same point, but unless this happens we are left with a tradition which splits into two families at say, the point *a,* with one of the two families dividing in its turn into two sub-families at the point *c.* The whole tradition thus develops in a dichotomous way, not merely as regards the families but also as regards the subordinate groupings within the families. Fourquet's argument in its turn appeals to uninstructed

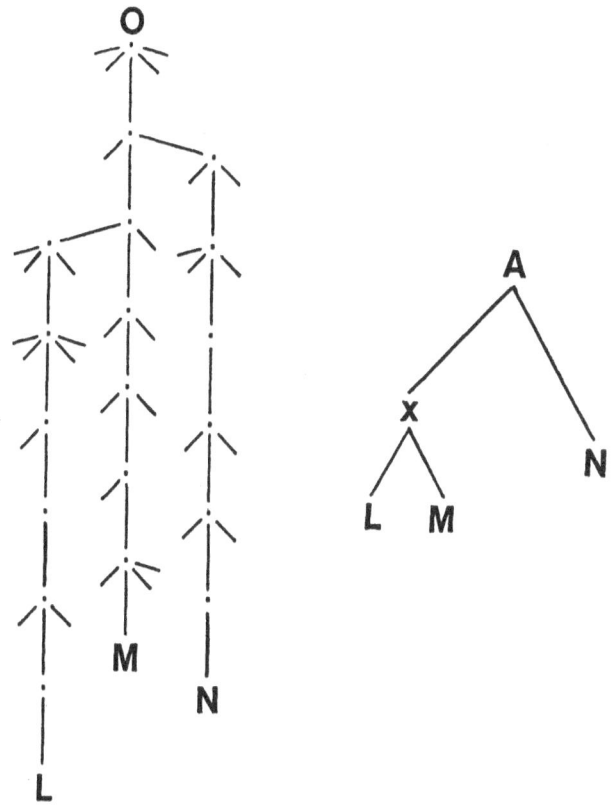

Fourquet's Diagram

common-sense, by arguing from a diagram and making certain implicit assumptions which the use of the diagram facilitates.

Our previous article on this subject in the *Bulletin de la Société internationale arthurienne* was directed to answering the question: under what conditions and making what initial assumptions, is the expectation that a manuscript tradition will survive in a two-branch form legitimate?[4]

We began by assuming the following case. A manuscript (o) containing the authentic version of a text has since been lost, but that before disappearing it gave rise to three families of descendants, going back to the three ancestors a, b, c, each of which was an independent copy of X. The three families were once of equal size, but in the course of time all the manuscripts that once existed have disappeared, except for three surviving MSS. P, Q, R. What is the probability that P, Q and R belong (a) to the same family, (b) to two different families, (c) to three different families?

The answer is given by the expansion of $(a + b + c)^3$, which becomes $(a^3 + b^3 + c^3 + 3a^2b + 3ab^2 + 3ac^2 + 3b^2c + 3bc^2 + 3a^2c + 6abc)$. Putting $a = 1$, $b = 1$, $c = 1$, the probability that P, Q, R all belong to the same family is $3/27 = 0.11$; the probability that they belong to two different families is $18/27 = 0.66$; and the probability that they belong to different families (i.e. the probability of a three-branch stemma) is $6/27 = 0.22$. The probability of a two-branch stemma on these assumptions is, it will be observed, three times as great as the probability of a three-branch one.

We can vary the assumptions by supposing that two of the original families (a and b) are each three times as large as the third. The probabilities of (i) a single family; (ii) a two-branch stemma; (iii) a three-branch stemma then become respectively $\frac{55}{343} = 0.16$; $\frac{234}{343} = 0.682$; $\frac{54}{343} = 0.16$. Similarly, with two families each twice as large as the third, the probabilities become 0.136, 0.672, 0.192 respectively. With the original families in the proportion of 3:2:1, the probabilities are 0.16; 0.66; 0.16 respec-

---

[4] F. Whitehead & C. E. Pickford, "The Two-Branch Stemma," *Bibliographical Bulletin* of the International Arthurian Society III (1951), pp. 83-90.

tively; and with the original families in the proportion of 4:3:2 they are 0.136; 0.66; 0.1975.

By assuming that we have four extant manuscripts (Q, R, S, T) the only survivors from three originally equal families, the expression $(a + b + c + d)^4$ allows us to find the probability (i) that they all belong to the same family; (ii) that only two of the original three families are represented among them; and (iii) that all three of the original families are represented. Expanding this expression, we obtain: $a^4 + b^4 + c^4 + 4(a^3b + a^3c + b^3a + b^3c + c^3a + c^3b) + 6(a^2b^2 + a^2c^2 + b^2c^2) + 12(a^2bc + ab^2c + abc^2)$. This gives the three probabilities as 0.037, 0.529, 0.454. It will be seen that with four extant manuscripts, the probability of Q, R, S, T forming themselves into a three-branch stemma is nearly equal to that of their forming themselves into a two-branch stemma. But again, marked disproportion in the size of the original families results in the probability of a three-branch stemma being distinctly less favourable. We give the probabilities for the proportions between the original families considered above:

3 — 3 — 1: (i) 0.068; (ii) 0.617; (iii) 0.315
2 — 2 — 1: (i) 0.035; (ii) 0.563; (iii) 0.384
3 — 2 — 1: (i) 0.076; (ii) 0.591; (iii) 0.33
4 — 3 — 2. (i) 0.054; (ii) 0.551; (iii) 0.395

With five extant manuscripts, the probability of the manuscripts forming themselves into a three-branch stemma is of course much higher. With three originally equal families, the probability that the five manuscripts belong to (i) the same family; (ii) two different families and (iii) three different families are respectively 0.012, 0.370, 0.617.

In practice, it is rare to find that more than five manuscripts are involved, since a partial grouping of the extant manuscripts is almost always possible and what we are really concerned with is the relationship between the primary groups (represented by their extant or presumed common ancestor). It is significant that the issue of the 'three branch' or 'two branch' stemma has been the really controversial one: the possibility of the occurrence of four branch stemmata is one that has been discounted in practice.

There is however a notion that we should like to introduce at this point. Decimation will not account for the large preponderance of two-branch stemmata unless we make certain assumptions about how a manuscript tradition develops. The important concept is that of the 'average reproduction rate' of manuscripts. With an 'average reproduction rate' of 3, the manuscripts of the tenth generation number around fifty-nine thousand. No one can suppose that the average reproduction rate was as high or as uniform as this. Fourquet's attempt to prove that the commonest type of classification will be a two-branch one assumes that the overall reproduction rate of medieval manuscripts is very low. Fourquet of course does not himself bring this concealed assumption into the light. But if we assume an overall reproduction rate of less than 2, and combine this with the effects of decimations, which when three families are concerned is very apt to leave only two of the three original families represented among the extant manuscripts, then is will be seen that the great preponderance of two-branch stemmata among the classificatory schemes proposed by modern editors is not surprising; nor should it provide by itself any grounds for rejecting the traditional methods of stemmatology.

Bédier's own explanation of the preponderance of two-branch stemmata implied no radical defect in the method but assumed that it was almost universally misapplied. Where groupings of the type *ab*)(*cd* occur frequently, as they do in the case of the manuscripts of the *Lai de l'Ombre*, and where it is clear that *a* and *b* share a common error that unites them into a family, while there is no decisive common error uniting *c* and *d* in the same way, then case will arise where an editor 'prefers' the reading offered by *ab* to that attested by *cd*. There is no decisive reason why *cd* should be treated as a family. But, on the other hand, there is no reason why they should not be, since, like a blood-test, the Lachmannian method of the indisputable common error can be used to *prove* a relationship between two manuscripts or families of manuscripts but it cannot be used to prove that *such a relationship does not exist*. If *cd* provide a common reading which seems inferior to that in *ab*, the editor will be tempted to regard *cd* as a family, and not as two independent groups.

The misapplication of the Lachmannian method of which Bédier complains was only possible as the result of a confusion of thought of which Bédier himself was equally guilty. The Lachmannian method of classifying manuscripts relies on what are in effect extrinsic criteria. It implies a distinction between the 'text' which a manuscript offers and external accidents which have affected that 'text.'[5] The loss of a number of lines resulting from mutilation of the manuscript, involuntary errors on the part of scribes during the copying process do not affect the intrinsic nature of the 'text' offered by the manuscript. Deliberate changes of the transmitted text, undertaken by a revisor or redactor for some definite purpose, literary or non-literary, of course do. By classifying manuscripts on the basis of common errors, and by defining 'error' in the strict sense to mean involuntary mutilation of the text either by external accident or scribal incompetence, the editor avoids making judgements on the quality of the 'text' embodied in the manuscript. Subjectivity is thus eliminated from the classificatory process. The ideal of classifying by purely objective criteria is one more easily attained by bibliographers, who dispose of a wealth of evidence, than by editors of medieval French texts, which were copied by scribes of great technical competence and freely altered and 'improved' as regards the language in which they were formulated. The consequence, in the Old French field, was a blurring of the distinction between the 'accident de copie' and the deliberate alteration by a revisor. Consequently, an obvious scribal error, a grammatical mistake, an illogicality of expression or of meaning, a poor rhyme, even a reading which was aesthetically unsatisfying could all be called 'bad' and pressed into service in the classifying process. Thus, in the *Lai de l'Ombre,* while it is clear that the two groups *a* (=AB) and *c* (=CG) are united by common error, there is nothing that can be called a common error in the proper sense of the term uniting the groups *d* (=DF) and *e* (=E). The question of a two-branch stemma therefore simply does not arise: there is

---

[5] A. C. Clarke argued that physical defects such as, e.g. *lacunae* caused by missing leaves, are the only recognisable errors for the purposes of classification in *The Descent of Manuscripts,* Oxford, 1912.

no proof that *d* and *e* form one family, even if there is nothing to prove that they do not.

When all is said and done, Bédier's case against stemmatology in the introduction to the *Lai de l'Ombre* amounts to no more than a claim that in the particular case of this text the evidence at our disposal simply allows to distinguish three groups of manuscripts, the A family (with its two sub-families *a* (=AB) and *c* (=CG) and the *d* (=DF) and *e* (=E) groups, both of which offer a type of text quite distinct from that of the A family. With this evidence, there is no possibility of producing a complete *stemma codicum:* no possibility therefore of an old-style critical edition. The questions that arise are (i) granted that this is the case, have we any right to generalise from this particular instance and (ii) even if we have, is Bédier's alternative to the old-style critical edition, i.e. the publication of one manuscript with apparatus and commentary the only practical alternative?

It should be remarkable that Bédier's hostility to the old-style critical edition, as displayed in the introduction to the *Lai de l'Ombre*, is not based entirely on methodological grounds but seems to also betray a certain subjective reaction. In the first place, the ideal of 'scientific stemmatology' based entirely on objective criteria and deciding the readings in a purely automatic way by reference to the *stemma codicum* seems to him to limit unduly the freedom of the editor and to dispense with taste and literary sensibility in favour of a purely mechanical process. In this, he may have been unduly influenced by his work on the *Chanson de Roland*. In the case of the *Chanson de Roland* it is a question of classifying not manuscripts but versions: it is also clear that the evidence, although of a different character from that involved in the classification of manuscripts, is amply sufficient to allow the construction of a *stemma codicum:* a two-branch stemma in which one family contains one member, the Oxford *Roland* and the other family all the other versions of the poem. But by applying in a mechanical and external way certain grammatical and logical criteria, Foerster and Stengel had produced a multi-branch stemma, in which the Oxford MS., together with V[4], constituted just one family among several, and on the basis of which Stengel, simply by following the consensus of the versions, was able to reproduce the text of the original poem of which the Oxford MS. was a much altered version! It is no doubt repugnance for the so-called objective and mechanical process which produced Stengel's edition of the *Roland* that inspired Bédier's distrust of the critical edition based on a *stemma codicum* which was wrongly constructed. The problem is also not the same: where it is a case of judging between isolated readings, involving a few words only and in no way affecting the structure of the work as a whole, the critic's taste, judgement and acumen is often completely powerless to decide. In l. 885 of the *Lai de l'Ombre*, where A has *n'en reprenderai*, the other members of the family *ne le retenrai* and *d* and *e n'en reporterai*, it is clear that the reading of *d e* has a point and a cogency that the other versions lack. But this, by itself, does not allow us to attribute it to the original author or to use it (since it is an *intrinsic* feature of the text we are trying to classify) in the construction of a *stemma codicum*. If we had irrefragable extrinsic evidence that *A, d* and *e* constituted three independent families, the reading could be automatically assigned to the common original. As it is, lacking a 'machine to do our thinking for us' we have no means of deciding whether *n'en reporterai* is a felicitous improvement on the part of a revisor or whether (as seems more likely) it goes back to the original version. Not only do the rules of the critical game sometimes forbid us to attribute the highly felicitous reading of one group of manuscripts to the author, they also require us to replace one entirely innocuous reading by another equally innocuous: *bonnet blanc* by *blanc bonnet*. What in effect, asks Bédier, do such trivial differences of formulation as *se merveillent* and *s'esmerveillent* or *pucele ne dame* and *dame ne pucele* really amount to?

It is perhaps the realisation that the critical edition of an Old French text need not necessarily result in a product which is aesthetically more satisfying than the version contained in any single manuscript that disgusted Bédier with what seemed to him an elaborate and pointless procedure. One impulse behind textual criticism since the time of the sixteenth-century Humanists was the assurance that the nearer one got to the *ipsissima verba* of the great authors of antiquity the more impressive and beautiful these words would become. Hence the formula 'authentic' means 'better.' Once this equation ceases to hold, as it may well do in the case of medieval French texts, then the textual critic is employing his acumen and imagination in what can only be a self-frustrating task.

But of course critical scholarship does not serve only aesthetic ends: the student of linguistics needs authentic texts for his syntactical and lexicographical studies. Trust in the readings of a given manuscript is no more justifiable than trust in the inerrancy of a critical edition. Moreover, it is exaggerated to represent a manuscript as preserving a state of the text that has enjoyed an authentic existence, since what we are dealing with is in most cases something quite as composite as any reconstituted critical text produced by a scholar in the quiet of his study. A manuscript generally presents us with several strata of alteration and behind many readings there is a complex history of change. In order to understand some aspects of the history of change, it can be helpful to consider closely some of the methods by which medieval manuscripts were copied. We have referred earlier to the average reproduction rate of manuscripts. This is essentially an abstract conception, and it is by no means certain that the reproduction of manuscripts can be seen in the uniform way that Professor Fourquet illustrates it. In his Inaugural Lecture, Professor Castellani considers the methods of copying literary texts from a theoretical point of view. He suggests that if an author wishes to produce multiple copies of his work as rapidly as possible, then the author's own copy will first of all give rise to a first generation descendant and then in the next instance will simultaneously give rise to a second generation descendant and to a second first generation descendant, and so on. In this way if a given text takes us one month to copy, seven copies can be produced within three months, but of these seven copies three will be first generation descendants of the author's original and one family will contain four manuscripts, the second two and the third only one.

THE INTRODUCTION TO THE "LAI DE L'OMBRE"   113

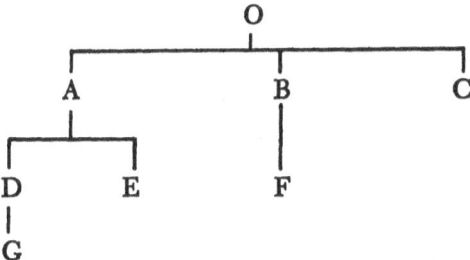

Castellani's arguments are interesting ones, but in truth we have little idea concerning the circumstances under which multiple copies of a work were made at the immediate request of the author. Rather more is known about the way texts were copied in times somewhat removed from the date of original composition. In the case of university texts, there is of course the technique of dividing a work up into several sections which could be hired out and copied individually. This system of *pecia* copying was not applied to medieval French literary texts. Again, multiple copies could be made by means of dictation, but once more there is no evidence to show that medieval French literary texts were reproduced in large numbers in this way. A further suggestion made by Professor Castellani is that if a manuscript were made for a private collector, it could prove to be completely sterile as far as future descendants or copies made from it are concerned. This suggestion is not however born out by a study of some literary texts, at any rate. Patrons of literature not only acquired texts, but also had copies made especially for themselves. It is interesting in this connection to notice that light may be thrown upon the classification of literary texts by the study of patronage and other known textual evidence such as illumination and decoration. To quote one specific example the arthurian prose romances collected in the private libraries of Jaques D'Armagnac show a close relationship in their texts. The copies of the prose *Tristan* which he owned, MS. B.N.fr. 99, and Nouv. Acqu. fr. 6579, are closely related as far as texts are concerned. MS. 99 was copied in the fifteenth century, and one wonders to what extent the copyist, Gonnot, worked from MS N.A.fr. 6579 which is a late thirteenth century copy that bears the signature of

Jaques D'Armagnac. The textual relationship of D'Armagnac's manuscripts in this collection is not limited to this point. One of the illuminators who worked for Jaques D'Armagnac, namely Evrard D'Espingues, also worked on MS. 315-317 in the Musée Condé at Chantilly. These manuscripts contain a text which is virtually identical with that in MS. 99. Furthermore Gonnot also copied MS. 112 in the French collection in the Bibliothèque Nationale and the text of 112 is very close to that of copies of the prose *Lancelot* and the prose *Tristan* which also belonged to Jaques D'Armagnac.

In other words when one comes to draw up a stemma of manuscripts, it is appropriate to take into account not only the text as such but also everything that is known about the other aspects of the manuscript as a book, namely copyist, illuminator and owner. If this is done, one sees that it is increasingly difficult to draw up a stemma which does not represent a considerable amount of cross-influences from one family of manuscripts to another. Furthermore these cross-influences are sometimes quite independent of literary or aesthetic considerations. The workings of pure chance have their part to play, and it is clear that a manuscript, once copied, does not become sterile, but may be used as the source of further copies, even centuries later.

These observations on methods of copying manuscripts refer, of course, to the copying of complete texts. The conditions which apply in the case of short works which are included in anthologies may well be somewhat different, but there again the taste of the compiler of the anthology may well play an important part just as an important part may be played by the availability of works for inclusion in the anthology. Thus in considering the establishment of a *stemma codicum,* one is in fact adding yet another weapon to our armoury which enables us to understand and define medieval literary texts. The real purpose of textual criticism is to question our easy faith in texts as they have been transmitted to us and to attempt to delimit the areas of our knowledge and our ignorance by determining what is certainly original, what is certainly a later improvement or corruption and what is of uncertain status, and even what may be a revised edition by the author. For this reason, as E. Vinaver [6] has declared, the most that an editor of medieval texts can aspire to is a partial reconstitution of original text. Perhaps the most notable change in the attitude of the textual critic in the Old French field in the period since 1939 has been the return to procedures familiar to textual critics in the classical field but completely lost to sight by editors of French medieval texts at the turn of the century. Most important of these is the principle that divergent readings have to be accounted for. If we believe that revisor v has replaced the reading a of his source by another reading b we ought not to rest content until we have formed some adequate hypothesis to account for his motives in doing this. Very often equally cogent reasons can be adduced for assuming that it is reading a that has replaced reading b, and very often a multiplicity of hypotheses can be found to explain a particular pair of readings. But in some cases, the editor may be fortunate enough to evolve a hypothesis that explains the genesis of a reading in a very illuminating way. The point surely is that by now textual criticism has moved decisively away from the phase of extreme conservatism inaugurated by Bédier's Introduction to the *Lai de l'Ombre* and that thanks to the insight of more recent textual critics and bibliographers, the textual critic can cheerfully assume the duty of finding out as much about any given manuscript tradition and any particular reading as he possibly can.

---

[6] "Principles of Textual Emendation," *Studies presented to M. K. Pope*, Manchester, 1939, pp. 351-70. See essay 7 below, pp. 139-166.

SHORT BIBLIOGRAPHY

1 J. Bédier, editor, *Le Lai de l'Ombre* 1890 (rev. by Gaston Paris, Romania XIX [1890] p. 609) and again in 1913 for the *Société des Anciens Textes Français* and as an Appendix to the reprint of his article "La Tradition Manuscrite du *Lai de l'Ombre*, Réflexions sur l'art d'Editer les Anciens Textes" *Romania* LIV (1928), pp. 161-96; 321-56.

2 Dom Henri Quentin, *Essais de Critique Textuelle*, Paris 1926.

3 P. Shepard, "Recent Studies in Textual Criticism" *Modern Philology* XXXIII (1930-1) pp. 130-i.

4 W. W. Greg, *The Calculus of Variants*, Oxford 1927, and "Recent Theories of Textual Criticism" Modern Philology XXVIII, pp. 401-4.

5 E. Vinaver, "Principles of Textual Emendation" in *Studies presented to M. K. Pope*, Manchester 1939, pp. 351-70.

6 Jean Fourquet, "Le Paradoxe de Bédier" *Mélanges 1949, II, Etudes Littéraires*, Strasbourg, Paris 1946, pp. 1-16.

7 E. B. Ham, *Textual Criticism and Jehan le Venelais*, Ann-Arbor, 1946.

8 F. Whitehead and C. E. Pickford, "The Two-Branched Stemma" in *Bulletin Bibliographique de la Société Internationale Arthurienne*, Vol. III (1951) pp. 83-90.

9 Arrigo Castellani, *Bédier avait-il Raison? La Méthode de Lachmann dans les éditions de texte du Moyen Age*, Fribourg, 1957.

THE PROBLEM OF CONTAMINATION IN PROSE TEXTS

by Cesare Segre

In this essay I wish to present as axioms the results of some personal and, therefore, limited philological investigations, which have their base in my study of the manuscript tradition of Richart de Fornival's *Bestiaire d'Amours*.[1] It is interesting to note that the Italian prose texts of the *Duecento* reveal far fewer instances of contamination than, for example, those in France during the same period. Perhaps, this indicates the less important and underdeveloped nature of philological activity in 13th-century Italy, which contrasts with the highly-refined craftsmanship of the French *scriptoria*. There is a remarkable correspondence between Richart's pre-Humanistic activity and the complex contamination that his masterpiece has undergone.

1. A procedural method with regard to contamination may more easily be determined by studying those manuscript traditions which contain both contaminated and uncontaminated codices. When the editor knows the source of errors and characteristic readings in the original groups or sub-groups, he obviously has a secure foundation on which to base his examination of subsequent junctures and, at the same time, avoids the pitfalls of unimportant conjectures, emendations, and overcorrections. Moreover, it should be noted that contamination of the sort that yields only correct readings (or those considered correct) in

---

[1] Richart de Fornival, *Li Bestiaires d'Amours e Li Response du Bestiaire*, ed. Cesare Segre (Milano-Napoli: Ricciardi, 1957).

a base text is extremely rare in the Middle Ages. At best the amount of collation involved in the establishment of a text may be considered to be inversely proportional to the degree of reliability accorded the text.

2. The contamination of exemplars should not be considered similar to other forms of contamination and, as such, should not be a part of the present discussion. This form of contamination occurs when the scribe copies first from one then from another text, either to supplement an incomplete exemplar or because he has found a more legible or authoritative one. In these instances his copy alternately presents readings which have their source in the separate traditions of the two exemplars.

3. The contamination of readings is the result of a collation performed on the ancestor of a manuscript and can be classified, according to its characteristics, as 1) simple (the result of one collation with one exemplar), 2) fractionated (successive collations with one exemplar), or 3) multiple (several collations with more than one exemplar), which can also be fractionated.

Three categories also emerge with regard to the amount of collation performed: 1) sporadic (readings taken from the second exemplar are desultory and isolated); 2) frequent (readings composed of words together with word groups and complete periods frequently inserted in the first exemplar); and 3) complete (when the collator has decided to note all the differences between the two exemplars). Although less categorical than the former, classification by amount of contamination does have, I believe, a certain value when compared to the pattern of errors and characteristic variants. To put it more clearly, in the case of sporadic contamination this pattern does not suffer noticeable deviations; however, in the other two divisions it is seriously distorted or interrupted.

4. Once a codex is identified as contaminated, many others then fall under the same heading; the contaminated codex, thus, may lead us to a focal point of the manuscript tradition. In fact, while simple collation can be the work of a scholar or a dilettante, the transcription of a collated codex is almost always ev-

idence of the work of a *scriptorium* (before the age of Humanism, that is, when the philologists themselves assumed the tasks of the scribes). Even if the *scriptorium* had two or more exemplars of the same text, an edition *ne varietur* was seldom prepared. However, we frequently find instances of multiple or fractionated contamination as well as the peculiar case of cross contamination, in which the text first incorporated as the second exemplar has been adopted in successive transcriptions as the base exemplar, and vice versa. Once the relationship between the groups of exemplars of a specific *scriptorium* has been determined, it is often possible to establish that the characteristic elements of the codices utilized appear in varying proportions and with varying distinctions.

5. The diffusion of a work increases the amount of contamination for three reasons: 1) there is a greater chance that more exemplars of the work will come together in the same *scriptorium*; 2) there is a greater probability that the codices used for the contamination are themselves contaminated; and 3) the person in charge of the collation by necessity makes note of the increasing differences between the exemplars.

6. As for the existence of a link between contamination and revision, it could be said that, while sporadic contamination corresponds to a desire for fidelity, frequent and multiple contamination suggest a sense of relativity and, moreover, allow one to obtain a certain fluency, albeit specious, through autonomous means. Forgetting his role as seeker of variants, the scribe becomes the creator of variants. It follows that, whenever very old, lost exemplars have contributed to the contamination, the faith placed in their contaminated representatives must be counterbalanced by a critical appraisal of possible conjectures and later revisions.

7. As one goes from simple to multiple contamination and from sporadic to complete contamination, there is less possibility of obtaining the true statement of the derivational relationships. In part this can be considered a consequence of section 5 above, but I should add that generally, given the characteristics of group

a, to which belongs the base exemplar, and given those of group *b* (and eventually of *c*, *d*, etc.), to which belongs the second exemplar, the system of the characteristic elements of *a* through the increase and entanglement of contamination becomes less and less clear, while those elements coming from *b* (and later from *c*, *d*, etc.) never attain the arrangement of a system because of the inherently free nature of collation.

From this one can deduce that the evidence valid for an analysis of simple and sporadic contamination (as *lacunae*, extraneous readings, etc.), which is always helpful and subject to further refinements, [2] is not completely sufficient.

8. The next step is a statistical analysis of the variants. This must be done with extreme care, for 1) it obviously precludes the distinction between errors and variants of equal weight and consequently 2) it runs the risk of taking into consideration concurrences that stem from regional and cultural similarities rather than from a direct relationship. On the other hand, it should be noted that, following the observations of section 6 above, the absence of a characteristic error, given the nature of the contamination, can often be the result (even the polygenetic result) of conjectural emendation.

Nevertheless, for a careful application of the statistical method, the following precautions will serve to render the results of such a study quite reliable. In essence, it is a question of 1) the incorporation of statistical analysis in the precise methods of examination currently in use or 2) the integration of statistical analyses defined in a different manner. While the first method needs no further illustration, I would like to pause for a moment on the second.

9. The collation from which the contamination derives is never uniform. Therefore, given the division of a text *A* in conventional sections, certainly those sections in which the system of derivational group *a* is more seriously distorted will be more

---

[2] For example, MS *A* contaminated with MS *B* will probably show a reading from *B* in place of a lacuna in its own group *a*, or MS *A* contaminated with MS *B* will probably show, in place of lacunae in its own group *a*, the readings of *B* moved from their original position, and so on.

densely populated with elements of group *b* (and then *c*, *d*, etc.) of the second exemplar. At the same time those sections rich in elements from group *b* will be richest in elements of the second exemplar *B*. If the second exemplar was already contaminated, the scarcity of elements of group *a* in *A* and the frequency of readings from group *b* and its representative *B* will coincide with the presence of readings from groups *c*, *d*, etc. (which have partially joined together in *B*). Conversely, if *A* is the already contaminated codex, the elements of the first contamination will be in inverse proportion to those of the contamination with *B*.

In the employment of these devices and others, which can be adopted according to the situation, the inversion of the statistical relationships that result from the contamination must also be kept in mind. Since characteristic errors are generally more numerous the farther one goes down the *stemma* of the manuscript tradition, then in MS *A* contaminated with *B* there will be more errors and characteristic readings of *B* than of its ancestor *b* (the reversal of the relationship). I note this fact here (and not in the first paragraph of this section), for, when hypothesizing a contamination, the errors of a group are more valid than those of its representative.

10. The study of contaminated codices not only satisfies the legitimate hope for completeness or the desire for an exhaustive historical study of the manuscript tradition, but often allows the editor to reconstruct lost authoritative manuscripts, or even archetypes or authorial redactions. If one thinks that manuscripts generally have a smaller lineage the closer they are to the original, that the establishment of a *vulgata* tends to eliminate isolated witnesses that are often the purest, and that finally the physical appearance of a codex (and therefore its fitness for diffusion) often depends on the fortune of the work transcribed therein (which consequently belongs to a period of time relatively far removed from the original date of composition), if one thinks all these things, then the possibility will become quite evident that some contamination, especially if it dates from a former era, constitutes the last trace of small elements of the textual tradition that have almost immediately disappeared. Contaminated "commercial" codices should have preserved the last words of those exemplars destined to a short existence.

In this essay I generalized this possibility in abstract terms only because I have established it concretely in the tradition of the *Bestiaire d'Amours*. However, I am convinced that it will be demonstrated again and again if research on contamination is continued and perfected.

THE ART OF EDITING LYRIC TEXTS

by † István Frank

We are all aware of the illumination shed by the Preface to the *Lai de l'Ombre* at the beginning of the century. Since that time, there has been no end to the responses provoked by Joseph Bédier's question: Are Lachmann's methods applicable, without reservation and without excessive risks of error, to the living tradition of the Middle Ages?[1]

If the common errors (Lachmann's phrase; Dom Quentin calls them "common variants"; M. Roques prefers "common innovations") permit us to rediscover the vanished archetype of each group of readings, they permit us, by the same token, to find relationships among them that lead us toward the original we are seeking (which Dom Quentin prefers to call "the common archetype"; and which M. Dain refers to more precisely as "the-closest-

---

[1] It is a simple matter to establish a bibliography of the subject. One should begin with the article by J. Andrieu, "Principes et recherches en critique textuelle," in *Mémorial des Études latines... offert... à... J. Marouzeau* (Paris, 1943), pp. 458-474; go on to the *Manuel bibliographique* of R. Bossuat (p. xxxi); and consult, for more recent publications, the chronicle of A. Roncaglia in *Cultura Neolatina*, XII (1952), 281-283. To the references found in these sources can be added those given in my *Trouvères et Minnesänger, Recueil de textes pour servir à l'étude des rapports entre la poésie lyrique romane et le Minnesang au XIIe siècle* (Saarbrücken: West-Ost-Verlag, 1952), p. xviii. Finally, one should consult the thesis of A. Micha, *La Tradition manuscrite des romans de Chrétien de Troyes* (Paris, 1939), as well as the articles by A. Norfeldt, in *Mélanges de philologie offerts à M. J. Vising* (Göteborg and Paris, 1925), p. 76, and by E. Vinaver, "Principles of Textual Emendation," in *Studies in French Language and Literature presented to Professor M. K. Pope* (Manchester, 1939), pp. 351-370 (see essay 7 below, pp. 139-166).

common-ancestor-of-the-tradition" [*sic*]). These ramified relationships constitute a genealogical tree, the *stemma*, which, when we reconcile its branches, prescribes a text.

It is this text, freed of the errors accumulated by successive copies, and amended by conjecture where the tradition as a whole is lacking, which will be attributed to the author — Aeschylus, Terence, or Chrétien de Troyes. It will be worthy of this ascription to the degree that the method has been applied with scientific rigor, with discernment, and with that philological instinct without which the attempt is not worth the effort. The procedure does not work when contaminations confuse the filiation or when the original is multiple: in the first case, the stemma either does not stand out clearly or does not lead anywhere; in the second, the originals act as archetypes and produce a synthesis of the versions that were written successively by the author.

In the last analysis, it was Bédier's repugnance toward a final contamination that led him to abandon the combinatory method, the so-called "critical" method. Each of the originals, in the guise of archetypes, would be valid; but their amalgam never had any legitimate existence. "What would we say of an editor of *Le Père Goriot* who combined in a single monstrous text variants taken from the three editions O^1, O^2, and O^3, all three of which were prepared by Balzac?" (*Romania*, LIV, 353). Translated into Lachmannian terms, Bédier's refusal signifies that the method is not applicable to the tale of Jean Renart because there was (or may have been) a multiple original. [2]

The stemmata of the manuscripts, moreover, were not unambiguous: there were four equally well-founded schemas, with which the editor found only one fault — *the fact of being four*. (*Romania*, LIV, 188). An examination of the schemas that gave

---

[2] On the subject of "Edizioni originali e varianti di autore," see the long and rich chapter bearing this title in G. Pasquali, *Storia della tradizione e critica del testo*, 2nd ed. (Florence: Le Monnier, 1952), pp. 397-465. This chapter, as L. Havet has said, is concerned more with pathology than with therapy, and questions of method are not examined. But, in view of what is pointed out in this chapter, every decision of a Lachmannian editor should carry with it an implicit clause conceived in the following terms: "Whereas it appears that none of the rejected variants can be traced to the author himself, we adopt the reading indicated by the stemma; and go on to the next question."

rise to the establishment of other texts, of more than one hundred other critical texts, led to the following observation, which has been called "Bédier's paradox": almost every stemma has two branches. Since it is improbable that all the manuscripts now known of all the literary works of the Middle Ages go back to two and only two initial copies, the stemma posited by the method of Lachmann becomes suspect. Particularly suspicious is the convergence of branches and their juncture in a trunk. (*Romania*, LIV, 356, 2nd paragraph).

Whatever may have been thought, said, or calculated, it is impossible to believe that dichotomy in the *real* transmission of texts could have occurred in the overwhelming majority of cases, as the genealogical schemas suggest. Born as a copy, every manuscript was capable, at a time when its contents were of lively interest and for a long time thereafter, of giving rise to copies in its turn. Apart from sterile copies, which were doubtless very frequent, the chances of a manuscript's being copied more than twice do not seem to me assimilable to the "double events" or "multiple events" of probability theory.[3]

The production of two new copies from a text that has already produced one (A > B, then C and D) is, clearly, a "double event" only if there is coincidence in time, and not temporal succession. The French *chansonniers* (KNPX, LV) and the Provençal ones (AB, A^a, A^b, m, z; IK) show clearly enough that multiple copies were not at all rare.

We are sometimes easily taken in by mathematical mirages. It has been demonstrated that the number of types possible in the filiation of three manuscripts is twenty-two, of which twenty-one are dichotomous and only one tripartite,[4] and this has seemed

---

[3] See two remarkable essays by J. Fourquet, as memorable as those of the master they tend to contradict: "Le Paradoxe de Bédier," in *Mélanges 1945, II: Etudes littéraires* ("Publications de la Faculté des Lettres de l'Université de Strasbourg," 105), (Paris: Belles-Lettres, 1946), pp. 1-16; and "Fautes communes ou innovations communes," in *Romania*, LXX (1948), 85-95, a response to the review by M. Roques appearing in *Romania*, LXIX (1946), 117-118.

[4] Cf. P. Maas, *Textkritik*, 2nd edn., (Leipzig: Teubner, 1950), pp. 27-31; Italian translation by N. Martinelli, *Critica del testo*, with preface by G. Pasquali ("Bibliotechina del Saggiatore," 9), (Florence: Le Monnier, 1952), pp. 53-62.

to afford a rigorously-calculated confirmation of the proportions noted by Bédier: 105 two-branched trees *versus* five three-branched trees. Is this not, to the highest degree of precision one could desire, the proportion of twenty-one bipartite types *versus* only one tripartite type? Such perfect agreement between the best opponent and the best proponent of the Lachmannian method has seemed to carry conviction.[5] In reality, this is only a mirage of numbers, an optical illusion, which confuses the mere enumeration of possible types with the probability of their actual realization. By this reasoning, if we posit the Dionne quintuplets as a limiting case, there is one chance in five of twins at every birth. The throw of the dice, the simple act of choosing a white ball, or a number, are hardly ever reproduced in their pure state within the complex network of natural phenomena or of human activity.

* * *

The lyric *chansonniers* of the Middle Ages result from just such complex activity; they are the surviving evidence of it. No general study has been made of them up to the present time.[6]

---

[5] Cf. *Cultura Neolatina*, XII, 281-282, for a viewpoint suggested by Maas, *Textkritik*, pp. 30-31 (pp. 60-61 in the translation cited).

[6] The basic bibliographies for the French and Provençal *chansonniers* are those of G. Raynaud, A. Jeanroy, A. Pillet and H. Carstens, and C. Brunel, as well as the essays by G. Gröber and E. Schwan cited in one of the following notes. In the field of Italian, the basic study remains that of N. Caix, *Le origini della lingua poetica italiana* (Florence, 1880); an excellent bibliographical orientation is given in the anthology edited by M. Vitale, *Poeti della prima scuola* ("Pubblicazioni del Sodalizio glottologico milanese," 1), (Arona: Paideia, 1951). For the Portuguese collections, see S. Pellegrini, *Repertorio bibliografico della prima lirica portoghese* ("Istituto di Filologia romanza della R. Università di Roma, Testi e Manuali," 15), (Modena: Soc. Tipogr. Modenese, 1939); and J. Filgueira Valverde, *Lírica medieval gallega y portuguesa*, in *Historia general de las literaturas hispánicas*, published under the direction of G. Díaz-Plaja (Barcelona: Ed. Barna, n.d. [1949]), I, 545-642; see especially pp. 554-563 and 634-635. For the Castilian *cancioneros*: C.-V. Aubrun, *Inventaire des sources pour l'étude de la poésie castillane au XVe siècle*, in *Estudios dedicados a Menéndez Pidal* (Madrid: C.S.I.C., 1953), IV, 297-330; and J. Simón Díaz, *Bibliografía de la literatura hispánica* (Madrid: C.S.I.C., 1953), Vol. III (cf. *Romania*, LXXIV, 544-545). For Catalan: J. Massó Torrents, *Repertori de l'antiga literatura catalana* (Barcelona: Alpha, 1932), of which only Vol. I has appeared.

These collections, whatever their language, constitute, however, a well-determined codicological type, and their diffusion can easily be discerned in broad outline.

Each of their linguistic domains would merit study from the viewpoint of verbal criticism. They present, of course, special problems: questions of linguistic transfer, especially, haunt the Italian manuscripts; the manuscript tradition of the Gallego-Portuguese school suffers from a paucity of evidence; the Castillian and Catalan collections, like the authors they contain, are late. The French and Provençal *chansonniers* are the oldest and most numerous, and have transmitted the largest number of copies of their texts. Italian, Spanish, and Catalan songs rarely appear in more than a few manuscripts; the *trouvères* and *troubadours* who enjoyed some reputation have left us very many pieces that have been preserved in more than ten or fifteen *chansonniers;* some figure in more than twenty copies.

This abundant tradition offers to textual criticism an instructive field of study. But it is not at all certain that what can be learned from it carries over perfectly to other manuscript traditions. In fact, it is clear that this tradition possesses certain features that are quite special.

It will be observed that, in editions of lyric texts, the *stemmata codicum* are bipartite, as they are elsewhere. This is only natural, if we keep in mind the explanation of stemmatic dichotomy that M. Roques suggested to Bédier, and which was expressed by Bédier as follows: "...the force of dichotomy, once unleashed, acts to the end. The Lachmannian system has launched [the editor] on a hunt for common errors, but has given him no way of knowing when to stop." (*Romania,* LIV, 175-176). This should not disturb us, if we recall, with M. Fourquet, that a bipartite schema can bind the editor, i.e., can serve him, as well as a tripartite schema. The stemma of manuscripts seems, then, for lyric texts as well as for others, to lead to an original or to the archetype which, within the limits of the accessible evidence, approaches most closely to the author's copy.[7] The question is:

---

[7] On the improbability of the exclusive productivity of a single copy and of two initial copies at a time when the literary tradition is still alive, see J. Marouzeau, *Térence* (Coll. Budé, 1947), I, 85-87.

did this author's copy composed by the combinatory method ever really exist?

A transcription of every lyric song known today was made at some point in time; that is obvious. Either the author wrote it down himself, or dictated it, or someone who heard it and liked it put it in writing or had it transcribed. Texts have been collected which testify to all these diverse practices. [8]

It would be imprudent to believe and rash to claim that all our copies go back to this first written copy. The *chanson courtoise* was intended for oral performance. There can be both an author's copy and an author's recital. When the recital is repeated, at places and times distant from the original one, variants can emerge, not only when the performer is the poet himself, but *a fortiori* when the performer — who may or may not be authorized — is someone other than the poet. And a new copy may of course be made at any recital. This is the phenomenon which confers a mark of singularity upon the tradition of the lyric *chansonniers*. Anyone who wishes to estimate the relative value of their valid variants must take it into account.

How, indeed, can we distinguish among the variants emerging from these performances, all of which are correct and authorized by the competence of the performers? Speaking of the dazzling beauty of his lady, Thibaut de Champagne says (ed., p. 17, verses 15-16):

> Car qui avroit le plus biau jor d'esté
> Lez li seroit oscurs a plain midi.

That, in any case, is the reading in the scrupulous critical edition made by Axel Wallensköld for the Société des Anciens textes français. But, of the seventeen known manuscripts, all offer some variant upon this summation of the tradition. For example, M has: "Car qui *veroit* le plus biau jor d'esté, *Vers* li seroit oscurs *en* plain midi"; K (the base manuscript) has: "Car qui avroit le

---

[8] G. Gröber, "Die Liedersammlungen der Troubadours," in *Romanische Studien*, II (1877), 377 ff.; E. Schwan, *Die altfranzösischen Liederhandschriften* (Berlin, 1886), p. 264. Cf. also *Mélanges de linguistique et de littérature romanes offerts à Mario Roques* (Baden and Paris: Didier, 1950), I, 69-70.

plus biau jor d'esté, Lez li seroit *oscur en* plain midi." The editor's explanation of the numerous crossings in his variants is that "most of our manuscripts are, evidently, 'contaminated,' that is, they go back directly or indirectly to several sources that were used at the same time" (p. xcviii). But what if, in addition to the obvious contamination (cf. *ibid.*, pp. cviii-cx), which in itself casts doubt upon the efficacy of the combinatory method, it was a question not of *"a copy already altered from the original"* (p. cviii, italicized in the text), but of a multiple original?

> Par Deu, Huet, ne m'en puis [plus] soffrir,
> Qu'en Bertree est et ma mort et ma vie.

So sang Gace Brulé [9] one day (ms. O). On another day, he sang (or will sing; mss. C and U):

> Par Deu, compans, ne vos os plus jehir
> Ke ma dame est et ma mort et ma vie.

How can we tell whether or not these are author's variants?

Marcabru,[10] in 1137, goes off on an Iberian tour, and announces his itinerary thus (ms. A):

> En Castell' e vas Portegau
> On anc non fo trames salutz:
>   E Dieus los sau!
> E vas Barcelon' atretau.
> Puois lo peitavis m'es faillitz [= Guillaume X],
> Serai mai cum Artur perdutz.

Then, upon his return from the peninsula, he modifies his text (mss. IKNa¹):

> En Castell' et en Portegal
> Non tarmetrai autras salutz
>   Mas: Dieus los sal!

---

[9] See H. Petersen Dyggve, *Gace Brulé, trouvère champenois* ("Mémoires de la Société néophilologique de Helsinki," 16), (Helsinki, 1951), p. 276, verses 53-54; and *Trouvères et Minnesänger, op. cit.*, p. 61, verses 49-50.

[10] Pillet, *Bibliogr.*, No. 293, 4, stanzas XI-XII; ed. Dejeanne, p. 13.

Et en Barsalon' atretal.
[...]
En Gascoigna, sai, ves Orsau [= Vallée d'Ossau],
Me dizo qu'en creis uns petits [= Pierre de Béarn],
O·m trobaretz s'ieu sui perdutz.

Are we to say, in this case, that ms. A alone presents innovations, and that the agreement of the other manuscripts (IK, on the one hand, N and a¹ on the other) testifies to the correct reading? We would then lose the precious allusion to Guillaume X, which is not the sort of thing that scribes could easily have substituted for corrupted verses.

Thus it would seem that Gace Brulé and Marcabru may have left us two versions of their poems. If we justifiably prefer the text of O in the first case (considering the banality of C and of U, their lack of signs of living reality as compared with O), such a choice cannot reasonably be made in the case of Marcabru. It is understandable that the more recent version had a wider diffusion (IKNa¹), since it is in this new version that the song was sung. What is striking, however, is the fact that the compiler of *chansonnier* A was so well informed about the *princeps* version.

There is surely nothing surprising in the fact that a song written in 1137 somewhere on the route to Santiago found its way across the terrain and the generations that separated it from the compiler of *chansonnier* A, seated before his desk in Provence [11] about the middle of the thirteenth century. This compiler must have had access to particularly trustworthy sources, dating from a time close to that of the literary event in question.

An excellent Lachmannian precept (Maas, 19) holds that an isolated reading that is authenticated allows us to presume that the other isolated readings of the same manuscript may likewise be true. Applied to the case of Marcabru, this means that all the isolated true readings of *chansonnier* A may stem from the author. The only question is, what are the limits of this enhanced authenticity of A: does it extend over a stanza? over a song? over a part or the whole of Marcabru's work? over wider sections still?

In reality, this *chansonnier* is often the only one to have preserved the true variant. For the most part, it gives the best

---

[11] See Bertoni, in *Archivum Romanicum*, II (1918), 396-397.

text of the hundreds of songs it contains concurrently with other collections, songs written on both sides of the Alps and of the Pyrenees, in the most diverse times and places. The excellence of its readings, as well as of its orthography, has been universally recognized for a long time. Thus it figures in a place of honor among the branches of genealogical trees drawn up for critical editions. It is A, along with C (to which we shall refer again presently), which has furnished for the majority of these editions the "base manuscript," whatever the editors may have meant by this term.

So here we have the "correct manuscript," revealed by the experience of numerous editors of texts, to which Lachmannian rigor must refuse all confidence, suspect as it is of systematic revision. Its virtues could be due, not to the authenticity of its sources, but to the thoughtful work of its compiler, a true philologist, a new Aristophanes of Byzantium. If we are to believe the editors' genealogical trees, the complex and varied diffusion of a large number of Provençal songs began with a copy "α" that reached the compiler of A. The latter would then no longer be Aristophanes, but rather the archivist of Lycurgus, charged with establishing the *ne varietur* version of the dramas performed at the Dionysian festivals.

Indeed, anyone who compares the stemmas of Provençal songs will find, in addition to the surprising fact of universal dichotomy (an expected surprise), a second surprise: it appears not only that every original copy gave rise to two and only two initial copies, but that, in a large number of cases, one of these two copies was to be transmitted directly to A.

Thus, for example, this song of Bernart de Ventadour (Limousin, 1145-c. 1175), reaching *Mon Francés* by way of *Mauren* (see ed. Appel, p. 60):

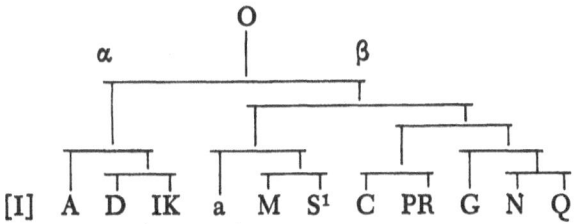

And this one, by the same poet (ed., p. 156):

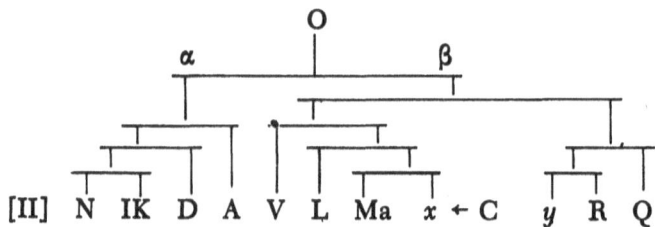

And these two compositions by Raimon Jordan, vicomte de Saint-Antonin (Languedoc, c. 1178-1200; ed. Kjellman, pp. 87, 111):

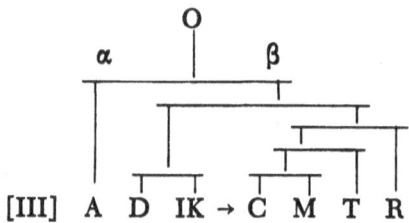

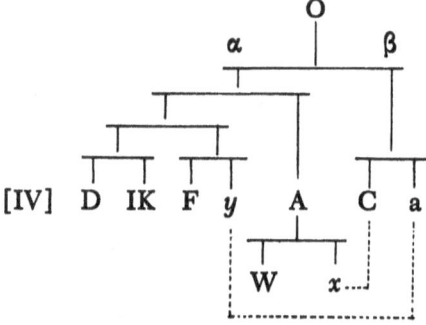

And these two poems of the Toulousain Aimeric de Péguilhan (c. 1190-1230), one written in Spain about 1190-1200 (cf. *Romania*, LXXIV, 121-122), the other in Italy about 1220 (ed., Shepard-Chambers, pp. 140, 168):

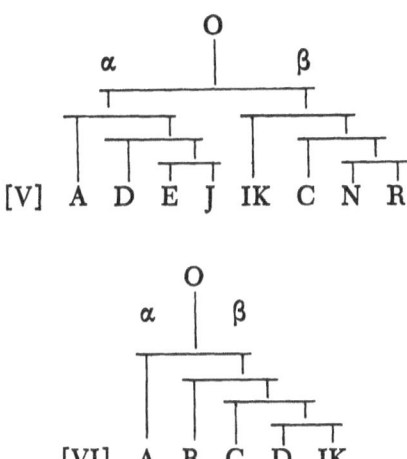

Clearly, it is not the real *filiation of texts* that these schemas reveal, but the *relationships of the variants* that a living tradition has been brewing beneath the surface of the mechanical transmission of texts. This living tradition constitutes a closed circle, in which we interrogate about thirty witnesses concerning the diffusion of two thousand songs, each with its own history; the contrast between the solidity of the base and the fragility of the apex of these genealogical constructions often appears in a glaring light. The need for a precise study of the *chansonniers*, of a *stemmatics*, is becoming urgent.[12]

The school of Pergamo, Alexandria's rival, is reflected in the work of another medieval philologist, the Narbonnais (?) author

---

[12] The order and disposition of the evidence does not rest upon clearly articulated principles. The slight transposition in the second schema, affecting manuscripts y, R, and Q, does not change their relationships. Of the six schemas reproduced above, three present contaminations (II, III, and IV, mss. C and a); in two schemas, some evidence has been omitted (I, mss. VW; II, ms. O); in the first case, the opposition of MS¹a to CGNPQRV is based on too frail a variant (verse 26 *esmai] esglai*); the same is true of III, of ADIK as opposed to CMRT (verse 36 *m'aucira] m'aura mort;* cf. *en breu d'ora] en pauc d'ora*); in IV, the derivation W < A (which, according to this stemma, is a *codex descriptus*) is based solely upon the weak evidence of verse 4 (*desiauzir] de iauzir;* but W contains only one stanza). The Lachmannian *iudicium* is not, as can be plainly seen, the most equitably distributed quality in the world, and it is only too true that "nous conduisons nos pensées par diuerses voyes, et ne considerons pas les mesmes choses."

of the voluminous collection C that belonged to the Counts of Foix. This modern Crates of Mallos doubtless did his work at the very end of the thirteenth century. His pen sometimes left marks that are too personal [13] upon the texts he transcribed; but it is these texts, always clear and coherent, and with homogeneous spelling, that Raynouard preferred. Ever since, his orthography has become a part of our habits: Romance philology owes to him especially the digraphs *lh* and *nh* which represent the palatalized sounds of Provençal.

The authors of such collections cannot be relegated to the rank of mere copyists, or even of experienced or well-informed copyists. They were editors, like the ancient librarians of Alexandria. They collected the best tradition; they concerned themselves with classifying their texts and with providing them, like Callimachus of the Πινακες, with a biographical and explicative apparatus; they employed a method that was simple, no doubt, and more or less effective, like ours; but, working at a time when Adam de la Halle, the *puys* of the North, the Cerveri, Sordello, the Guittonians and the poets of the *dolce stil nuovo* were still flourishing, they had an immediate acquaintance with things.

Thus there are some manuscripts that are more correct than others in the tradition of Provençal *chansonniers*. This is true also of the French *chansonniers* (M and T, which are Artesian; C, which is Messinian; K and N, which form a family with P, X and with L, V, all of the thirteenth century); it holds also for the Italians (the *Libro de Varie Romanze volgare*: A). There are others which, without being *codices descripti*, reveal to us identifiable composite sources, either because they provide texts of which only one part is closely related to another manuscript (Prov. S and P), or because they have been corrected by collation (Prov. L by S; cf. also Fr. B, F, O, P, S, V, X).

Contaminations may have been produced by oral transmission; coincidences of variants must be more frequent than is generally assumed. Just as in the manuscripts of the works of Antiquity we note "error traps," so in medieval songs there are words and expressions that provoke variants. When we read *bone amour* in one manuscript, we expect to find *fine amour* in another, whatever

---

[13] Cf., for example, *Romania*, LXXIII (1952), 227-234.

its family; for *li desir: li penser* or *li sospir;* for *le: cil, cist;* for *douz vis: cler vis*. The conjunctions often present a very complete range of variants: *car, que, quant, et, si*. We will never know the succession of changes that preceded, in any given manuscript, the reading (Prov.) *que'm*, which may have alternated, in a straight line, through the abbreviation q̄ū or q̄, with *que, qu'en, qu'eu*.

These are, of course, variants which, for diverse reasons, are not only negligible, but must be ignored: to serve in the establishment of a stemma, a variant must, as we know, be "apt and sure."

* * *

In like manner, application of the Lachmannian method with any chance of success requires that the tradition be *apt*, i.e., resulting from the written transmission of a single text, and *sure*, i.e., free from contamination.

The tradition constituted by the lyric *chansonniers* of the Middle Ages seems fraught with every sort of difficulty for the scholar who wishes to establish a stemma: (1) a multiple original (real, virtual, or possible); (2) variations and contaminations stemming from oral transmission; (3) contaminations due to the use of several divergent sources by the copyists; (4) and finally, the existence, in the *chansonniers* themselves, of editions resulting from thoughtful work, employing conjecture. How far we are from the mechanical transmission that guarantees the efficacy of the stemma!

This being the case, and in view of the special nature of the evidence, the very notion of the author's copy is fallacious. The selective method alone rests upon a reliable tradition. The combinatory method should be used with moderation and with extreme caution. For the criticism of variants, we must have recourse to Lachmannian principles. As Aurelio Roncaglia advises, in the beginning "it is better to make an effort out of all proportion to the attainable results than to accept a 'solution by laziness'" (*Studi medievali*, XVII, 361). But once the effort has been made (cf. *Lai de l'Ombre*, ed. of 1890 and of 1913, introductions, and *Romania*, LIV, 161-169 and 321-356), it is preferable to accept negative conclusions (cf. *Lai de l'Ombre*, ed. of 1913, text) rather than to set out on a road of illusory certainty paved with uncertainties that are quite real. On the basis of groups established according to Lachmannian principles, the genealogical tree will take shape unambiguously only if the tradition is "apt and sure"; for it will be suspect if the contamination that has surely occurred introduces suspect relationships; and it will be arbitrary if the editor eliminates contaminated or unclassifiable readings.

In practice, however, the selective and combinatory methods, however irreconcilable they may be in principle, must agree on several points: (1) in their evaluation of the readings; (2) in the selection as the base manuscript of the one presenting the fewest clear-cut errors, or other advantages; (3) in the variants chosen to replace faulty readings in the base manuscript. The two methods will diverge with regard to the role they assign to the base manuscript, and especially with regard to the way they treat its valid readings: the selective method will keep them all, and in the largest number possible; [14] the combinatory method will reject them, and in the largest number possible, when they are contradicted by the agreement of other readings.

Some cases are more suitably treated by one method, some by the other. Bédier held that the combinatory method was not viable for the *Lai de l'Ombre;* some scholars have disputed this. M. Delbouille considered the *Lai d'Aristote* unsuited to the selective method; we must agree. As he writes in his edition of 1951 (p. 13): "If we were to disregard the corrections forced upon us by the critical [combinatory] method, and slavishly follow a single manuscript — even the best of them —, we would be accepting, in the full awareness that we were doing so, a text that is certainly corrupt, and with its full share of weaknesses and

---

[14] A less rigorous formulation of the selective method might be offered, in which valid but isolated readings in the base manuscript would be abandoned, especially if they are contradicted by evidence contained in manuscripts closely related to the base manuscript. It is important, however, not to abandon the tradition that is followed in the case of variants which, at the moment of the *recensio*, cannot be legitimately retained as "apt and sure." There is no reason to "contaminate" (in the spirit of the selective method) the tradition followed by synonymous variants, which oral transmission may have multiplied and permuted *ad libitum,* like *tengues* for *tenga* and *cug* for *cre* in a *chanson* by Guilhem Ademar (cf. *Studi medievali,* XVII, 362-363).

fantasies." In the tradition of the lyric *chansonniers*, this "best manuscript" may have its weaknesses, even its fantasies (cf. Prov. C), but on the whole it is never "certainly corrupt."

But even if corrupt, the text of every *chansonnier* deserves monographic study. The Hellenists, masters as well as pupils, would write painstaking dissertations on a *Pluteus* or a *Bodleianus* which the editor of just one book was going to be able to put to immediate use. *A fortiori*, then, when we are dealing with collections of lyrics containing numerous authors and diverse works, we surely may hope to see such collections studied with the utmost precision possible. They should be situated in time and space, in their literary and diplomatic particularities, in their interrelationships, in the psychology of their scribes. If we think of the problems of orthography, of dating (external and internal; paleographic and literary), of localization, of sources, that remain unresolved, we can begin to realize the contribution that could be made towards perfecting our methods by detailed research, even of limited scope. The most urgent preliminary work will be the study of "good manuscripts" and their families. This will be, indeed, the study of archetypes — surely an indispensable means of approaching more closely to the originals, the most ancient forms of the tradition. Often, in fact, this will be the final and decisive step in our progress toward the originals.

Whichever method we use, however, when we are confronted by the peculiar complexity of the tradition of the *chansonniers*, we are inclined to brush aside too many valid variants, which just might be true. Their divergences are often such that they cannot be summarized in a combined critical text. We shall have to accustom ourselves to devote more attention to the valid branches of the tradition — to more frequent and more complete commentaries, glosses, and interpretations of them. The narrow scope of a lyric *chanson* should facilitate this task. This is the only way to attain that transcendent philology called for with so much verve by A. Roncaglia: "This fidelity to the internal evidence, even when it contradicts the external evidence, seems to us the soundest scientific position. The critic who takes such a position — whatever his understandable modesty in the face of the difficulties of historical reconstruction, however great his fear of failing to adhere positivistically to the brute reality of the 'datum' — will not be misled into renouncing criticism, reconstruction, and even history itself" (*Cultura Neolatina*, XII, 282). It is not so much a matter of creating a new but inadequate "datum" that a new but equally inadequate positivism will accept where it refused the primary data, which alone were really historical. What is essential is that we take a broader view of the texts of the past, and treat them with greater flexibility.

PRINCIPLES OF TEXTUAL EMENDATION

by Eugène Vinaver

> La dernière démarche de la raison est de reconnaître qu'il y a une infinité de choses qui la surpassent. Elle n'est que faible, si elle ne va jusqu'à reconnaître cela.
>
> PASCAL

Recent studies in textual criticism mark the end of an age-long tradition. The ingenious technique of editing evolved by the great masters of the nineteenth century has become as obsolete as Newton's physics, and the work of generations of critics has lost a good deal of its value. It is no longer possible to classify manuscripts on the basis of "common errors"; genealogical "stemmata" have fallen into discredit, and with them has vanished our faith in composite critical texts.

This in itself is a welcome change, and nothing has done more to raise textual criticism to the position of a science than the realisation of the inadequacy of the old methods of editing.[1] But the reform has so far been largely negative. The modern school of criticism has trained us to be cautious and has warned us against the dangers of Lachmann's method; but it has failed to

---

[1] Cf. J. Bédier's Introduction to his edition of *Le Lai de l'Ombre* (S.A.T.F., 1913) and his articles in *Romania*, April and July-October 1928; Dom Quentin, *Essai de Critique Textuelle*, Paris, 1926; M. D. Legge, *Recent Methods of Textual Criticism* (*Arthuriana*, vol. II); A. Ewert, *On Textual Criticism with special reference to Anglo-Norman* (*ibid.*). In the classical field a similar movement began at a much earlier date.

produce a technique of its own.[2] Faced with the task of editing a work preserved in a number of imperfect copies, the critic is no longer expected to base his text on a combination of variants; he is supposed to choose a single version and edit it as best he can. But he has acquired no reliable method of dealing with it, no substitute for the wonder-working mechanism of classifications which gave so much confidence to his predecessors.

There is a significant remark to this effect in M. Joseph Bédier's Introduction to the *Lai de l'Ombre*: "Puisque," he says, "selon cette façon de procéder, le choix entre les variantes n'est plus déterminé d'avance, une fois pour toutes et mécaniquement, par un classement des manuscrits, puisqu'il est remis, en chaque cas douteux, au jugement, au tact, à la prudence de l'éditeur, et, pour dire le vrai mot, à son goût, qui est la chose la plus faillible du monde et la plus précaire, il convient qu'en chaque cas douteux l'éditeur s'applique à justifier son choix."[3] Is this an adequate alternative to the method so brilliantly refuted by M. Bédier himself? Is the critic to be left in the end at the mercy of his own "taste," — "la chose la plus faillible du monde et la plus précaire"? One of the main reasons for rejecting Lachmann's technique was that the notion of "error" being largely a matter of the critic's preference, a classification based upon "common errors" could have no objective value. Are we likely to do any better than the partisans of Lachmann's school if we rely on an equally subjective criterion? "Il convient qu'en chaque cas douteux l'éditeur s'applique à justifier son choix." But if we are to avoid the initial mistake which mars all composite texts, is it not vital that we should determine on strictly objective grounds what considerations *should* dictate the editor's choice, and how far he is entitled to go in emending his text?

This is the problem with which I am here concerned. Needless to say, its solution lies far beyond the limits of this essay. I have endeavoured merely to suggest a possible theoretical approach to

---

[2] The only notable exception is Dom Quentin's *Essai*, but the method he suggests can only be applied under certain conditions which are by no means common to all texts.

[3] *Op. cit.*, p. xliv.

the technique of emendation, and I have based my remarks on my own experience of editing which is naturally limited: chiefly on the work I have done in connection with my edition of Malory's Arthurian Romances. But it seems reasonable to suppose that the critical issues they involve have a much wider bearing.

THE MECHANISM OF TRANSCRIPTION

The term "textual criticism" implies a mistrust of texts. It presupposes that in any copied text errors are inevitable and that the critic's main function is to correct them. But no error can be properly corrected, just as no illness can be scientifically treated, without a knowledge of its origin. And the first question we must ask ourselves is, what are the definable conditions under which a copy may deviate from its original?

The human agency which is responsible for errors in copied manuscripts is the usually anonymous person known as the scribe, and we naturally assume that a scribe has certain characteristics which distinguish him from any author; otherwise we should not hold him responsible for altering the author's work. What are those characteristics? The people who copy manuscripts do not belong to any distinct human type. They may have the same sympathies and idiosyncrasies, the same tastes and reactions as the authors themselves. But in one respect they are unquestionably different: the *mechanism* of their work is quite unlike that of original writing.

Mechanically speaking, original writing is a process limited to one plane — that of the page facing the writer. It is on this plane and on this plane alone that he moves his hand and fixes his eye, and there is no necessity for him ever to separate his line of vision from the movement of his hand. Not so with the copyist: his object is to transfer the text from the original to the copy, and his eye must travel at regular intervals from one to the other. While looking at the original he will endeavour to retain as much as possible of what he sees. The visual or mental impression thus received must then be transferred to the copy, and while the scribe's eye goes from one to the other this impression must remain intact. Once it has been placed on the copy, the scribe must look again at the original. This time he has to bear in mind the last letter, word, or words he has written down, so as to find in the original the point at which he left it a moment ago. Thus the process of transcription requires a constant shifting of the line of vision from one plane to another, and with each movement of his eyes the copyist has to carry mental or visual impressions which help him, first to reproduce part of his text, and then to find his way back to it. This may be shown by the following chart: —

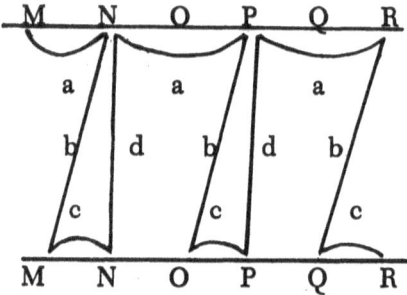

If it is admitted that this mechanism is the only distinctive feature of the process of copying, all we have to do is to discover the possible irregularities in its working. Our chart shows that the scribe's eye must perform four distinct movements: *(a)* the reading of the text; *(b)* the passage of the eye from the text to the copy; *(c)* the writing of the copy; and *(d)* the passage of the eye from the copy back to the text. Any accident that may legitimately be called a "scribal error" must, therefore, occur in the course of one of these movements, and in each case the character of the error will be determined by the conditions and the nature of the movement performed.

These, then, are the outside limits of our interference with any given text, and they can only be extended if we happen to know more about the scribe. When, for example, we know the peculiarities of his language and orthography, it is theoretically possible, though not always easy in practice, to eliminate them from the text. But such cases lie outside the scope of the present enquiry. We are here concerned with a scribe whose individual characteristics are completely unknown, and with the extent to which the work of *any* author may be reconstructed from a copy made by *any* scribe.

ERRORS ARISING FROM MOVEMENT *a*

Movement *a* — the reading of the text — may lead to two different kinds of error: —

1. The scribe's palæography may be at fault; he may mistake one letter for another or one abbreviation for another.[4] The resulting error would be an unconscious one: the scribe would think that he had read his original correctly.

2. He might think, on the other hand, that the original needed correction. He would then act as its editor and consciously emend it.

There is a passage in Malory's *Merlin* which provides an illustration of both these kinds of scribal deficiency. The reading varies in the two earliest versions of the text: Caxton's edition of 1485, and the manuscript recently discovered in the Library of Winchester College. The Winchester MS reads as follows: "Sir Lucas saw kynge Angwysschaunce that nyght had slayne Maris de la Roche." This does not prevent Maris de la Roche from reappearing in Malory's narrative; moreover, the French *Merlin* (Malory's immediate source) makes it abundantly clear that although Maris was severely attacked, he escaped death owing to the timely assistance of Lucas the Butler. The reason for the strange statement in the Winchester text is not far to seek. Malory's own reading must have been: "that *nyghe* had slayne," etc. Someone who copied his text in the first place must have mistaken *e* for *t* and made *nyghe* ("almost") into *nyght*. The error was a purely palæographical one.

---

[4] This occurred, for instance, when the writers in one mediæval *scriptorium* were unfamiliar with contractions used in another, or when some of the contractions familiar to them allowed of several possible readings. Cf. A. C. Clark, *Recent Developments in Textual Criticism*, Oxford, 1914, p. 7.

But when Caxton saw it in his copy he took it for a grammatical, not a palæographical error, and changed "that nyght had slayne" to "that *late* hadde slain." In this form the sentence has been reproduced in all the subsequent modern editions of Malory. Until the discovery of the Winchester MS the miraculous resurrection of Maris de la Roche had remained unexplained.

One could easily fill volumes with examples of errors due to an imperfect performance of movement a, and in any representative collection of such examples both varieties — a^1 and a^2 — would probably have an equal share.

Errors arising from movement d

Movement d is again purely "scribal" in the sense that it can never take place in the course of original writing. It can produce *three* main varieties of error:

1. It will be remembered that in performing movement d the scribe carries in his mind some element of the text that helps him to find the place at which he left his original. If, as is often the case, the word or letter he is looking for occurs twice within a comparatively small space, he may easily go wrong and pick up his text not from the place at which he left it, but from another place, at which the same "key-word" occurs. In terms of our chart this process may be represented as shown on the following page.

The error in this case will be the omission of O and P, and its cause — the recurrence of N in the original. This process is known in textual criticism as *saut du même au même*, and a few examples will suffice to illustrate it.

Malory's version of the *Quest of the Holy Grail*, as reproduced by Caxton, contains the following sentence: "The sonne shall not beare the wyckednesse of the fader nor the fader shall not beare the wyckednesse of the sonne." The recurrence of the word *wyckednesse* caused the scribe of the Winchester MS to omit *of the fader nor the fader shall not beare the wyckednesse*, and to write: "the sonne shall not beare the wyckednesse of the sonne." In another instance the Winchester MS reports a remark by

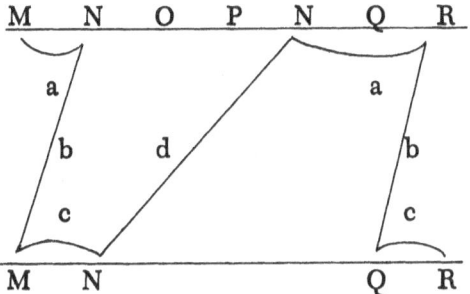

Bodwyne who has been accused of treachery by king Mark and tries to explain to him that he had to start fighting the Saracens without waiting for Mark's return: "Sir," sayde prince Bodwyne, "hit was so that, and I had sente for you, tho myscreauntes had distroyed my contrey." If Bodwyne had really nothing more convincing to say to explain his breach of discipline, one would almost sympathise with Mark who in a fit of fury "stroke hym to the herte wyth a dagger." But the absurdity of Bodwyne's answer is merely the result of a scribal error. What he did say in Malory's text was: "and I had *taryed tyl that I had* sente for you, the myscreauntes," etc. The recurrence of *had* caused the Winchester scribe to omit the words italicised in our quotation.

It is comparatively easy to detect mistakes of this kind and to supply the missing words from a parallel text when the corruption is as blatant as in the two cases we have quoted. But there may be much less obvious cases of an "eye skip" such as the one I came across in Malory's description of Elayne. According to Caxton, she was "the fayrest and the best bysene lady that ever was sene in that Courte." The Winchester MS has instead: "the beste beseyne lady that ever was seyne in that Courte." Assuming that Caxton's reading is correct, the Winchester reading can be explained as a *homœoteleuton* caused by the recurrence of *the*. But this need not be the case: Caxton was quite capable of adding an adjective, and the shorter of the two readings *(brevior lectio)* may easily be the original one. The problem can only be solved with the help of a third witness, namely Malory's French source, where we find the statement that "*il n'avoient oncques mais veue si biele feme comme ele estoit,*" which clearly justifies Caxton and points to a *homœoteleuton* in the Winchester text.

It is by no means necessary that the "recurrent element" which causes the omission should always be a word or a letter. It may be any feature of the text that the scribe happens to use as a *point de repère*. He may, for example, remember that to find the right place in his original he ought to look for the beginning or the end of a line, or he may have a rough visual recollection of having copied say half or three-quarters of a line and look for the remaining half or quarter as the case may be. He would then be liable to omit a passage of corresponding length; a line, if he is thinking in terms of complete lines, half a line, if he is thinking in terms of half-lines, etc. In studying the Vatican MS of Cicero's speeches, A. C. Clark noticed that certain passages omitted by it and found in the other family of MSS contained the same number of letters. He then found that longer passages contained multiples of that number, and naturally suspected that this number of letters might represent a line in the archetype. Further study turned his suspicion into a certainty. He was then able to restore to the text passages which earlier critics had regarded as interpolations but which, in fact, were mere victims of mechanical omission due to the scribe's use of "linear" technique in performing movement *d*.

2. The next category of errors due to movement *d* may be shown on our chart as follows:

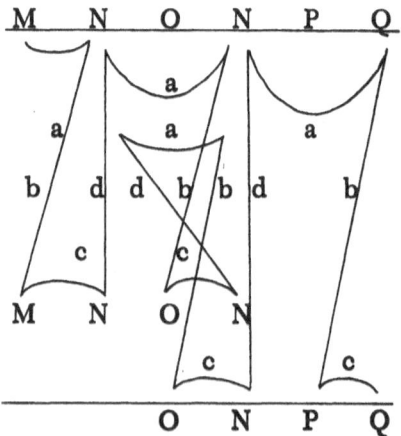

Here recurrence of N has the opposite effect to what we observed in the previous category: instead of causing omission it causes repetition or *duplication*. The original text consisting of M N O N P Q becomes M N O N O N P Q. Cases of this kind are not as frequent as omissions, but they are infinitely easier to diagnose. For it follows from our formula that whenever a deviation of this sort occurs, the copyist has to write the key-word *(N)* three times. To take a hypothetical example, if in the *Grail* passage quoted above the Winchester scribe had committed this kind of error instead of a *homœoteleuton*, he would have written: "The sonne shall not beare the wyckednesse of the fader nor the fader shall not beare the wyckednesse of the fader nor the fader shall not beare the wyckednesse of the sonne." The word *wyckednesse* occurs here three times: the first two times it is in keeping with the original, but the third time it comes as the inevitable result of a mechanical error. This is what distinguishes this particular variety of movement *d* from ordinary repetition or "dittography": the latter may be due to the author, but the former is an exclusively scribal error, and we feel justified in laying down as a general rule that *the symptom by which it can always be recognised is the triple occurrence of the keyword in the copy*.

3. Lastly, movement *d*, in causing the scribe's eye to wander off the line he is transcribing, may bring into the copy parasitic elements from any part of the original. This can best be illustrated by the following lines from the Oxford MS of the *Folie Tristan* (99 ff.):

> Tiltagel esteit un chastel
> Ki mout par ert e fort e bel,
> Ne cremout asalt ne engin ki vaille.

In editing the poem, M. Bédier was puzzled by the length of the third line and transcribed it as follows:

> Ne cremout asalt ne engin
> ....
> .... [engin?] ki vaille,

thus adding two hypothetical lines to the text.[5] We venture to suggest a much simpler emendation:

> Tiltagel esteit un chastel
> Ki mout par ert e fort e bel,
> Ne cremt asalt ne engin ki vaille.

Assuming that this was the original reading, the scribe in copying the word *cremt* would first write down *crem* (movement *c*); then, looking back at the original (movement *d*), he would bear in mind the last letter he wrote down, namely *m*, but instead of going back to where he left off, his eye would wander to the line above, seize upon the *m* of *mout* and carry the whole word to the copy (movement *b*). This would produce *cremout*. Having written *cremout* (movement *c*), the scribe would again go back to the original. This time he would look for the *t* which he has just copied; he would find it, not in line 2 from which he took it, but in line 3, at the end of *cremt*, and then proceed to transcribe the remaining part of the line. The process may be visualised thus:

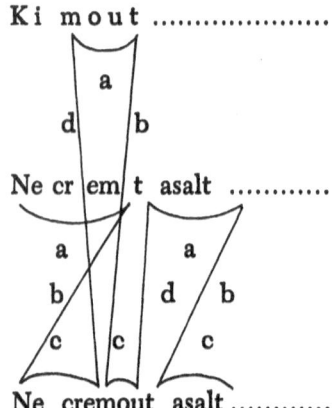

It will be observed that we have in this instance corrected a corrupt line in the *Folie Tristan* by a mere reproduction of the

---

[5] The same reading appears in M. E. Hoepffner's recent edition of the poem.

mechanism of copying, without the aids of versification and grammar, but that our emendation has produced a reading which is both linguistically and metrically sound.[6]

The process leading to this type of error may be described as *contamination*. The following sentence in the Winchester MS provides another illustration of it:

> "I wolle take this shylde and the adventure uppon me what and I wyste whothirward my journey myght be. For because I was this day made knyghte I wolde take this adventure uppon me." "What is youre name, fayre yonge man?" seyde the damesell.

This can only be explained as follows: having written *adventure uppon me*, the scribe looked two lines lower down and, finding these same words, followed by *what*, introduced the latter into his copy. Had he continued with *is youre* etc. he would have committed a *homœoteleuton*; but immediately after writing the parasitic *what* he returned to the right place in the text.

THE MIDDLE MOVEMENTS

We now come to movements *b* and *c*. It stands to reason that movement *c* is not peculiar to the technique of transcription: it is the actual writing of the copy — a process which belongs equally to scribal and authorial technique. Its working will be much the same whether the writer finds the words in his own mind or in a written document. An infinite variety of accidents may occur in the course of this movement — omission, dittography, misspelling, etc. — but we can never be quite certain what the accident is due to.[7] Movement *b* appears at first glance

---

[6] Linguistically *cremt* (Anglo-Norman form of *criemt*) is distinctly preferable to *cremout*.

[7] The only kind of purely scribal error we can detect in this category is that which is due to dictation, but dictated manuscripts form a separate class with which we are not concerned here. Their mechanism is simpler in the sense that it is limited to line *c*; but at the same time the possible errors are infinitely varied, as varied, in fact, as the chances of phonetic confusion in a spoken language.

to belong to scribal technique; it consists in transferring to the copy an image received from the original, and, if imperfectly performed, it may lead to the loss or to a distortion of the image. But this process is essentially a mental one, and its efficiency depends on the scribe's retentive capacity, in other words, on the number of things he can remember at a time, and on the length of time he can keep them in mind. Something very similar takes place when the author forms words and sentences in his mind and then transfers them to the written page. To do this he has to resort to a retentive action which is not unlike that of memorising: he has to carry in his mind whatever he intends to say. And just as a scribe may lose some of the impressions he received from the original, so the author, on the way to his own text, may lose parts of the mental or verbal concepts that he had meant to record in writing.

Since the two processes are similar in the case of movement b and identical in the case of movement c, the errors are bound to be of much the same kind whether they are due to the author or to the scribe, and, as a general rule, we must refrain from correcting them. There is, however, one important exception: errors may be scribal in character without being necessarily scribal in origin. The fact that the author performs two of the four movements which constitute the technique of transcription means that to that extent he acts as a scribe: in remembering what he wants to say and in actually writing it down he does much the same thing as if he were copying his text. And if we can detect those of his errors which are due to his "scribal" action, we can quite justifiably correct them and restore, if not what he actually wrote, at least what he had intended to write. When we find in Béroul's *Tristan* the lines:

Toz a genoz sōt enligliglise,

there can be no doubt that this is a case of unconscious dittography, and that what Béroul meant was:

Toz a genoz sont en l'iglise.

This is a typical scribal error due to the b movement: whether it was committed by the author or by the scribe, it certainly resulted from the "scribal" action of the man whose mind was slowly transmitting to his hand each word of the text, syllable by syllable. A slight acceleration in the movement of the hand or a slight slowing down in the transmission could easily break the rhythm of either of these processes and upset their co-ordination; in this way the same syllable would naturally appear twice on the written page.

The reverse can happen just as easily. When the Winchester MS says that "*Arthur lette bury this knyght rychely and made mencyon his tombe how here was slayne Berbeus,*" we are justified in supposing that this is a scribal error and that either the author or the scribe has left out *on* after *mencyon*. The reason for the omission is a mechanical one: the *on* ending of *mencyon* has been telescoped with the preposition *on*, either because the two were too quickly transmitted from the mind to the hand, or because *mencyon* took longer than usual to write, and "absorbed" the following *on*.

These two examples illustrate the type of scribal error arising from a break in the rhythm of writing, which we may describe, for the purpose of our classification, as *arrhythmia*.

Combinations of Errors

It follows from the foregoing remarks that the "emendable" errors fall into six main categories.

(1) *Misunderstanding of the original* (Movement a^1).
(2) *Conscious correction* (Movement a^2).
(3) *Homœoteleuton* (Movement d^1).
(4) *Duplication* (Movement d^2).
(5) *Contamination* (Movement d^3).
(6) *Arrhythmia* (Dittography and omission due to break of rhythm in movements b and c).

In manuscripts copied not from the originals but from earlier copies, it is possible to find readings resulting from two or more successive mistranscriptions of the same word or sentence. In such cases the reconstruction of the original reading depends on the possibility of detecting the particular combination of errors that has led to the extant reading.

The six types of error indicated above may combine in many different ways, but the most common combinations may be classified as follows:

(A) *Error 1 followed by Error 2.* This we have already illustrated by the word *nyghe* first changing to *nyght*, then to *late*. [8] The following example from Caxton's text may show how such combinations of errors can be discovered without the aid of external evidence:

And the meane whyle word came vnto sir Launcelot and to sir Trystram that sire Carados the myghty kynge that was made lyke a gyaunt that fought with sir Gawayn and gaf hym suche strokes that he swouned in his sadel (Book VIII, ch. 28).

The main clause here has no verb and the whole sentence is therefore meaningless. But if we only assume that instead of *gyaunt that* Caxton's original had *gyaunt whyche* (error 2 in Caxton), and that in a still earlier version the reading was *gyaunt whyght* (error 1 in Caxton's original), we can reconstruct and punctuate the sentence as follows:

And the meane whyle word came vnto sir Launcelot and to sir Trystram that sire Carados, the myghty kynge that was made lyke a gyaunt whyght, fought with sir Gawayn, etc.

It so happens that the Winchester MS supports our emendation: it has *whyche* instead of *that* and represents, therefore, the first degree of corruption. But the emendation would have been legitimate even if Caxton's text had been the only one in existence.

(B) *Error 3 followed by Error 2 or 6.* Assuming that in the first stage of transcription a scribe commits a *homœoteleuton* (error 3), the next scribe will, in all probability, be faced with an unintelligible reading which he will naturally want to correct (error 2). If the original reading was $M \ N \ O \ P \ N \ Q \ R$, it would become, as a result of error 3, $M \ N \ Q \ R$, presumably with a

---

[8] See above, pp. 143-44.

break after *N*. *N* would probably strike the second scribe as either meaningless or redundant, and he would be inclined either to replace it by another word or to delete it altogether as the case might be. The result would be either *M X Q R* or *M Q R*. If, on the other hand, a *homœoteleuton* were followed by *arrhythmia* (error 6), the same reading *M N O P N Q R* would become either *M N N Q R* or again *M Q R*.

These particular combinations of errors cannot, as a rule, be discovered without the help of parallel readings, for in so far as the second error deletes all traces of the first, neither of them can be ascertained on internal evidence alone. But once we have a collateral version, i.e. a version not derived from the one we are editing, the chances are that the two scribes will not have made the same mistakes in the same places, for, as the old school of textual criticism solemnly laid down, "common errors must have a common origin." It is therefore most likely that each time we find a reading such as *M Q R* or *M X Q R* in one of our texts, the collateral text will show a less advanced degree of corruption and help us to reinstate the original reading *M N O P N Q R*.

An interesting example of a passage to which this method of reconstruction can be successfully applied is found in Malory's *Tristram*. When Blamor has been defeated by Tristram he says that he prefers death to shame and asks Tristram to kill him. Tristram appeals to "the kings that were judges" who refer him to Bleoberis, Blamor's brother. Much to their dismay, Bleoberis supports his brother's proud request. In the Winchester MS (f. 168 verso) his speech is reported as follows:

My lordys seyde sir Bleoberys thoughe my brother be beatyn and have the worse in his body thorow myght of armys he hath nat beatyn his hearte.

Caxton's reading is:

> My lordes said Bleoberys though my broder be beten and hath the wers thorou myghte of armes I dare saye though syre Trystram hath beten his body he hath not beten his herte (Book VIII, ch. 23).

Although both readings make perfectly good sense, it can be shown on purely mechanical grounds that they are both corrupt, each in its own way.

We notice, first of all, that the words *his body* are attested by both texts, but occur in different places: if we put the two quotations side by side we shall observe that *his body* comes in the Winchester MS roughly a line above the same phrase in Caxton. We shall also observe that most of the matter in between those two points is omitted in Winchester. Barring a coincidence which in this case would be nothing short of a miracle, we have to infer:

(a) that the words *his body* occurred *twice* in the original and caused a *homœoteleuton* in the Winchester MS (error 3); and (b) that Caxton omitted the first *his body* (error 6).

We must, therefore, restore both omissions to our text. But here another problem arises: if we correct the *homœoteleuton* in the Winchester text and at the same time keep the first *his body* exactly where it occurs, the result will be:

> the worse in his body *thorow myght of armys I dare saye though syre Trystram hath beten his body*.

Now, if this had been the original reading, the *homœoteleuton* would have swept away all the italicised words, including *thorow myght of armys*. Since these four words are in the text, the *homœoteleuton* must have occurred at a time when they stood outside its sphere of action, i.e. somewhere *before* the first keyword (*his body*). The reading at that time must have been as follows:

> the worse thorow myght of armys in his body *I dare saye though syre Trystram hath beten his body*.

The italicised words then dropped out by *homœoteleuton*, but *thorow myght of armys* remained intact. In the next stage of transcription the scribe simply changed the order of words, and instead of *thorow myght of armys in his body* wrote *in his body thorow myght of armys*, as in the Winchester MS. The Winchester reading is, then, the result of a combined error; it clearly indicates **the second degree of corruption.**

PRINCIPLES OF TEXTUAL EMENDATION

I have dwelt on this example at possibly needless length, because it seems to me to illustrate a vital aspect of the problem: it shows that the "mechanical" approach to textual emendation is not a purely negative one, and that in some cases it can lead to the discovery of readings which no amount of "rational" editing could have revealed.

The detection of "combined errors" may also serve to assess the *critical value* of extant copies: each time we discover a "second degree of corruption" in a copy we may be quite certain that it is *at least twice removed from the original*. The "genealogical tree" then works itself out by purely mechanical means. To take again the last example we have quoted, it is clear that neither of the two extant readings could be derived from the other. They must, therefore, go back to a common original X. But since, as our analysis has shown, there is a "combined error" in the Winchester MS, there must have been at least one intermediary between that manuscript and X. And as in a number of other cases we find equally striking "combined errors" in Caxton,[9] Caxton too must be at least twice removed from X. This may be graphically expressed by the following stemma which expresses as accurately as our present knowledge allows the relationship between the two extant versions of Malory's work:

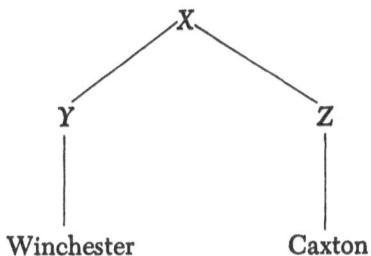

THE PLACE OF "RATIO"

Most of the individual phenomena described above have long been familiar to critics, and the real object of our account has been

---

[9] See above, p. 152.

to reduce them to general principles and so to facilitate their analysis in each particular case. If the principles we have formulated are correct, their application may be two-fold: they may serve to widen the scope of "mechanical" emendation, and to narrow the limits of "rational" editing. But in either case the use of the method we suggest would imply an attitude to textual criticism far different from that which largely prevails in spite of the recent advance towards a more objective treatment of texts. No one could afford nowadays to follow the example of Bentley who, we are told, treated manuscripts with a high hand, "as though they had been Fellows of Trinity"; nor could anyone agree in theory with his maxim: *nobis et ratio et res ipsa centum codicibus potiores sunt*. But nothing is in fact more painful to the critic than to accept the opposite view. For it means that no matter how strongly he may condemn his text on "rational" grounds, he has to leave it intact as long as it is possible that the author, not the scribe, is to blame for it. It is easy enough to admit that since we are not divinely inspired we must not correct a reading simply because we do not like it; but when it comes to applying this truism in practice, our mind revolts against the limitations which it inevitably imposes upon our reasoning faculty. It seems unnatural to distrust our intelligence, our power of guessing the truth, and few can imitate the wisdom of Casaubon who said in discussing a doubtful line in a Greek poet: "I can point out that this place is corrupt; emend it I cannot, without the help of manuscripts." [10]

Our ability to accept the implications of this remark and to apply the method outlined above will depend in the last resort on a correct understanding of our aims. When a critic edits a text represented by one of several corrupt copies, what must he endeavour to achieve? Are his *ratio* and his *rei ipsius scientia* to be used in such a way as to yield a complete reconstruction of the lost original? If so, he must work on two assumptions: (*a*) that his *scientia*, i.e. his sense of what is right and his knowledge of the "thing itself," is *infallible*; and (*b*) that his judgment is in every case *identical* with that of the author. The temerity

---

[10] Cf. R. C. Jebb, *Bentley*, London, 1882, p. 213.

of the first assumption will be obvious to anyone who has studied the history of critical texts and knows how often the most ingenious emendations based on rational principles have been invalidated by subsequent research. But the second assumption is no less erroneous, for to say that our taste and logic are identical with the author's means forgetting (a) that the author is liable to err, witness the story of Don Quixote ordering Sancho to dismount and tie up his ass just after it has been stolen; and (b) that the author and the critic may both be right without necessarily agreeing.

In face of these obstacles there is but one possible course open to the critic, and that is to define his task as a *partial* reconstruction of the lost original; to aim, not at restoring the original work in every particular, but merely at lessening the damage done by the copyists. An analogy with the visual arts might perhaps make this clearer. Historians of art, who have over textual critics the advantage of dealing with more tangible material, have long since realised that to "restore" does not mean to reconstruct an object in its entirely, but to clear it as far as possible of adventitious and foreign matter. A textual critic should proceed likewise: he should reproduce what is extant with such modifications as a strictly scientific "cleaning" process would allow. He should approach his task in much the same spirit as if he were an archaeologist anxious to preserve every shade of color that can possibly be authentic in a dilapidated mural painting, every detail of the sculptor's design in a broken statue, every stone in a battered building that may conceivably belong to the original structure.

A misinterpretation of this fundamental aim of criticism may lead to disastrous results; it has in fact caused infinite damage to most of the old texts "rationally" edited. But it is perhaps fortunate that the moment "rational" critics begin to rationalise their own behaviour, they supply excellent arguments against themselves. There is no better example of this unconscious self-condemnation than A. E. Housman's Preface to his edition of Juvenal.[11] It is a spirited but unnecessarily bitter attack on modern editors who, in Housman's opinion, are "afflicted with lack

---

[11] Cambridge, 1931.

of understanding," "destitute of discriminating faculty, so destitute that they cannot conceive it to exist." They must, he affirms, "have a rule, a machine to do their thinking for them." And he concludes by a delightfully appropriate formula: "In enquiring whether a given reading is right, we behave as if we really wanted to know, and we ask whether it is probable: they ask only whether it is possible, and unless it is impossible they believe it to be right."

The indictment can serve as a vindication of the school of thought which it purports to condemn. Much depends, of course, on what "they believe it to be right" means in this context. If it means "they regard it as authentic," i.e. if any editor seriously thinks that because a reading is possible it should be *ascribed to the original*, the case against him is unanswerable.[12] But if the sentence means — as it obviously does in this case — "*they want to keep it*," Housman's formula justifies the very method he attacks. For it *is* right to preserve a reading as long as it is *possible* that it comes from the original, and it is wrong to replace it by what is merely *probable*. "Impossible" readings are those which can be shown to result from scribal errors; such readings

---

[12] Some of the earlier editors of Juvenal did in fact take this view and acted as though they had heard a voice from heaven saying, "P is the best MS of Juvenal." Housman rightly remarks that by doing this they were sapping the very ground on which they stood, for "if nobody can tell a true reading from a false reading, it follows of necessity that nobody can tell a truthful MS from a lying MS" (*ibid.*, p. xiv). But blind faith in the goodness of the base MS is by no means the only alternative to Housman's theory, and the use of a single MS for the purpose of an edition of the text need not imply a belief in the superiority of that MS to others. M. Bédier has put the case very clearly in his Introduction to the *Lai de l'Ombre*: "Nous avons choisi, entre nos sept manuscrits, le manuscrit A, pour servir de 'base' à notre édition. Ce n'est nullement que nous le tenions pour le plus voisin de l'original, puisque, comme nous l'avons vu, il se peut fort bien que D, ou E, représente le dernier état du texte, tel qu'il plut à Jean Renart de le constituer. Si nous avons choisi le manuscrit A, le précieux manuscrit 837 de la Bibliothèque nationale, c'est de façon tout empirique, et simplement parce que, offrant d'ailleurs un texte à l'ordinaire très sensé et très cohérent, et des formes grammaticales très françaises (à part quelques 'picardismes'), et une orthographe très simple et très régulière, il est, entre nos sept manuscrits, celui qui présente le moins souvent les leçons individuelles, celui par conséquent qu'on est le moins souvent tenté de corriger. L'ayant une fois choisi, nous avons pris le parti d'en respecter autant que possible les leçons."

it is our duty to correct. "Improbable" readings may or may not be due to the author, and those we have obviously no right to alter.

The acceptance of such a criterion is not in any sense a refuge for those whom Housman suspects of suffering from "intellectual infirmity." But it puts the editor in a position which is substantially different from the one he generally claims. He can no longer indulge in a disguised collaboration with the author, borrow his pen, and profess to speak for him. The editor's function becomes that of a referee in the strictly mechanical conflict between the author and the scribe, and his judgment will only be required if there is evidence of the scribe's guilt.

There is a vital corollary to this restriction. For the ultimate task of the critic lies not so much in the difficult and uninspiring process of subduing his *ratio*, but in diverting it to other, more promising channels; in using it for the purpose of a better understanding of texts as they are, instead of letting it invade the province of emendation in which it can do so little. By making rational interpretation begin where mechanical emendation ends we should render a less doubtful service to the texts left in our hands; and we should certainly bring textual criticism much nearer the real object of any science, which is to explain, not to alter, reality.

A striking instance of the advantages of interpretation over emendation is M. Bédier's work on the Oxford manuscript of the *Chanson de Roland*. His edition of the text and his masterly commentary show that in the majority of controversial cases it is possible to keep and to justify the uncorrected readings of the manuscript. A similar rehabilitation of manuscript readings ruthlessly rejected by editors should be attempted for a number of other texts. And each attempt will be an inspiration and a lesson: for, by putting the critic's virtues to the test of real understanding, it will reveal once more that the greatest of these is humility.

1939.

APPENDIX

Lancelot's Two Steps

When a cart driven by a dwarf appears suddenly before Lancelot proceeding on his quest "armed with shield and helmet," and the dwarf offers him information about the Queen if he will ride in the cart, Chrétien de Troyes explains that carts in those days took the place of the pilory; every good town possessed only one, in which to bear through the streets in shame criminals caught in the act. Will Lancelot accept the dwarf's offer and allow himself to be carted about like a common criminal, just to avoid any delay in saving the Queen imprisoned in the kingdom of Gorre? At once there takes place a debate in his mind between Reason and Love; meanwhile the dwarf continues on his way without waiting any longer.

> Tantost a sa voie tenue (= *the dwarf*)
> Qu'il ne l'atent ne pas ne ore,
> Tant solemant deus pas demore
> Li chevaliers que il n'i monte.
> Mar le fist et mar en ot honte
> Que maintenant sus ne sailli. [1]

This is how the initial episode of the *Chevalier de la Charrette* appears in the first critical edition published by Wendelin Foerster in 1899. [2] The dwarf rides on without concerning himself further with the knight, who "delays mounting the cart no more

---

[1] *Der Karrenritter (Lancelot) von Christian von Troyes*, ed. Wendelin Foerster, Halle 1899, vv. 362-7.

[2] Unjustly described as "médiocrement critique" by Mario Roques in the Introduction to his edition of the text published in the series Classiques français du moyen âge in 1958 (p. iv). Foerster is the only editor of the *Chevalier de la charrette* to provide all the variants of any value and a detailed commentary.

than the time necessary to take two steps." And Chrétien adds: "It was unfortunate for him that he did so, unfortunate that he felt shame at mounting it instantly."

Now, in Roques' edition, the most recent to date and the only one to appear in France since 1849,[3] we read:

> Tantost a sa voie tenue
> Li chevaliers que il n'i monte;
> Mar le fist, etc.[4]

Here, the subject of the verb *tenir* is no longer the dwarf, but rather the knight who, overtaken by the cart, continues on his way without mounting it. It is therefore with no little surprise that in v. 377 of the same edition we see him mount it anyway, as if the cart had been waiting for him all the time. And when Guenevere (vv. 4486-7) reproves him for hesitating with the words:

> Molt a grant enviz i montastes
> Quant vos demorastes deus pas,

one wonders what two steps *(deus pas)* she may be referring to. Roques' edition shows no trace of them.

His edition, like Jonckbloet's much earlier one,[5] follows Guiot's copy faithfully, that is B.N. fr. 794, the best according to Roques of all the manuscripts that transmit to us the romance of Lancelot, since the others are "assez gravement lacunaires."[6]

---

[3] In 1849 there appeared at Rheims an abridged and modernized transcription of ms. T (B.N. fr. 12560), together with a preface by P. Tarby, entitled *Recherches sur la vie et les ouvrages de Chrétien de Troyes et Godefroy de Laigny*. V. 364, a syllable too long in T (*Tant solemant deus pas ne demore*), is reduced in the Rheims edition to *Tant solemant pas ne demore* (p. 14).

[4] *Op. cit.* (reprint 1965), vv. 360-362.

[5] *Roman van Lancelot*, The Hague, vol. I (1850), pp. 1-51.

[6] Roques' edition, p. iii: "les autres copies... sont assez gravement lacunaires, peu soignées, ou diversement contaminées, et nous aurons peu d'occasions de recourir à leur témoignage." Of the 7112 lines in the romance, I have counted only twenty where the evidence of those texts has been used to correct Guiot's copy. They all date from the thirteenth-century, and all are incomplete except for ms. T (B.N. fr. 12560). Except for Guiot's copy, the passage which concerns us appears only in mss T, A (Chantilly 572), and E (Escurial M. III 21).

This manuscript has obvious qualities: a careful hand, adherence to the rules of declension, accurate revision of the entire text. Nevertheless, one may wonder just how far our respect for "good" manuscripts ought to be carried. Roques does not correct vv. 360-361 (*Tantost a sa voie tenue/ Li chevaliers*, etc.), doubtless because he admits in principle the possibility of an imperfect, or even incomplete, reading in the original text. To his way of thinking an internal contradiction in the text we are provided with does not suffice to make it inauthentic. It is of course possible in theory that Chrétien never wrote the two lines missing in Guiot's version, and that a scribe added them to explain the narrative sequence. The unanimous agreement of the three other manuscripts against Guiot's copy on this detail is no proof of authenticity. Roques cites in his notes two other lines not found in Guiot — vv. 3700 *a* and *b*; these he finds "utiles," but fails to take them into account in establishing his text.[7] The problem therefore comes down to this: is it right in a case like this one to respect the base manuscript for fear of corrupting what might just bring us back to the original reading?

This characteristic refusal to impose on a work a reading that *appears* good or useful, but which just might be wrong, derives from Bédier's conservative method, a method that has proved to be highly beneficial in textual editing. One reservation must be

---

[7] The Guiot version reads:

    Or te veons si antrepris.
    Torne toi, si que de ça soies
    Et que adés ceste tor voies.

In Foerster's edition we have:

    Or te veons si antrepris
    Qu'arriere main gietes tes cos,
    Si te conbas derrier ton dos.
    Torne toi si que de ça soies
    Et que adés ceste tor voies. (3716-20)

This is the scene of the combat with Meleagant. Lancelot, told by a maiden to look behind him in order to see Guenevere, can not take his eyes off the Queen, scarcely bothering to protect himself against his opponent, who continues his relentless attack. "We see you," the maiden exclaims to Lancelot, "distracted *so much that you are striking blows from behind and fighting with your back turned*. Place yourself where you belong so that you'll be on this side facing that tower." The italicized words do not appear in Guiot.

made however, a reservation suggested in an especially perceptive note by Bédier himself, which I cited over 25 years ago in a booklet written in his honor.[8] He wrote there concerning his edition of the *Chanson de Roland:* "Mon principe est de ne pas corriger *Malprimes* en *Malpramis, Marganices* en *l'algalife*, etc., parce que je ne sais pas ce que le poète a écrit; — mais de corriger *la labaille* (v. 1653) en *la bataille* parce que je suis sûr que le poète a écrit *la bataille* (ou du moins que le scribe O, écrivant *la labaille*, n'a pas fait exprès)." But is one ever sure that the scribe did not act intentionally? Roques did not hesitate to change *besoigne nest* to *besoigne en est* (v. 290), *antrevient* to *antre vienent* (859), *dou savez* to *don savez* (1879), *m'amez* to *m'amet* (4891), etc.,[9] because he saw in them undeniable "scribal" slips. But in order to determine whether there actually was such a slip, should one not first ask oneself under what circumstances inadvertancies may occur which would produce a scribal error? The mechanics of copying are known. There are four steps, each one of which involves certain obvious risks: reading, passage from the original to the copy, transcription, and finally return to the original at the stopping point chosen in the initial reading of the text. The last step is the most precarious of the four, since it is there that the copyist *inadvertantly* commits errors that are the most difficult to recognize. Imagine, for example, a text containing the elements ABCBD, in which B is taken as the stopping point; in the copy, this text could be reduced to ABD, if the copyist skipped the original stopping point and picked up a similar one further on in the text *(saut du même au même)* — in this case the involuntary passage from the first to the second B. Elements BC or CB would thus disappear without a trace, BC if the scribe stopped after A, CB if he stopped after AB. When one encounters a variant like that for v. 6589 in Guiot's copy:

Que je toz mes serai vostres,

one may be sure that the copyist, not the poet, omitted the word *jorz* after *toz*, the *z* of *toz* having furnished him with a stopping

---

[8] *Hommage à Bédier* (Editions du Calame, Collection "La Belle Feuille"), 1942, p. 15.
[9] *Op. cit.*, p. 220.

point and the *z* of *jorz* having caused his eye to move to the following word. And it is perfectly natural for Roques, who otherwise follows Guiot so faithfully, to adopt in this case the common reading of the other manuscripts:

> Que je toz jorz mes serai vostres.

All this means that the discovery of a slip which by its very nature can occur only while copying, authorizes a correction in the base text, no matter how "good," how trustworthy it may be. Now, there are two circumstances that can divert the eye of a copyist. In the case of v. 6589, the scribe rightly sought a *z*, since he had just copied a *z*. The "key letter" remained fixed in his memory; he erred merely in *locating* that letter when he returned to it. But it happens that, after transcribing a letter, a word, or a line of verse, the scribe looks in his model, not for a particular verse, word, or letter, but rather for *something that resembles them*. So, after copying the line

> Tantost a sa voie tenue,

nothing prevented Guiot or the author of the copy he was following from saying to himself that he now had to seek in his text what came directly after a line of verse in which the initial letters were TANT. He had to tell himself thus only once for his eyes to fall immediately on *Li chevaliers que il n'i monte*. He thereby unwittingly suppressed the two intermediate lines of verse, that is the very lines that are missing in the Guiot copy:

> Qui ne l'atent ne pas ne ore,
> Tant solemant deus pas demore.

If, in our formula ABCBD we substitute for the second B an element similar to, but not identical with it — say B^1 — the fate of our passage might be represented by a skip from B to B^1, resulting in the loss of CB^1. This kind of haplography, which has been the object of very little study, has been defined in very precise terms by Professor George Kane, in a recent edition of *Will's Vision of Piers Plowman*, as a *retreat from what the scribe thinks he has already copied*, or — what amounts to the same thing — a move towards that which follows the letter or group of letters the scribe believes he has already copied; [10] a movement which resembles the skip from one element to another similar to it, with the single difference that in place of the identity of the two elements in question, we have only the *impression* that they are identical. [11]

This should suffice to explain what happened in vv. 360-2 of the Guiot copy. One might object that a scribe of Guiot's quality would have quickly noticed the absence of anything so essential. This is of course true. But we still need to know what the essential elements of a text are for the best of scribes. Guiot's text was syntactically and logically impeccable. The verb *tenir* has a subject, although not the one Chrétien gave to it; the conjunction *que* in v. 365 meant something different from what it did in the original text, but its meaning was still perfectly clear. Like a good scribe, Guiot was content with that. The sentence he had just copied sufficed; even its immediate context mattered little to him. He could very easily fail to discern in vv. 365-377 a development of those he had just suppressed. [12] The initial seven lines of this passage — one of the very first interior monologues — correspond to Lancelot's first step; Reason opposed Love, and urged Lancelot not to act in any way prejudicial to his honor:

> Que rien ne face ne anpreigne
> Don il ait honte ne reproche.

But Reason dwelt only on his lips, while Love held sway in his heart. And thus in the six lines that follow, Love, symbolized in Lancelot's second step, *li comande et semont*

---

[10] *Will's Vision of Piers Plowman and Do-Well, an Edition in the Form of Trinity College MA. R 3.14 Corrected from Other Manuscripts, with Variant Readings* (London 1960), p. 121 ff. See as well my second edition of the works of Malory (*The Works of Sir Thomas Malory*, Oxford 1967), pp. cxix-cxx.

[11] The disappearance of vv. 3700 a and b (see above, note 7) can be accounted for in the same way, if one supposes that the second verse began with *Or te* rather than *Si te*.

[12] Cf. Foerster's note on this passage, which, he says, explains "why he hesitated for two seconds: 'Reason, whose judgment differs from Love's, and is thereby distinguishable from Love in this respect'" (*op. cit.*, p. 367).

> Que tost an la charrete mont,
> Amors le vialt et il i saut,
> Que de la honte ne li chaut
> Puis qu'Amors le comande et vialt.

The use of the chiasma strengthens further both the parallel and the contrast. We move, in the seven lines of Reason's speech, from her counsels to the position she occupies with respect to Lancelot himself: *n'est pas el cuer, mes an la bouche;* and, in the six lines of the following movement, from the place occupied by Love in his heart to the orders she gives to her faithful servant.

Guiot perceived none of this, no more than did the author of the prose version of the "Conte de la charrette" a half-century after Chrétien's work. In version α, [13] Lancelot does not hesitate a second. When the dwarf promises to take him to a place where he will hear word of Guenevere, Lancelot exclaims: "Creantes le me tu?" And after being reassured, he *saut maintenant en la charete*. [14] In the more complete version β, he first says to the dwarf "qu'il iroit plus volontiers aprés la charrete qu'il ne montera dedenz." But as soon as the dwarf points out to him that "ja par lui ne sera avoiez (= directed) s'il n'i monte," the dialogue links up with that found in version α. "Creantes me, fait Lancelot, que tu me menras tresqu'a ma dame se je i monte?" The dwarf promises as much, and Lancelot springs into the cart *ausi legierement c'une merveille*. [15] Was the author of the Prose Lancelot following a copy similar to Guiot's? We do not know. But nothing prevents us from supposing that the abridged variant version of the cart episode was as widespread in the thirteenth-century as the authentic version. The symbolic two steps of Lancelot were then only an ill-defined memory. The scribes and adaptors of Chrétien's romance were in danger of being unable to grasp its meaning. It behoves us to restore that meaning, by putting back into the text what distraction in some instances, incomprehension in others, have so ruthlessly removed from it. (Translated from the French by F. Douglas Kelly)

---

[13] For a more detailed discussion of this classification, see *Le Roman en prose de Lancelot du Lac: le Conte de la Charrette*, ed. Gweneth Hutchings, Paris 1938, pp. xxx-xlvii.

[14] Ibid., p. 15.

[15] Ibid., p. 16.

TRANSCRIPTION ERRORS

by Arrigo Castellani

The best advice one may give to a transcriber of old texts seems to me this: Do not trust yourself.

Even where the reading does not present any difficulty, it is inevitable that some errors are made. The editor need have patience, he should return to the original, possibly at a distance of weeks or months, and check the transcription word for word. It would be desirable to stop only when there are no errors present in the last collation... I don't want to insist too much on this point, for I fear that in this case we would all be guilty.

There are errors, however, that are not due to mere carelessness. At times the editor transcribes poorly because he misunderstands or because he becomes fond of the first explanation that comes to mind and fails to go beyond that. I will present three examples that give an idea of the consequences of such an attitude, with regard to both the modern presentation of the text (division of words, etc.), and to its orthographic representation (letters and abbreviations rendered inaccurately):

> 1. "messer Lapo d'esta," for "messer la podestà." GUIDO ZACCAGNINI, "Il volgare pistoiese dall' VIII al XIV secolo," in *Bullettino storico pistoiese*, XI (1909), p. 127 (statement of 1335).
>
> 2. "Dissemi che dedens Lancia dell'Oro mi drebbe lo più che potesse." Note to *Lancia dell'Oro*: "Possibly a Bolognese member of the dell'Oro family."
>
> LUIGI CHIAPPELLI, "Una lettera mercantile del 1330, e la crisi del commercio italiano nelle prima metà del

Trecento," in *Archivio storico italiano* s. 7ª, I (1924), p. 252, lines 88-89 of the edition of the document. The correct reading is "dedens la Ciandelloro" ('before the end of the Candlemas'). In the manuscript the nasal is indicated by the abbreviational hyphen [lacīa], referred to by Chiappelli as pertaining to the first *a* of the *lacia* group (which is detached from *delloro*) instead of to the second.

3. "Quie finiscie lo libro de la doctrina del dire edel tacere ... stralactato di latino involghare permano di ser soffredi del grathia inprovano di santo Aiuolo." Note to *provano*: "for *plebano - plebania, pievania* (cf. *chiesa plebana*)."

GUSTAV ROLIN, *Soffredi del Grathia's Uebersetzung der philosophischen Traktate Albertano's von Brescia* (Leipzig, 1896), p. 16, lines 21-5. In his introduction Rolin observed that "the words *improvano di santo Aiuolo* permit us to conclude that this city is the place the translator sojourned since the word in question *(pievania)* continues to exist in Pistoia" (p. iv), and he cited *provano* as an example of *pr* from PL (p. xxvii).
The reading of the codex, which is preserved in the Forteguerrian Library of Pistoia, A. 53, is "in Provino di Santo Aiuolo" (division of the words and the capitals according to modern usage).
The error was revealed by Francesco Torraca "Per la storia letteraria del secolo XIII," in *Rassegna critica della letteratura italiana*, X (1905), and later in *Studi di storia letteraria* (Firenze, 1923): "I believe it should be read *in Provino* ... Therefore, if I am not greatly mistaken, Soffredi translated the first treatise of Albertano ... while in France" *Studi* etc., p. 58. In the *Giornale storico della letteratura italiana*, LXXXIII (1924), p. 211, Zaccagnini confirmed that the manuscript has *Provino*. As for the connection between Soffredi and Provins, I cite, moreover, the article by Erwig Gabotto, "Un prosatore delle origini in documenti liguri-subalpini," in *Bollettino storico-bibliografico sub-alpino*, XV (1910), pp. 14-16.

I don't know if there is much value in differentiating between errors of transcription in a broad sense, such as "Lapo d'esta" (the reader is deceived, but the symbols found in the original are not altered), and errors of transcription in a narrow sense, such as the last two. The errors of the first type could disappear in diplomatic and semi-diplomatic editions, remaining, however, in the commentary. For example, let's examine the following passage, taken from Rolin's already cited edition of the treatises of Albertano (in which, unlike the edition by Sebastiano Ciampi (Firenze, 1832), the original word groupings of the codex are reproduced):

> "OR finisce lolibro del conso la mento edel consiglio loquale Albertano giudice dibresca dela contrada di saneta agata conpuose ne lianni D. M.CCXLVI del mese dabrile ed imago regato insuquesto volgare ne lianni D. M.CCLXXV, del mese di sectembre" p. 80, lines 17-21. Note to *imago regato*: "i.e. *imagorecare*: to translate." In the introduction, with regard to the sonorization of the intervocalic *K*, Rolin observes: "The obscure word *imagoregato* 80.20, probably belongs here, according to Ciampi, for *imagine recato*, in the sense of *volgarizzato*. However, I see in the ending *-egato* the suffix *-eggiato* from *-eggiare*" p. xxxix.
>
> The correct interpretation is obviously: "del mese d'abrile e di mago ('di maggio') regato in su questo volgare...".

It is, as in the above-mentioned cases, a gross blunder. And from time to time anyone may make a mistake, even the most experienced and learned transcriber. The error, however, should disappear when the editor examines the text with a critical eye. If what he would like to write or what has already been written does not offer a satisfactory meaning, or, moreover, if a given form is not quite probable, linguistically or historically, he must stop and attempt other possibilities.

Let us take, for example, the edition of a brief Sangimignanese document of 1236 (or before 1236), which appears in the Appendix to the "Illustrazioni linguistiche dei Frammenti d'un libro di conti fiorentino del 1211," compiled by Ernesto Giacomo Parodi, in *Giornale storico della letteratura italiana*, X (1887), pp. 195-6 (Parodi has relied on a copy by Pio Rajna, later collating it with the original):

> Item diede palmieri iiii l. e x. f. per la gonela marie. Item diede in I sottana xviii f. Item 1 paria di chalzari

vi f. Item palmieri porttoa ala molie sasetti vno iscaciale d'ariento, che costoa iii l. e v f. Item le portoa vna benda che costa xvii f. Item inn una paria di iscalzari viii f. Item uno iscagiale che costa xxxvi f.[1]

Linguistically, 1 *paria* or *una paria*, and *iscalzari* are quite improbable. And the abbreviation *f.*, if it were actually written thus, could only refer to the large silver florins, whose existence is recorded since 1237.[2] But in other cases silver florins are never identified with such an abbreviation; and furthermore, it would be unusual to find mention of it, in the same account, together with 'libbre.'

In short, the forms contained in this transcription, *paria* s., *iscalzari*, and *F* 'fiorini,' should have been considered strongly suspect and thus presumably erroneous even before reading the manuscript. On close examination one can ascertain that the accurate readings are *pario, chalzari* and *s.* (slashed *s*, a common abbreviation for *soldi*).[3]

In regard to 'libbre,' 'soldi' and 'danari,' it may be recalled that in the edition of the *Frammenti del 1211*, edited by Pietro Santini (and in other more recent ones), one can read at a certain point "lib. xj and sol. xxiij,"[4] in which *xxiii* should be substituted with *xviii*. Santini mistook the upper part of the *v* — the only part that can be distinguished in the manuscript — for the upper part of an *x*. If, after he had transcribed the individual figures, he had glanced at the whole, he would have certainly become aware of the error (eleven 'libbre" and twenty-three 'soldi' is like saying eleven dollars and one hundred-fifteen cents), and, upon reexamining the text, he would have realized that even from a paleographical point of view it cannot be understood as anything other than *xviii*.

In the excerpts from *Ricordi di Mattasalà di Spinello*, collated by Enrico Molteni for Monaci's *Crestomazia*, we observe:

---

[1] This edition is reproduced in the *Crestomazia italiana dei primi secoli* by ERNESTO MONACI (Revised by FELICE ARESE, Roma-Napoli-Città di Castello, 1955), n. 38. Monaci, who has not consulted the original, resolves *f.* in *fiorini* and writes *isciacale* instead of *iscaciale*.

[2] Cf. my *Nuovi testi fiorentini* (Firenze, 1952), Gloss., s. *fiorino*.

[3] I published the document in my *Testi sangimignesi*, Firenze (pp. 54-6).

[4] Ms: 4.13 (Cf. *Studi di filologia italiana*, XVI (1958), p. 37).

"Questi so li denari que io Matasala e Spinello diemo ne lo chartelacio..." *Crestomazia*,[2] 37.162. The glossary explains *chartelacio* as 'cartolaccio, a book in which documents and contracts were recorded'.

The edition of 1847,[5] edited by Niccolò Tommaseo and Gaetano Milanesi, contained:

"Questi so' li d. que io Matasala e Spinello diemo nele cartelacio" p. 68, lines 4-5.
Notes: "Possibly *cartolaccio (cartholacium)*, a book in which documents, contracts, etc. are recorded [Milanesi];[6] "It does not convince me, all the more so because it says *nele*, agreeing only with *carte*, not with the rest, which is probably a poorly comprehensible abbreviation of some adjective" [Filippo Polidori]; "Possibly *nelle carte fece*, the *che* being usually omitted" [Tommaseo].

Believing the *cartelacio* of the preceding edition to be correct (except for the *c-*, corrected in *ch-*), Molteni has gone so far as to see *ne lo* in the place of *ne le*. And yet he should have been put on his guard by Polidori's reasonable suspicions. If I am not mistaken the original should read:[7]

"Questi sono li d. que io Matasalà e Spinello demo ne le charte d'ano" 48 v. 1-2 (interpretative transcription).

The proper solution, in the case where the meaning is not clear, can be indicated by an apparent irregularity in the writing of the original. Permit me to refer to the first verse of the *Detto del gatto lupesco*, of which I have already spoken in the *Studi di filologia italiana*, XVI (1958), pp. 15-17. The traditional "Dico mal... uomini vanno" obviously is not satisfactory. By adding the letters *tr* (which may be clearly recognized in the codex) in place of the dots, previous editors were still unable to reach a persuasive result. I resolved the problem by noting that the initial

---

[5] *Archivio storico italiano*, App., V, 1847, n. 20.
[6] The unusual *cartholacium* of Milanesi, accepted by Monaci as the base for *cartelacio*, is probably a misread *cartholarium* or *chartolarium*.
[7] The ink is faded at various points. In my photocopy the form *demo*, especially, appears to be uncertain (but there is no doubt that *dieno* is to be excluded).

D is not at the same level as the rest, but slightly lower: it is an *S*, slashed vertically in both loops, of which the upper part has disappeared (but not completely, however: Once one knows what to look for, one can still see a small part of the slash). The correct text is: "Sì com'altr'uomini vanno."

When the editor must deal with proper names, it is more difficult to note possible errors on rereading his transcription. The criterion remains the same, but it is not always possible to evaluate the likelihood of certain forms. He should examine the manuscript with the utmost care at all points where there are onomastic indications that do not seem to correspond to the norm.

Perhaps it would be helpful to recall what I said in a review on the *Studi di antroponimia fiorentina (Il libro di Montaperti, an. MCCLX)*[8] by Olof Brattö: "The author not infrequently bases his text on anomalous forms, witnessed only once or in only one document. One must always distrust such forms; they could be errors of writing or of transcription, one's own or someone else's."[9]

Examining carefully the family names of the *Libro di Montaperti* that recur only once, we are able to correct various errors of the edition by Cesare Paoli (Firenze, 1889), errors which Brattö accepts, expressing some suspicion now and then, in his *Nuovi studi di antroponimia fiorentina (I nomi meno frequenti del Libro di Montaperti)*.[10] For the examples I refer you to a forthcoming article of mine *(Note critiche d'antroponimia medievale)*,[11] in which I will in fact discuss, first of all, the *Nuovi studi* by Brattö. I limit myself, here, to mention the instances where the error appears evident even prior to collation with the manuscript: *Bonigia* p. 30 in place of *Bomgia*, shortened form of *Bongianni* (Brattö proposes *Bonigia*, admitting that there is "no way to explain this name other than as either a wrong spelling or a misreading," and that "the correct form is *Bomgia*"), *Grisus* p. 343

---

[8] Göteborg, 1953.
[9] "Nomi fiorentini del Dugento," in *Zeitschrift für romanische Philologie*, LXXII (1956), p. 71. Among errors of transcription I cited three made by Brattö in his selections of Tuscan documents and two due to other authors (but authors on whom he relies).
[10] Stockholm, 1955.
[11] This article has subsequently been published (*Zeitschrift für romanische Philologie*, LXXVI (1960), pp. 446-98).

in place of *Grifus* (*Grisus* could only equal *Grižus* 'gray,' but ž is never indicated with *s* either by the notary to whom the passage in question is attributed, or, to my knowledge, in the remainder of the *Libro di Montaperti*), *Marczanellus* p. 106 in place of *Morczanellus* (the context is "Morczanellus Stephani populi Sancti Michaelis de Morczano"), *Tottovieni* p. 140 in place of *Tostovieni* (Brattö: "it is probably a wrong spelling or a misreading").

In the *Studi*, p. 7, n. 2, Brattö corrects a dozen inexact readings of Paoli. It is strange that we are able to find an error, and precisely one of those which can be spotted at first sight, even in this list of corrections. On p. 65, it is stated, the correct transcription is not *Gualunghi* ("Iacopus Gualunghi"), but *Gualvighi*, as on p. 30. Except that the codex contains neither *Gualunghi* nor *Gualvighi*, names, both of which are not at all convincing, but *Gualinghi* (p. 30 of the edition), written also *Gualimghi* (p. 65).

Up to now I have cited errors made by others. Here is one I made in the transcription of a surname: *Marsilio de' Venchi* (ms. *vēchi*), instead of *Marsilio de' Vecchi* f. 1277-96, 49 v. 28. To have avoided it, I would only have had to consider that in Florence we do not expect to find a form with *e* instead of *i* before *n* such as *Venchi* (moreover, to my knowledge, neither has V*inco*, *-chi* ever been attested)...

In summary, it is extremely hazardous to neglect the warning bell sounded by a peculiarity, of whatever kind, which does not appear to be normal. The unusual should be considered with suspicion. Nine times out of ten, an oddity should not be attributed to the author, but to the transcriber.

As a conclusion I believe it appropriate to append a caveat to those working with difficult texts. The editor must abstain from interpreting too hastily, for once he has accustomed himself to see something in a determined way, it is difficult to abandon that idea for another. He should not let his imagination run rampant; he should make the final decision only after he is certain of having considered every possibility. The meaning must originate from the material which he has before him, without solicitations or prefigurations; it should never be imposed on the text, but rather spring forth from it spontaneously and with the strength of proof.

INTRODUCTION TO THE EDITION OF MEDIEVAL VERNACULAR DOCUMENTS (XIII AND XIV CENTURIES) *

by Egidio Rossini

The transcription of the text of any Medieval document, independent of the writing material on which it is found (papyrus, parchment, paper, stone, etc.) and of the content (petition, will, statutes, etc.), implies giving it a modern appearance so that the reading may be facilitated. Moreover, the text should be free of linguistic and syntactical problems that have been posed and resolved in previously published editions of documents in the particular language. This transformation of the text, however, concerns only the external aspect, for the content must never be altered.

Having accepted his responsibility, the editor also indicates from time to time the numerous other details inherent to the nature, to the terminology, and to the goals of his edition of the document in question. When necessary, he describes the type and the characteristics of the script, as well as the places in which the reading may be uncertain or present particular difficulties. In these cases he proposes reasonable emendations and indicates whether his interventions are attributable to changes in the writing material, to the mutilation or the omission of folios, or to the fading of the ink, and so on. He also calls the reader's attention to those places in which he has encountered a lapse in content, in form, or in the transmission of the document. [1]

---

* Tr. by Christopher Kleinhenz with the approval of the author.
[1] These are essentially the guidelines for the preparation of a critical

In short, by means of appropriate measures he attempts to present the most faithful version not only of the text, but also of all the other elements, both internal and external, of the same document.[2] In practice this reworking is essential to the verification of the document as a historical and linguistic source, one that the scholar may use, on future occasions, within certain limitations of form and measure. The validity of the critical edition depends directly on the experience, knowledge, care and judg-

---

edition of archival documents (notarial acts or those of legal character). Although there is no general acceptance of one system among scholars, most do agree at least on the basic principles involved. As is usually the case, all institutes and foundations that are dedicated to the publication of historical documents (for example, the Monumenta Germaniae Historica that publishes the charters of various Emperors) establish their own editorial principles. In Italy two such organizations are the F.I.S.A. (Fondazione Italiana Studi Amministrativi) and the Istituto Storico Italiano, both of which distribute to their collaborators informative pamphlets containing editorial regulations. For further information see the following works that relate primarily to Italian documents:

"Norme per le pubblicazioni dell'Istituto Storico Italiano," *Bollettino dell'Istituto Storico Italiano*, 28 (1906), vii-xxiv.

"Norme per le pubblicazioni documentarie della Società Storica Subalpina," *Bollettino Storico Bibliografico Subalpino*, XXXV (1933), 542-545.

Masai, F., "Principes et conventions de l'édition diplomatique," *Scriptorium*, IV (1950), 177-193.

Cencetti, G., "Progetto di unificazione delle norme per la pubblicazione delle fonti medievali," *Atti del Convegno di Studi delle Fonti del Medioevo Europeo* (Roma, 1957), 25-34.

Pratesi, A., "Una questione di metodo: l'edizione delle fonti documentarie," *Rassegna degli Archivi di Stato*, 3rd series, XVIII (1957), 312-333.

Petrucci, A., "L'edizione delle fonti documentarie: un problema sempre aperto," *Rivista Storica Italiana*, LXXV, no. 1 (1963), 69-80.

Carli, M., "Norme tecniche per la edizione critica delle pergamene pisane dei secoli VIII-XII," *Bollettino Storico Pisano*, XXXIII-XXXV (1964-1966), 569-615.

Rossini, E., "Documenti per un nuovo Codice Diplomatico Veronese — Dai fondi di San Giorgio in Braida e di San Pietro in Castello — (803ca. -994)," *Atti e Memorie dell'Accademia di Agricoltura Scienze e Lettere di Verona*, XVIII (1966-1967).

[2] The study of thirteenth and fourteenth century documents includes the examination of internal characteristics, that is, those relating to the use and position of formulas in the text, to the dating, to the language and to the subject matter (legal, economic, etc.). The external characteristics regard the writing material, the calligraphy, the format, and so forth. Additional information can be found in any manual of diplomatics (for example, G. C. Bescapé, *Sommario di diplomatica* (Milano-Varese, 1946), 29-55).

ment of the editor who, in his edition, expands all abbreviations, clarifies the meaning of other symbols, integrates the defective parts, and provides an interpretation of those troublesome words whose meaning, through excessive use or other circumstances, has become at best uncertain.

Although the editor in his work necessarily remains faithful to the text, he nevertheless gives it a personal interpretation; for example, while noting the original punctuation (in those texts where it occurs), he is duty bound to present the document in a modern form. However, his interventions are valid, if they always enable the reader to distinguish what he has brought to the text from what is actually in the written document, and in most cases this is accomplished by the use of appropriate indications (as round and square brackets[3]) and footnotes.

In the modernization of old texts the editor, of necessity, has frequent recourse to numerous and highly-specialized disciplines, such as paleography, diplomatics, epigraphy, sphragistics, heraldry, codicology, and so forth. In addition he must incorporate certain modern techniques, such as photography, the use of monochromatic lights to differentiate the color of the faded ink from that of the writing material, for with time the contrast with the writing tends to lessen, and X-rays are used to penetrate the writing material in the hope that at least some of the tannic or metallic substances contained in the ink filtered down to the parchment. Moreover, whenever the editor requires assistance in his work, he is at the same time contributing to the advancement of the auxiliary disciplines (history, linguistics, jurisprudence), because every newly-edited document of the past is an additional contribution to the knowledge of those centuries so far removed from us in time.

* * *

In these brief, but comprehensive notes we will consider only non-literary texts which are either directly or indirectly linked to the archives. Therefore, we will not discuss any texts, even

---

[3] As a general rule, the expansion of abbreviations is presented inside round brackets ( ), while emendations supplied by the editor are included in square brackets [ ].

in the vernacular, which assume a literary character. However, we will also examine those documents which, even though appearing as inscriptions preserved in stone, have their origin in a transaction of legal character. For epigraphs too, as well as parchment and paper documents, have their natural home in the archives. A rather late example of this is the inscription on the portal of the church at Marcellise, which we present in the Appendix. [4]

Only after these documents written on stone, paper and parchment have appeared in a modern critical edition can they be examined, either individually or in a series or in much larger groupings, in order to gather data of a linguistic or juridical nature. However, the information that we may obtain from them, either from the documents themselves or through mechanical or electronic processes, is limited to a synthesis, a sample as it were, that indicates in a general way certain basic tendencies.

Using these indications revealed by modern research tools, we are able to propose other problems in order to acquire new and important data. But first we must turn our attention to the selection and simultaneous utilization of non-Latin texts and, then, to the examination of the various difficulties that the scholar encounters on a first analysis of a manuscript, an analysis that is completely divorced from the eventual study that he will make of the edited text.

One thing appears certain, that the preliminary work of textual criticism and transcription cannot be performed with mechanical devices except in extremely restricted cases. In this area of research the difficulties to overcome are primarily manual and two-fold in nature:

1) Difficulties of a diplomatic nature, that is, those inherent in the internal and external characteristics of the document. The science of diplomatics, even in the case of private transactions, is always able to recognize the authenticity of a document under examination, which is considered to be a primary source, by

---

[4] For the edited text, see E. Rossini, "Persistenza di tradizioni pagane nel Veronese (L'iscrizione di Marcellise del 1407)," *Vita Veronese*, XVII, no. 1 (1964), 1 ff.

establishing the limits within which one can use such a document for a study conducted along rigorously scientific lines.

2) Problems of a paleographical nature, which must be resolved in order to clarify the content of the text with the greatest accuracy possible. Paleography helps us to expand the various abbreviations in the appropriate manner and to interpret scribal annotations and similar signs contained in these documents. Moreover, together with the information gathered in the diplomatic process, the paleographical study establishes the limits for a valid undertanding of the text, by giving it a completely modern appearance.

To these difficulties others, of a linguistic nature in our case, are added, in so much as the transcriptions are very often the sole arbiters in the resolution of the thorny problems inherent in the subdivision of words and in the occurrences of lexical forms and syntactic modes in a wide range of variants. In addition, it is necessary to clarify the relationship among the various components of the period, especially when they do not conform to normal patterns. In the thirteenth and fourteenth centuries the syntactic and morphological structures of the vulgar tongues were essentially weak, and when they became separated from the structures of the Latin forms, very often they would completely fall apart. In short, transcription requires patience, perseverance, constant checks, and continuous comparisons that always must be performed with scrupulous care and, above all, with calm and a clear mind, which should always be open to possible comparisons, to more specific analyses based on new knowledge, and to new and old experiences alike, until each part fits into the linguistic and juridical logic of the text itself.

* * *

At this point, while taking for granted the wealth of knowledge inherent in the diplomatic and paleographical processes, [5] we must

---

[5] For diplomatics, see the following fundamental works:
Giry, A., *Manuel de diplomatique* (Paris, 1894 & 1925).
De Boüard, A., *Manuel de diplomatique française et pontificale*: Vol. I, *Diplomatique générale* (Paris, 1929); Vol. II, *L'acte privé* (Paris, 1948).

advise the reader that very often certain methodological procedures, already adopted by related sciences (as, for example, codicology) and valid for them, are not appropriate for documents of a juridical nature and lead to blatant errors.

In many ways codicology is very similar to paleography and diplomatics; in fact, it often makes use of them in the study of written documents. However, in many respects it differs greatly from them not only because of the subject matter, but also because of the modes of expression, as in the case of abbreviations. Codicology studies problems peculiar to codices, diplomatics those relating to documents in the archives. Paleography teaches us how to read codices and archival documents. However, we must not forget that the latter are and will remain documents of a legal nature that attest to an event, which has either occurred or which probably occurred within a fixed period of time. Therefore, in reading these texts, we must become familiar with the abbreviations derived from the *notae iuris* that are, in fact, the symbols first used in the oldest legal manuscripts and then adapted to new situations according to the need. This system of abbreviations is quite often greatly different from the one used in the codices which treat specific arguments. Therefore, if paleography teaches us to read a text, then it assumes at the same time the task of situating it in time and place. If the calligraphy and systems of abbreviations were uniform, this undertaking would be impossible; fortunately, they are not. Consequently, it is in these two elements that we must find the clues regarding the dating and the provenance of a given document. While it is true that in such studies there are common areas, in others there are only differ-

---

Bresslau, H., *Handbuch der Urkunden für Deutscheland und Italien*, 2 vols. (Leipzig, 1912-1931).

For paleography, among the most recent and best informed is the work by G. Battelli, *Lezioni di Paleografia* (Città del Vaticano, 1949[8]). Other helpful volumes are:

Thompson, E. M., *Handbook of Greek and Latin Paleography* (London, 1906[3]);

——, *An Introduction to Greek and Latin Paleography* (Oxford, 1912);
Madan, F., *Medieval Paleography* (Oxford, 1907);
Sauders, W., *Ancient Handwritings* (London, 1909);
Hector, L. C., *The Handwriting of English Documents* (London, 1966).

ences, and from the study of these differences we can deduce many useful things.

In searching among thirteenth and fourteenth-century documents in the archives of Western Europe, we are almost always confronted with great piles of folios, either loose or bound, which are of various juridical types and almost always written in Latin. However, these volumes are not codices, but rather public records, which are structurally different from the former. In some of the latter ones, also called *libri copiali* ("copy books"), we find integral copies of documents: imperial commands, papal bulls, royal and feudal charters, public permits, and the like. In addition, we encounter private records: bills of sale and purchase, leases, donations, exchanges of property, wills and other papers concerned with the patrimony. Besides these copy books, we find the so-called *libri actorum*, which record the normal administration of legal privileges: accounting records, payments and collections, records of expenditures, and similar documents. Often these books are reserved for specific subjects: *libro scodirol* (accounting books), roll-books, and so forth. Therefore, because of their legal and administrative nature these books are indeed different from codices.

In archival acts of the Middle Ages, particularly in those of the thirteenth and fourteenth centuries, we observe the almost constant use of Latin. However, it is a Latin with far different structures than that of Antiquity. Scholars have called and continue to call it "corrupt Latin," "decadent Latin," "low," or better, "Medieval Latin." To be sure, they are inappropriate names, because they refer to a language that, after having been the means of universal communication for centuries, was incorporated primarily in dealings of the chancellery and in legal affairs. As a result, Latin became the vehicle of expression among public officials and men of law (such as judges, lawyers, and notaries). Through these individuals this variety of Latin entered into the chancelleries, into public and private offices, and, consequently, into daily commercial activity. For the most part, these men of law, be they notaries or scribes, used as a means of graphic expression the cursive miniscule, called precisely "corsivo cancelleresco," and in the syntactic-lexical forms of the learned language we note a great influx of neologisms and technical terms that have specific sources in the local *patoi* or in formularies. The latter were standard phrases, learned very often by rote, either at school or in practice, and applied sometimes in so rigid a manner as to forget the relationship between the various elements of the sentence, which in Classical Latin were bound together in inflexible patterns.

This juridical tendency can also be found, through natural osmosis, in non-literary texts, as for example in the following lexical forms: *sucessores* in place of the dialectal *rexi* ("heirs"); *factor* instead of the German loanword *gastaldius* ("administrator"); *factione/fatione* instead of *colta*, which indicates a tax that must be paid; and many others that could be easily listed.

To aid our understanding of these terms, we possess reliable reference works, such as the new edition of *Du Cange* and other extensive compendia of recent issue. However, these formulas and terms are not used everywhere. Generally speaking, we can say that every chancellery, just as every judge or notary, depended on the local *scole juris* or else on different university centers, which were distinguishable by both the calligraphy and the terminology, as well as by the abbreviations and the similar format of separate documents. Today, we are able to establish with certainty whether this or that notary was inspired by this or that law school; but a complete study of this remains to be done. Here is one example:

The notaries who studied at the Bologna Law School dated documents in a manner completely different from those who attended other schools, like those at Padua and Venice. While the latter were accustomed to date their papers according to the traditional Roman calendar that was composed of calends, ides and nones, the Bolognese notaries, on the other hand, divided the month in two parts. The first consisted of the first fifteen days, which were indicated as *primo, secondo*, etc., and followed by the word *intrante* and the name of the month in genitive case. The second half, which ran from the sixteenth day on, was tabulated from the end of the month, for which February 28 (not in leap year) became the *die prima exeunte februarii* and, thus, February 20 was the *die IX exeunte februarii*. However, this is only one of the features that relate to the formulas. For individual schools differed also in abbreviations, lexical forms, and the format of single documents. Nevertheless, it is possible to determine some constant factors, for which a notary in Verona was perfectly capable of reading and understanding one from Milan and vice versa. This diversity, while present everywhere, did not create insurmountable difficulties.

* * *

In the study of thirteenth and fourteenth-century documents, despite the normal use of Latin, it is not uncommon to find passages in the vernacular and sometimes even in various local dialects, which were sometimes inserted in Latin texts. In our many investigations of documents from the Venetian region, we have found that vernacular passages occur with greater frequency in the numerous statutory regulations and acts of the "Associazioni di mestiere" ("trade guilds"), as well as in the dealings of individual citizens and governmental bodies. The latter items are usually in the form of petitions, banns, *ambaxate* (i.e., ordinances of the "Lord" that have the same legal value as laws), and letters, which are difficult to fit into the orthodox patterns of diplomatics.

In many civil codes compiled during these centuries, we find it written that some procedural steps in the administration of justice should be translated into the vernacular so that the defendant could understand their content. However, in the individual tribunal matters that we have observed, we have never found a suitable counterpart to this order. All parts of a trial (testimony by witnesses, official reports, accusations, sentences) are always given in Latin. It appears, then, that the notary, who functioned as court clerk in the administration of justice in these centuries, limited himself to an oral translation into the vernacular of certain parts of the trial.

Vernacular documents in the archives are almost always of a legal nature and are rarely separated from other texts written in Latin. This is generally the case, even though we possess evidence that in some chancelleries, as in the one of the Scala family, the petitions and statements sent by private citizens to their Lord were transcribed in special copy books. Since these volumes have not come down to us, the texts in the vernacular and of a non-literary nature can be singled out either among the parchment pages of a manuscript or in individual registers.

In the collections of administrative acts (accounts, expenses, receipts, earnings, and the like), the annotations in the vernacular are as frequent as those which can be found in parchment texts. From these observations we see that the first problem to overcome lies in the identification of these documents, because, if they are not uncommon, they are neither very frequent.

* * *

Once the individual texts have been chosen, it is necessary to determine the nature of each document and to establish the limits within which they can be used as reliable sources of linguistic information. In fact, whoever works with a document of this kind must modify his approach methodology according to the circumstances and the conditions in which the text has survived, and this should be done without taking the writing material (paper, parchment, stone, metal, etc.) into consideration.

The document under analysis, be it a notarial act, constitutional code, banns, *ambaxata*, or letter, may have come down to us in the original (in one or more copies) or else in later copies. The term original means that text which was composed by a notary in public office at the same time as the realization of the ordinance or contract, of which the document itself is an acceptable witness in the eyes of the law.

In the tradition of single documents, the originals are easily distinguishable from the copies by the presence on the text of precise annotations: for example, *exemplum ex autentico relevatum*. In other cases the copy can be identified by an annotation of the notary-scribe, who would declare *scripsi*, if he had written the text immediately after having witnessed the transaction described in the text itself; or else he would write *exemplavi*, if he were only copying the document. Moreover, in the second case he would note that from the original he had transcribed the copy *bona fide sine fraude*, that is, without having removed or added anything that might change the sense of the original document.

When dealing with a copy, it is first necessary to identify the notary-scribe and, at the same time, to establish the date in order to determine, if possible, its relationship with the original, and this is not always easy. Here is an example:

On January 15, 1324, a certain Antonio Zentillis, son of the late Pietro and resident of Verona in the district of Santo Stefano, made his will. In the extant parchment we note the preliminary annotation, *exemplum ex autentico relevatum;* therefore, we know that we have in front of us a copy and not the original.[6] The problem that confronts us, then, is the dating of his copy, if possible, in view of the fact that there are no precise indications. However, our examination of the context has revealed linguistic peculiarities that can be considered to be phenomena completely abnormal in a document of 1324. For example, the presence of the letter z in place of a voiced sibilant which could also have been represented with x or $ç$. In addition, there are the forms *stimare* (instead of the more frequent *stimaro*), *quegi* (for *quigi*), and others. A further examination revealed that three notaries had signed the document, two of whom declared *interfui,* which indicates that they were the witnesses; however, the third notary stated: *Ego Alexander notarius, filius domini Bernardi de Sancto Paulo, bona fide, sine fraude, exemplavi.* With this evidence in hand, we searched in the roll-books of the notaries of Verona[7] and, in the one of 1348, found: *Alexander domini Bernardi de Sancto Paulo,* who registered after this date. From this we know that the document under consideration, although perhaps valid as a historical source, is not valid as a linguistic one. The language of this document is at least thirty years removed in time from the date of the event, that is to say a generation later. In this regard we can justify the orthographical characteristics which, if they can be justified after 1350, are hardly ever found before this date.

With this information we are able to provide a brief conclusion to this story. Antonio de Zentillis first composed his will in his

---

[6] This document has already appeared in my study, "Testi non letterari in volgare Veronese (1235-1361)," *Studi Storici Veronesi Luigi Simeoni,* Vols. XVI-XVII (1966-1967), 9-14. The original is preserved in the private archive of the Pellegrini family of Verona.

[7] Archivio di Stato di Verona, *Collegio dei notai,* reg. 2, f. 84r.

own hand before 1324. On January 16, 1324, he was ill, for which he called a notary to whom he gave the holograph, and from this the notary himself made a *publicum instrumentum*, which was a valid document in the eyes of the law. Toward the middle of the fourteenth century and surely after 1348, this testament, perhaps for reasons of succession, was recopied by the notary Alexander. The scholar interested in linguistic problems must take these transcriptions into account, because, even though the notaries assure us of the legal accuracy of the text, they do not similarly guarantee its linguistic elements; and, consequently, this failure on their part must always be considered by the scholar.

Let us turn our attention to another case:

On August 3, 1361, [8] Giovanni, the town herald, was entrusted by the Comune of Verona with the text of an announcement, in which were outlined new regulations regarding the commerce, consumption and sale of wine. A few days later, Giovanni returned to the offices of the Comune and declared to the representative of the Mayor of Verona that he had completed his assignment according to the current practices and, then, returned the text of the announcement which he had read in public. Here we are confronted with an original document which bears the transcription of the very words that the Veronese citizens, who were present in the market square and in other popular places, had been able to hear.

We also encounter some problems in transmission when dealing with petitions, which may be extant either in the original text of the author or in a copy of it. In a parchment document of January 18, 1345, the monks of the Ospedale of SS. Giacomo and Lazzaro, located in the community of Tomba outside the city walls of Verona, asked Mastino II della Scala, who was at that time the Lord of Verona, to exempt them from paying certain taxes, which had been levied on their property. [9] As stated in the document, the notary Giovanni Favaccia had asked two of his colleagues, Costanzo and Maxio, to come to the City Hall of Verona and serve as witnesses. In the presence of these three people there

---

[8] Archivio di Stato di Verona, Carlotti Trivelli, busta V, perg. 177.
[9] See document I of the Appendix.

appeared Manfredo da Sommacampagna, the *factor generalis* (a sort of "secretary general") of Mastino II, who ordered the Mayor, Nicolò de' Rimbaldesi da Firenze, to study the request, which had been sent to the Lord of Verona, and presented him with the text of the same. The Mayor then summoned his advisors and, having heard their opinions, commanded that the orders of Mastino II be carried out.

From this we see that the extant text is not the letter that the Prior of the Monastery of SS. Giacomo and Lazzaro sent to Mastino II, but rather a copy of it. Therefore, we may assume that the *iter* of this document is the following:

After having met with the Brothers of his Order, the Prior sent a letter to Mastino, which, once received in the chancellery, was transcribed in the registers of the petitions. From this register or from the original, which had been put on file, more copies were made, two of which are extant, and at least a third copy should be somewhere in the Archivio del Comune.[10]

While it is true that, when dealing with notarial acts, we can be certain of the historical or legal content of the specific transaction, we cannot, on the other hand, be equally certain that such an act has been transcribed scrupulously, with particular attention to the orthography and morphology of the text. Although he does not alter the meaning, the notary often inserts slight variations so as to "improve" or, at least, to modernize the text, thus rendering it more comprehensible and, perhaps, less antiquated. So, even if these variants do not alter the legal value of the document, the same is certainly not true with regard to the linguistic reality of the text itself. Consequently, in the above example we may consider the testimony to have been linguistically filtered by a notary, whose culture was far different from that of the Prior and monks of the Monastery at Tomba.

However, there are other cases in which the extant text is the autograph. For example, we possess in the original a letter that the Mother Superior of the Monastery of San Michele in Campagna sent to Tedis, the canon of the Cathedral chapter, on whom the Monastery depended. Without doubt, it is a linguistically

---

[10] The two copies are found in the Archivio di Stato di Verona, *Istituto Esposti*, perg. 117 (Diplomi), and *Istituto Esposti*, perg. 2367.

original document which was written by the nun and which lends itself well to a detailed examination. [11]

On the other hand, the situation is much less complex when the linguistic source material is taken from the registers, which we have classified as *libri actorum*. While it is true that registers generally contain less complete texts (annotations of various types, references to sums spent, acquisitions of objects, etc.), they nevertheless reflect the characteristics of real, colloquial speech, and, consequently, these documents are extremely useful for a variety of studies.

* * *

Another thorny problem on which we will briefly pause, without pretending in the least to have resolved it, centers on the criteria followed by these copyists (scribes, notaries, judges) with regard to the representation of phonemes. Whoever transcribes documents, both those mentioned above and those in the vernacular, must have the sounds and the characters of the Latin alphabet as constant points of reference. At that time, the predominant pronunciation was the one which, from the fifth century on, spread throughout the Romance language area and was marked by local peculiarities that tended to become, in the course of centuries, more and more individualized and autonomous.

A major factor in these changes was the constant pressure of the local *patoi*; phonemes underwent rapid transformations even in the short space of a generation. Therefore, if in the fifth century Latin presents a spirant *u*, general palatalization of the *c* and *g*, and *ti* plus vowel as a sibilant, then its stabilization in the thirteenth and fourteenth centuries can be attributed to the *scole iuris* and to the general method of textual transmisison. But in the encounter between Latin paradigms, which had been set forth in accordance with fifth-century phonetics, and the new sounds of the vernacular languages, the educated and non-educated scribes alike almost always had recourse to "aural impressions" (*impressioni d'orecchio*), that is, to transcriptions without fixed

---

[11] The document has already appeared in my study, "Testi non letterari...," 14-15.

norms. For example, the unvoiced sibilant was represented by *x, ss, xs, xss*, and so forth; the voiced sibilant, on the other hand, was usually written with a single *s*, but more frequently with a *ç*, which toward the middle of the fourteenth century was written *z* in Veronese. Thus, we can see the large number of possible variants in any given text.

* * *

As we have already stated, the transcription must be absolutely faithful to the original manuscript; however, the editor must adopt certain modern conventions, such as the subdivision of words and punctuation. Although punctuation is very often indicated in manuscripts, it is completely different from our contemporary practices. The same can be said for the use of capital letters. In general, while there are seldom any difficulties with capitals and punctuation, frequent enigmas do crop up in the subdivision of words. There are no rules to follow in their resolution, except, of course, a good knowledge of the language or dialect of the document; the greater the mastery of the language, the less the chance for error. Consider the following example:

In the petition that the Prior of the Monastery of SS. Giacomo and Lazzaro sent to Mastino II, the phrase *che torto palexo* appears, in order to show that the tax was not just. However, this phrase is rather ambiguous, because the sense depends on the subdivision of the words. It could read: *ch'è torto palexo* ("which is an obvious injustice") or *che torto palexò* ("which manifested the injustice").

A second example of these insidious cases follows:

On August 3, 1331, the nuns of the Dominican Monastery of Acquatraversa at Verona elected a new Prioress.[12] Having listed those voting, the text continues as follows: *Leto e publica lo scrutinio la sor Elena chavo la prima vosce....* The problem lies in the meaning of the phrase *chavo la prima vosce*, which can be understood as *ch'avo la prima vosce* ("who had the floor first") or as *chavò la prima vosce* ("was chosen to speak first").

---

[12] The document has already appeared in my study, "Testi non letterari...," 15-16.

Difficulties of this nature are the most troublesome, because they can distort the meaning of a document. To overcome them, the editor has no other choice than to read and re-read the text itself, perhaps spacing his readings so as to approach them with a clear mind; he should also attempt to imagine all possible combinations, always keeping in mind the general sense of the document and making use of his experience with other texts. Here, as in other dubious cases, the editor should put all possible combinations in the notes.

Once the problems inherent in the subdivision of words are resolved, those relative to the expansion of abbreviations must be considered. These are similarly problematic, for even if they do not threaten to obscure the meaning of the text, they at least cause confusion and errors in the variants. In these cases the editorial work should be conducted with frequency tables in mind. Consider the following example:

The text reads *cōpito*. Do we write *conpito* or *compito*? If a certain vocalic or consonantal combination has a very high frequency, we should use the more prevalent form to expand this abbreviation. However, if the phenomenon is an isolated occurrence or one of very low frequency, the editor must indicate such a form when the reading leaves no doubts. For example, after having determined the frequency rates, he will write *ha* (verb) or *he* (verb), if such forms are present in the text. If these verb forms are abbreviated, he will write *à* and *è*, as he would do in all other cases.

Since we find many abbreviated words in our texts, the first problem is to determine their precise value. Fortunately, the frequency of abbreviations is lower in vernacular manuscripts than in Latin texts. But, while in Latin we are able to recognize words by certain orthographical conventions, in the vernacular tongues we can not benefit from such indications, for which reason the possibility for error is much greater.

According to the rules that we find in paleographical manuals, abbreviations can be classified as follows: [13]

---

[13] For these distinctions we follow the outline given by A. Cappelli in his preface to the *Dizionario di abbreviature latine ed italiane* (Milano, 1961). However, we should advise the reader that this very useful manual

1. Abbreviations by apocopation.
2. Abbreviations by syncopation.
3. Abbreviations with a specific meaning.
4. Abbreviations with a generic meaning.
5. Abbreviations with superscript letters.
6. Conventional symbols.

However, we must remember that this system of abbreviations, whose origin is Latin, had been used for centuries solely in Latin manuscripts, and, only long after the birth of the Romance languages, did it find its way into vernacular texts. This is essentially the reason for the rather restricted use of these conventions by scribes and notaries. They were convinced that, if they had applied this system in its entirety, they would have created numerous unsolvable enigmas.

Abbreviations by apocopation (i.e., when the last part of the word is missing) are indicated by a sign that, according to Cappelli, can be:

1. A general sign —, ‑, ⌒ , ∼ , placed above the word.
2. A sign of apocopation ʇ , ⁄ , ₹ , ⋅ , which cuts diagonally across the last letter of the abbreviated word. The last of these signs is usually attached to the final letter in the word. In vernacular texts the following rarely cause problems:

    V. = Verona
    ſ = ser

Abbreviations by syncopation are those in which one or more letters are missing in the interior of a word:

    domāda = doma(n)da
    p̄metro = p(ro)metro (= "promettere")
    doña = don(n)a (= "signora")

However, do we put *m* or *n* in front of *p* and *b*? In Italian it is always *m*, but in the Veronese dialect the phenomenon is the opposite:

---

is not complete, nor is any other manual, because the system of abbreviations depends not only on the school or the city, but also in many cases on the personal preference of the scribe, especially in cursive texts.

Italian	Veronese
te*m*po	te*n*po
ca*m*po	ca*n*po
To*m*ba	To*n*ba (a place name)

In a document that we will reproduce in the Appendix we find *enbrigamento*, as well as *Tomba* and *sempro* (= "sempre") in another text.

In the transcription of a manuscript, we are confronted with the following problems: Do we transcribe *chōpraro* as *conpraro* or *compraro*? Similarly, *tēpo* as *tempo* or *tenpo*? At this point we are unable to judge adequately. Only when a frequency table for the two instances has been compiled, can a judicious solution be reached. For the present we will limit ourselves to writing *tenpo* and *conpraro*, when we encounter the indication —. On the other hand, when the word is written in its entirety, we must follow the spelling of the text.

Another rather common example is provided by the abbreviation *cõe* (= "comune"). When it occurs in a Latin text, we know that we must write *commune*. However, the Italian equivalent of this word is *comune* (with a single nasal), and this is also true in modern Veronese, for this dialect tends to simplify geminates. Thus, in Latin texts we write *commune*, in vernacular ones *comune*. The same problem of *m* in front of *p* and *b* is also present in the abbreviation 9 (= *con* / *com*).

In vernacular texts the following abbreviations with a specific meaning occur:

1. — , ⌒ = *m, n*
2. ⟩ , 9 = *con, com, cun, cum*
3. ⟩ = *e, et*

Abbreviations with a generic meaning include the symbol —, which in ꝑ can indicate *per, par* or *por*, while p equals *pre* or *pro*. Other signs are 3 = *-que, -sis*, and the like.

There is also a certain frequency in the use of small, superscript letters, as for example: ꝑ^a = *persona*.

Finally there are the conventional symbols (as 7 = *et* and 9 = *con/com*), which attest to the persistence of Tironian signs.

For additional information on the above, the reader should consult specialized handbooks, as those compiled by Cappelli, Battelli, Thompson, and others.

As we have indicated, abbreviations in vernacular manuscripts do not present many problems; nevertheless, in our discussion of the texts in the Appendix, we will pause to consider those that lend themselves to important observations.

In any case, we must insist on this fact: that the principal problem in transcription is one of patience and continuous revision. A first reading is never sufficient to allow a complete and exact understanding of a text.

APPENDIX

In order to clarify the substance of the above essay, we present for the reader's examination three documents, of which the first is written both in Latin and in the vernacular and the remaining two solely in the vernacular. The first is a petition, the second a letter and the third a will. They are written respectively on parchment (extant in two copies, both original), on rag paper (made of cotton fibres), and finally on stone. Obviously, the writing material has no relation to the subject matter of the text.

I

The document that we present below is dated February 8, 1345, and is written in accordance with the simplified, fourteenth-century form of the *instrumentum notarilis*, which was used by the Veronese notaries and, therefore, also by almost everyone who worked in the chancellery there. It is a typical example of an original document, written and signed by the notary, Giovanni Favaccia, who added his *signum tabellionatus*, which certified it at that time as a completely reliable public document. In the compilation Giovanni Favaccia rigorously followed the usual formalities: he used an outline that he had learned at school and inserted the appropriate formulas.

In this type of *instrumentum notarilis*, we are able to distinguish three parts: the protocol or initial protocol, the text, and the final protocol or "escatocollo."

In the initial protocol we note the following:

1) The *Signum Tabellionatus* that, from the beginning of the thirteenth century, became a truly individualized mark, one which identified the notary and guaranteed the authenticity of the documents signed by him. The rule was that every notary

Verona, Archivio di Stato, *Istituto Esposti*, busta 102, perg. 117

Verona, Archivio di Stato, Carlotti-Trivelli collection, box IV

Inscription above East portal of the parish church of Marcellise, Comune di San Martino (Verona). [Photograph by Egidio Rossini.]

Inscription (continued) above East portal of the parish church of Marcellise, Comune di San Martino (Verona). [Photograph by Egidio Rossini.]

should put his *signum* on file in a special register kept at the guild of which he was a member.

2) The *invocatio*. This act of respect toward the Divinity always precedes a transaction and, in this document, is represented by the formula *in Christi nomine*.

3) The first part of the *datatio cronica* (day and month of composition). In this document, *die veneris octavo februarii*. The rest of the date is found at the end of the final protocol and precedes the signature of the notary.

4) After the *datatio cronica* comes the *datatio topica*, in which is stated the place where the transaction was concluded (here, *Super sala domus nove Communis Verone*).

5) Finally, there are the names of the witnesses who were present at the termination of the transaction. In this case, they are the notary Costanzo and Maxio da Firenze, *miles et socius* of the Mayor of Verona.

At this point we find a *signum paragraphi* that indicates the beginning of the second part of the *instrumentum*, the text, which is divided as follows:

1) The *narratio* (also called the *expositio*), wherein are stated the preliminary and formal circumstances that have determined the following *dispositio*.

2) In this document the *dispositio* contains the declaration of the Mayor of Verona who, having heard his advisors' opinions, orders that the monks of the Monastery of SS. Giacomo and Lazzaro at Tomba be excluded from the payment of taxes.

3) The *minatio* is the fine of 100 *lire* (in Veronese currency), payable by those who do not observe the order of the Mayor of Verona.

In conclusion we find the final protocol (or "escatocollo") which consists only of two parts:

1) The completion of the date with the indication of the year, calculated from the birth of Christ and followed by the current indiction period.

196   EGIDIO ROSSINI

2) The signature of the notary who executed the transaction, together with the titles relative to his office (here, the notary of the Mayor).

In the *narratio* of this document the text of the petition that initiated the Mayor's official decree is written in the vernacular.

The transcription of the part in Latin presents no problems, because it is based on well-known words and formulas, as well as common abbreviations.

We possess two contemporary copies of this document, both in the hand of the notary Giovanni Favaccia and written on the same day. They are preserved in the Archivio di Stato di Verona, *Istituto Esposti*, busta 102, perg. 117 *(diplomi)* and busta 22, perg. 2367. (Fig. 1 § 2) Although basing our transcription on perg. 117, we have indicated interlinearly the variants of perg. 2367.

(S.T.) [1] In Christi [2] no(m)i(n)e. Die {ven(er)is. Decimo / veneris}

octauo [3] februa(r)ij. [4] sup(er) Sala {domus / dom(us)}

noue Co(mmun)is veron(e). P(re)sentib(us) s(er) Constantio

Nota(r)io de S(an)cto {Silu(est)ro. Ac d(omi)no / Siluestro}

Maxio de florenc(ia), milite (et) socio d(omi)ni Pot(est)atis i(nfra)sc(r)ipti, testib(us) ad hec. /

₡ [5] D(omi)n(u)s [6] Manfredus de {Sum(m)acampan(e)a g(e)n(er)alis / factor / Sum(m)acampan(ea)}

---

[1] (S. T.) = *signum tabellionatus*.

[2] XPI is the famous Constantine symbol that serves as the abbreviation for *Christi*. This sign may be reduced to X with a superscript i: X̽.

[3] The use of capital letters in this text is far different from that currently in use. We can observe that: Ꝼ alternates at the beginning of a word with ſ . Ꝼ is only used at the beginning, while ꝭ can be both initial and final. Therefore, Ꝼ should be capital, as we have indicated. Ꝗ should be the initial sign both for *v* (*veneris; Verone*; etc.) and for *u* (*universis*). However, we also find *uiro*.

[4] The mark ~ indicates an *r*, sometimes accompanied with a vowel. The final *i*'s of februarij are differentiated so as not to be confused with *u*. This notary rarely dots the *i*.

[5] The mark ₡ is the typical *Signum Paragraphi*.

[6] Many editors prefer the abbreviated form *domnus* for *dominus*, which to us seems incorrect.

{Magnifici d(omi)ni d(omi)ni [7] /
{magnifici

Mastini. de Lascala. Civitatum veron(e), vinc(encie) (et) c(oetera), do(min)i g(e)n(er)alis. Ex pa(r)te p(re)fati /

d(omi)ni Mastini, dixit (et) ambaxatam fecit {Nob(i)li uiro
{d(omi)no
{nobili

Nicolao de Rimbalde [8] /

xijs de florenc(ia), honorab(i)li Pot(est)ati veron(e). [9] Q(uo)d idem

d(omin)us {Mastinus uult [10] (et) ma(n) /
{Mastin(us)

dat, q(uod) sup(er) quadam Supplicatio(n)e ip(s)i d(omi)no

Mastino {Porecta
{porecta

p(er) d(omi)nos P(ri)orem /

(et) {fr(atr)es hospitalis s(an)cti Jacobi ad Tumbam. Cui(us)
{fratres

Supplicat(i)onis tenor talis est. /

Segnor nostro, Nuy {auemo afaro en Bagnollo. e cossi a ce(r)ti
{Auemo

Citayni [11] de que /

sta {ter(r)a. Bagnollo sie extima, vna octaua. de vno fogollaro. [12]
{t(er)ra

E tuti i Citayni /

i quali gea afaro {se defendo dalesoe fatione. Anuy fi sempro
{se defe(n)do daLesoe

{tolleto i pigni /
{toleto

del tuto. E {cossi enfi fato A Colegnolla. {Siando nuy {Sempro
{cosi {siando {sempro

ip(r)imi che paga /

---

[7] *Dominus* is not repeated through error, but rather functions as a form of respect.

[8] The name of this Mayor is found in many other documents.

[9] Here, too, it is possible to transcribe *Veron(ensis)*. Cf. line 2.

[10] The second *u* is closed at the top, for which it appears to be an *n*.

[11] *Citayni* is an over-corrected form. The notary refrains from using *i* so as to avoid faulty readings (Cf. *nuy, vuy,* etc.).

[12] *Fogollaro*: Italian *focolare*. In this case it indicates a tax that every family had to pay.

a veron(a) ogna Colta che fi metua. E questo no fi fato alogo de veron(a). {Seno / seno

{A La Tumba, che to(r)to palexo. vndo nuy ve doma(n)demo p(er) Deo che vuy mande / ala

che questo to(r)to no en fia fato. El p(r)ioro vostro {e ifray, da La Tumba. / ei frai

{P(er) ip(s)um / p(er)

d(omin)um pot(est)atem non p(er)mittat(ur) fieri d(i)ctis d(omi)nis P(ri)ori (et) {fratrib(us) Cont(ra) Jus. Q(ua)m / fr(atr)ib(us)

{Ambaxatam idem d(omi)nus Pot(est)as volens obs(er)uare, (et) ab ambaxata(m)

alijs obs(er)uari face(re) h(ab)ito /

p(ri)mit(us) Consilio cum Sapiente viro, d(omi)no Bellengerio de Guiscardis di Cre /

{mona Judice g(e)n(er)ali, vica(r)io ip(s)ius d(omi)ni Pot(est)atis Cremon(a)

{ac plu(r)ib(us) alijs Sapientienti(bus) ei(us)de(m) / ac cum pluribus

d(omi)ni Pot(est)atis, hui(us) publici Jnstrume(n)ti tenore, districte p(re)cipiendo {mandat. / ma(n)dat

Vniue(r)sis (et) {Sing(u)lis Judicib(us) Nota(r)ijs, viato(r)ib(us), sing(u)lis

beroe(r)ijs, cet(er)is q(ue) Officialib(us) /

Co(mmun)is veron(e) p(re)sentib(us) (et) futuris quat(enu)s Jncontin(enti) visis p(re)sentib(us). nullo modo {v(e)l / u(e)l

i(n)genio audeant u(e)l presuma(n)t impedire u(e)l molestare, d(omin)um p(r)iorem (et) fr(atr)es /

hospitalis s(an)cti Jacobi ad Tumbam, seu fratres (et) {familliares, familiares

ac eor(um) bona, exi /

stentes. et existentia, ad p(re)sens u(e)l in {futur(um). futurum

in {Domib(us) domib(us)

p(re)fator(um) d(omi)ni p(ri)oris /

(et) fr(atru)m in {Domo Tumbe {Sortis Bagnolli. et in domo s(an)cti domo so(r)tis

Jacobi ad Tumbam {pen(es) / penes}

Colegnollam. p(re)textu {aliquar(um) fa(c)t(i)onum. Scuffor(um). aliq(u)ar(um)}

Lar(ium)[13] (et) Oner(um). realium, (et) p(er)(son)alium, /

{impositor(um) (et) impositar(um), Ac imponendor(um) (et) imponendar(um). i(m)positor(um)}

Juratis (et) ho(min)ib(us) dom(us) /

Tumbe Sortis Bagnolli et {Dum(us) s(an)cti Jacobi ad Tumbam dom(us)}

pen(es) {Colegnollam / Colegnolla(m)}

tam p(er) Co(mmun)e veron(e) q(uamque) alia {qua(m)cu(m)q(ue) ratio(n)e u(e)l quac(um)q(ue)}

causa. Ban(n)o .C. l(i)b(arum) p(ro) q(u)oq(ue) c(ontra)facie(n)te /

Et siq(ui)s p(re)dictor(um) Officialim. {contra p(re)d(i)cta u(e)l c(ontra)}

aliq(ui)d p(re)dictor(um), in aliquo face(re), {At / At}

{tentare(n)t. te(n)tare(n)t} Ex nunc {mandat idem d(omin)us pot(est)as fr(atr)ib(us), ma(n)dat}

familijs {Ac ho(min)ib(us) stantib(us) / ac}

(et) habitantibus in p(re)dictis Domib(us) d(i)ctor(um) domini P(ri)oris

(et) fr(atru)m. {quat(enu)s p(re)dictos talles Offi / q(ua)t(enu)s incontinenti}

ciales p(erson)aliter debea(n)t detinere, et coram ip(s)o d(omi)no

Pot(est)ate, {Seu Successorib(us) suis / seu}

destinare

Ann(o) D(omi)ni mill(esim)o trecentesimo quadragesimo q(ui)nto, Indic(ione) t(er)ciadecima

Ego Johannes de Favacia de ponte petre, p(re)fati d(omi)ni po(test)atis notari(us) sc(ri)ps(i).

---

[13] *Larium* is written above the line in the same hand and with the same ink as the rest of the document. This, too, was a tax.

As we can see, there are very few abbreviations in the vernacular text, and those present are among the most common and, as such, do not cause misunderstandings or erroneous readings. Among these we note the omission of *r* in *certi*, *terra* and *torto*, of *ri* in *primi* and *prioro*, and of *er* in *per*.

* * *

The above is a diplomatic transcription. However, in a modern edition we must omit all parentheses, except those that contain deviations from the standard language, and provide the text with a modern punctuation and capital letters, as follows:

(S. T.) In Christi nomine. Die veneris decimo octavo februarii; super sala domus nove Communis Verone; presentibus ser Constantio notario de Sancto Silvestro ac domino Maxio de Florencia milite et socio domini potestatis infrascripti, testibus ad hec. Dominus Manfredus de Summacampanea generalis factor magnifici domini, domini Mastini de la Scala, civitatum Verone, Vincencie etc. domini generalis, ex parte prefati domini Mastini dixit et ambaxatam fecit nobili viro domino Nicolao de Rimbaldexiis de Florencia, honorabili potestati Verone, quod idem dominus Mastinus vult et mandat quod super quadam supplicatione, ipsi Mastino porecta per dominos priorem et fratres hospitalis sancti Iacobi ad Tumbam, cuius supplicationis tenor talis est:
Segnor nostro,
    nui avemo a faro en Bagnollo e cossì a certi citaini de questa terra. Bagnollo si è extimà una octava de uno fogollaro a tuti i citaini i quali ge à a faro se defendo da le soe fatione. A nui fi sempro tolleto i pigni del tuto e cossì en fi a Colegnolla, siando nui sempro i primi che paga a Verona ogna colta che fi metua. E questo no fi fato a logo de Verona se no a la Tumba che torto palexò. Undo nui ve domandemo, per Deo, che vui mandé che questo torto no en fia fato.
    El prioro vostro e i fray de la Tumba
Per ipsum dominum potestatem non permittatur fieri dictis dominis prioris et fratribus contra ius. Quam ambaxatam idem dominus potestas volens observare et ab aliis observari facere, habito primitus consilio cum sapiente viro domino Bellengerio de Guiscardis de Cremona, iudice generali vicario ipsius domini potestatis ac pluribus aliis

sapientibus eiusdem domini potestatis, huius publici instrumenti tenore districte precipiendo mandat universis et singulis iudicibus, viatoribus, beroeriis, ceterisque officialibus Communis Verone presentibus et futuris, incontinenti visis presentibus, nullo modo vel ingenio audeant vel presumant impedire vel molestare dominum priorem et fratres hospitalis sancti Iacobi ad Tumbam, seu fratres et familiares ac eorum bona existentes et existentia ad presente vel in futurum in domibus prefatorum domini prioris et fratrum in domo Tumbe, sortis Bagnolli et in domo Sancti Iacobo ad Tumbam penes Colegnollam, pretextu aliquarum factionum, scufforum, larium; et onerum realium et personalium impositorum et impositarum ac imponendorum et imponendarum iuratis et hominibus domus Tumbe, sortis Bagnolli et domus Sancti Iacobi ad Tumbam penes Colegnollam, tam per Commune Verone quamque alia quacumque ratione vel causa. Banno C librarum pro quoque contrafaciente.
Et si quis predictorum officialium contra predicta vel aliquid predictorum in aliquo facere ac tentarent, ex nunc mandat idem dominus potestas fratribus familiis ac hominibus stantibus et habitantibus in predictis domibus dictorum domini prioris et fratrum quatenus predictos talles officiales personaliter debeant detinere et coram ipso domino potestate seu successoribus suis destinare. Anno Domini millesimo trecentesimo quadragesimo quinto, indictione terciadecima. Ego Iohannes de Favacia de Ponte Petre, prefati domini potestatis notarius, scripsi.

* * *

A translation of the document follows:

    In the name of Christ. Friday, February 18, in a room of the new town hall of Verona. Present as witnesses, the notary Costanzo of the district of San Silvestro and Masio da Firenze, *milite et socius* of the Mayor named below. On behalf of Mastino della Scala, Lord of the cities of Verona and Vicenza, Manfredo da Sommacampagna, who is Mastino's secretary general, ordered the noble Nicolò dei Rimbaldesi da Firenze, the honorable Mayor of Verona, to study, following Mastino's wishes, the petition presented to him by the Prior and Brothers of San Giacomo at Tomba. The text of the petition is as follows:
    Our noble Lord,
We own property in Bagnolo and some of it is in the hands of certain citizens of that town. Bagnolo levies a

tax on our holdings *(una octava de uno fogollaro)*, but all the citizens who are in possession of our property are exempt from taxes, because these taxes were collected completely from us. The same thing happens at Colognola, even though we are always the first to pay the levies at Verona when requested. However, now we are not asked to pay taxes only at Verona, but also at Tomba, which is an obvious mistake. Therefore, in the name of God, we request that you prevent this injustice from being perpetrated against us.

(signed) the Prior and Brothers of Tomba

On behalf of the Mayor it is declared that no illegal activity will be allowed to the detriment of the Prior and Brothers.

Thus, wishing to observe this ordinance and desiring that it be observed by others, and having heard the advice of the nobleman Bellengerio dei Guiscardi of Cremona, judge and deputy to the Mayor, and of many other learned men, the Mayor orders all the judges, lawyers, and public officials of the Comune of Verona, present and future, that they must in no way bother or presume to bother the Prior or the Brothers of San Giacomo at Tomba. Nor must they bother their servants or their property, present and future, in the dwellings of the Prior and Brothers: the residence at Tomba, the property at Bagnolo, and the edifice of San Giacomo at Tomba located near Colognola ai Colli. No one must molest these individuals with the pretext of claiming taxes and obligations, both real and personal, to be imposed on the petitioners and people at Tomba, the property at Bagnolo, and the house of San Giacomo at Tomba in the vicinity of Colognola, either on behalf of the Comune of Verona or for any other reason or cause, under penalty of a fine of 100 *lire* levied upon every violator. And if any of the said officials, from this time on, tries to bother the Brothers, servants and other individuals living in the said residences, it is the Mayor who orders it, that these individuals may personally restrain him and, subsequently, hand him over to the Mayor and his successors.

The year of the Lord, 1345, indiction XIII.

I, Giovanni di Favacia from Ponte della Pietra, notary of the said Mayor, wrote this.

II

The document transcribed below (fig. 3) is found in the Archivio di Stato di Verona on a folio of cotton rag paper inserted in box IV of the Carlotti-Trivelli collection.

There are no signatures or dates; therefore, even though we know the names of the authors, we have no information about the scribe or the date of composition. The entire text was written in one hand with one ink by an individual who, we believe, was a notary attached to the chancellery. In fact, from the document it appears that he was familiar with the offices of the Comune, for he mentions the *massaria* (the present Office of the Treasury) and the office of the Procurators (among whom he recalls by name a certain Andrea). The text mentions by name Guglielmo, who was the superintendent of public business and private estate of the Scala family. In addition, the notary knows that the goods claimed by his client are a part of the possessions of the estate itself.

By comparing the rather elegant script of this folio (notarial cursive of the mid-fourteenth century) with that of other documents in the Carlotti-Trivelli collection, we have been able to identify the scribe as the notary Giovanni Guastalex, who lived in the district of Mercatonovo and who conducted affairs for the same office.

The text of this letter offers a few indications regarding the date. There is the mention of Cansignorio who was Lord of Verona from December, 1359, to October 19, 1375, the day of his death. However, we may be more precise, for the document states that Tebaldo Trivella sold a house to Valeriano di Cardin in 1361. In looking among other manuscripts in the same collection, we found one from May 3, 1369 (No. 19), which contains a copy of the bill of sale of 1361. From this we are able to establish the missing data: the document, which we present, is in the hand of Giovanni Guastalex from Mercatonovo and was written a few days before or after May 3, 1369.

We present two transcriptions of this document, the first being a faithful reproduction of the manuscript, with the retention of upper and lower-case letters and the original division of words. A slash (/) indicates the end of the line in the original.

We have limited our interventions in this first phase to the expansion of abbreviations within parentheses. In the second transcription, we have given the document a modern appearance: besides adding punctuation, we have altered the linear format of the text and imposed on it a system of capital and small letters, according to current usage. In this phase we have also subdivided words, keeping in mind present-day lexical and syntactical exigencies.

* * *

Al magnifico segnor mess(er) Cansegnor (et) c(oetera). / Notifica el vostro Citain'[1] e fidel s(er)uior ' thealdo triuella'che madon(n)a Desira soa mare'sicomo tuerise de Anth(on)io so neuo /
e fiiol coçaendre de Bonaue(n)tura frell[2] freello del dito thealdo' E el dito thealdo' de .m. III. LXIII. vende vna soa Casa la q(u)ala /
e en v(er)ona en la Co(n)tra de san martin aquaro' a valeran de Cardin per millo e Cento l(i)br(e). E alora en c(on)tene(n)to el dito valeran per /
si ' e per soi successori ' p(ro)mete p(er) amor e p(er) gracia speciala ' a la dita do(n)na en nomo predito ' e al dito thealdo ' de farge vençea en dre /

---

[1] In this first transcription, we have kept the punctuation of the original, considering the apostrophe (') as a comma and the (.) as a period. We have retained the original lines of the text and placed the expanded portion of abbreviated words within parentheses. At the same time, we have left superscript letters as they appear in the manuscript. Some uncertainties can be observed in the use of capitals, but problem would be better treated at length elsewhere. The following abbreviations occur in the text:

— indicates the omission of *m* or *n*, and in one case *on* (*Anth(on)io*).
ſ is read *ser*, since the generic sign ⁊ stands for *er*.
₽ = *pro*.
q^a = *qua*.
q^{a}la = *quala*.
v, vona = *Verona*.
III (with superscript c) = *trecento* ("three hundred").
7 = *et* (Latin), *e* (vernacular).
7 ꝯ = *et coetera*.

[2] The word *frell* has been expurgated.

de la dita Casa pagando igi ' o altri p(er) igi ' al dito valeran ' o a i soi successori ' le dite millo e Cento l(i)br(e). en fina a .X. an(n)i ' mo per /
lo mal far del dito Valeran ' la dita Casa cu(m) li altri soi Beni ' e scrita a la vostra fatoria la quala fi reta p(er) mess(er) guio. vndo el /
dito thealdo per si ' e per lo dito so neuo ' doma(n)da gracia a la vostra segnoria che da vostra parto fio fata ambaxa a mess(er) guio /
e a mess(er) Andrea p(ro)curaor del Comun de v(erona).
e a çaschaun altro che besognesso ' che igi ' o algun digi ' segondo che megi poesso valer ' /
façça la vençea en dre de la dita Casa a la dita don(n)a en nomo del dito Anth(on)io so neuo ' e al dito thealdo ' o sio al dito thealdo pe(r) si ' /
e per lo dito Anth(on)io' segondo i pati ' en ogna modo e forma che megi possa ualer'pagando la dita don(n)a en nomo predito ' e el dito /
thealdo' o uer el dito thealdo per si ' e per lo dito Anth(on)io ' le dite .m. e Ce(n)to l(i)br(e) [3] en la massaria del Comun de v(erona)' o al dito mess(er) guio' o uer a altri a chi /
piu piasa a la vostra segnoria ' E che la dita casa debia fir cançella de su i libri de la dita Vostra fatoria ' e de su çaschaun altro /
libro en lo qual la dita casa fosso scrita soto cason del dito fallo del dito Valeran' si e talmentre che i diti thealdo ' e Anth(on)io ' ne /
i soi resi ' no en poesso auer per algun te(n)po' enbrigame(n)to ne dan(n)o /.

* * *

Al magnifico segnor messer Cansegnor etc.
notifica el vostro citain e fidel servidor Thealdo Trivella che madonna Desirà, soa mare, si come tuerise de Anthonio so nevò e fiiol Coçaendrè de Bonaventura, freelo del dito Thealdo, e el dito Thealdo, de MCCCLXIII, vendè una soa casa la quala è en Verona en la contrà de San Martin Aquaro a Valeran de Cardin per millo e cento libre. E alora encontenento, el dito Valeran per sì e per i soi successori prometè, per amor e per gracia speciala, a la dita donna, en nomo predito e al dito

---

[3] *Le dite.m. e Ce(n)to l(i)br(e)* has been written on the left margin of the folio with a special mark for its insertion in the text.

Thealdo de farge vençea en drè de la dita casa pagando igi, o altri per igi, al dito Valeran o a i soi successori, le dite millo e cento libre, enfina a X anni. Mo', per lo mal far de lo dito Valeran, la dita casa cum li altri soi beni è scrita a la vostra fatoria, la quala fi reta per messer Guio. Undo el dito Thealdo, per sì e per lo dito so nevò, domanda gracia a la vostra segnoria, che da vostra parto, fio fata ambaxà a messer Guio e a messer Andrea procuraror del comun de Verona e a çaschaun altro che besognesso, che igi o algun d'igi, segondo che megi poesso valer, façça la vençea en drè de la dita casa a la dita donna, en nomo del dito Anthonio so nevò e al dito Thealdo, osio al dito Thealdo per sì e per lo dito Anthonio segondo i pati en ogna modo e forma che megi possa valer, pagando la dita donna, en nomo predito e el dito Thealdo, over el dito Thealdo per sì e per lo dito Anthonio, en la massaria del Comun de Verona, o al dito messer Guio, o ver a altri a chi più piasa a la vostra segnoria. E che la dita casa debia fir cançellà de su i libri de la vostra fatoria, e de su çaschauno altro libro en lo qual la dita casa fosso scrita soto cason del dito fallo del dito Valeran. Si è talmentre che i diti Thealdo e Anthonio, né i soi rexi no en poesso aver algun tempo enbrigamento né danno.

* * *

A translation of the document follows:

To the magnificent Lord Cansignorio,
Your subject and faithful servant Tebaldo Trivella declares that his mother madonna Desiderata, being the protectress of her grandson Antonio, son of Cossaendrè de Bonaventura, brother of Tebaldo, and the said Tebaldo sold in 1363 one of their houses located in Verona, in the district of San Martino in Aquaro, to Valeriano de Cardin for 1100 *lire*. At that time, on behalf of himself and his heirs, Valeriano promised the said lady and Tebaldo, out of love and particular alleviation, to give them the possibility of repurchasing the said house, either by paying by themselves the sum of 1100 *lire* to Valeriano or to his heirs, or by having others pay it for them within ten years. Now, because of the improper action of Valeriano, the said house with all its property is registered among the possessions of your estate, which is at present administered by Guglielmo. Therefore, for himself

and for his nephew, Tebaldo asks the favor that your Lordship order Guglielmo and Andrea, the procurator of the Comune of Verona, and anyone else necessary, to provide for the resale of the said house to the said lady, in the name of Antonio her grandson, and to Tebaldo, or else to Tebaldo for himself and Antonio according to the best possible arrangements, either having Tebaldo and the lady, in the name of Antonio, pay, or having Tebaldo pay for himself and for Antonio the sum to the Treasurer of the Comune of Verona, or to Guglielmo, or to others according to the desire of your Lordship. In addition, it is requested that the said house be removed from the rolls of your estate and from every other book in which it had been registered erroneously by Valeriano, in order that Tebaldo and Antonio, as well as their heirs, incur no difficulty or penalties.

III

Above the East portal of the parish church of Marcellise, in the Comune di San Martino Buonalbergo about ten kilometers from Verona, there is an elaborate inscription, measuring 194 cm. by 64 cm. and written in elegant Gothic capitals about 5 cm. high.

In addition to the usual abbreviations found in archival documents, this text presents ligatures, that is, two letters joined together. This rather inconveniently-located inscription has never been edited, even though it is known to many scholars. Since it was not possible to take a complete picture of the inscription, we have reproduced only a part of it, with the warning that the angle (the only one possible for a camera) has distorted some of the letters which appear to slant.

Here is the text:

MCCCCVII IN D̂IE XV ADI. V. ꝑ OTTOVRE FAXO 9DADE FR̂ACESCO DALAVAGNO PSO TES-TAM̂ETO /

ORDENO ELASSE ĈH LVCIA SOA MUIERO E STE-VANO ꝑ ANDREA E GASPARO ꝑ MARCHIOROSOI REXI DEBIA /

OGNI ANNO ĨLAFESTA ⱭSAN PERO Ɑ FEBRARO
Ĩ MARCELIXEFAR VNALIMOSI ... A Ɑ IIII MINALI
Ɑ FŌMEŌ E IIII BRĒTI Ɑ VIN /
CHE FIA DISTIBUIĨ DI SACĒDOTI CHE VEGNI-
RAALA DICTA FESTA Ĩ MĀCELIXE ELAVANCO Ĩ
Q̃LE PSONE CHE VEGNIRA ALA GIEXIA /
Q̃L DI EAI POVERI DELA DITA TERA ECHE AFAR
Q̃STO SE INOL FESO I FIA 9STRITI P LO MASARO
E P IOMENI Ɑ MARCELIXE /
LA QVAL LIMOSINA OBLIGO EL DITO FAXO LA
CAXASOA CHE ZAXO Ĩ 9TRA DEL BORGO E LE
TERE· SOE CHE ZAXO ĨLE 9TRE /
DELPRE Ɑ PIAZOLO E Ɑ PGNOLO E COSI STA PĨS-
TRVMĒTO FATO DA GVIELMO D AVAZO DA LA-
VAGNO NOARO E PIS ... E SCRITA.

* * *

The text with the abbreviations in expanded form follows:

M C C C CV I I IN DI(cion)E XV ADI .V. D(e) OTTO-
VRE FAXO C(on)DA(m)DE FRA(n)CESCO DALAVAG-
NO P(er)SO TESTAME(n)TO /
ORDENO ELASSE CH(e) LVCIA SOA MVIERO E
STEVANO D(e) ANDREA E GASPARO D(e) MAR-
CHIOROSOI REXI DEBIA /
OGNI ANNO I(n)LAFESTA D(e) SAN PERO D(e) FE-
BRARO I(n) MARCELIXEFAR VNA LIMOSI ... A
D(e) IIII MINALI D(e) FO(r)ME(n)TO E IIII BRE(n)TI
D(e) VIN /
CHE FIA DISTRIVII(n) DI SACE(r)DOTI CHE VEG-
NIRAALA DICTA FESTA I(n) MA(r)CELIXE ELA-
VANCO I(n) Q(ue)LE P(er)SONE CHE VEGNIRA ALA
GIEXIA /
Q(ue)L DI EAI POVERI DELA DITA TERA ECHE
AFAR Q(ue)STO SE INOL FESO I FIA C(on)STRITI
P(er) LO MASARO E P(er) IOMENI D(e) MARCE-
LIXE /

LA QVAL LIMOSINA OBLIGO EL DITO FAXO LA
CAXASOA I(n) C(on)TRA DEL BORGO E LE TERE
SOE CHE ZAXO I(n)LE C(on)TRE /
DELPRE D(e) PIAZOLO E D(e) P(ro)GNOLO E COSI
STA P(er)I(n)STRVME(n)TO FATO DA GVIELMO D
AVA(n)ZO DA LAVAGNO NOARO E P(er)IS ... E
SCRITA.

* * *

In the third and last phase of our edition, we will remove the parentheses and give a modern subdivision to the words. Moreover, we will attempt to integrate the two lacunae of the text, placing our conjecture in square brackets. Finally, we will provide capital letters and adequate punctuation.

MCCCCVII, indicione XV, a dì V de ottovre, Faxo, condam de Francesco da Lavagno, per so testamento ordenò e lassè che Lucia soa muiero e Stevano de Andrea e Gasparo de Marchioro soi rexi débia ogni anno, in la festa de san Pero de febraro, in Marcelixe, far una limosi[n]a de IIII minali de formento e IIII brenti de vin che fia distribuì in di sacerdoti che vegnirà a la dicta festa in Marcelixe e l'avanço in quele persone che vegnirà a la giexia quel dì e ai poveri de la dita tera. E che a far questo se i no'l feso i fia constriti per lo masaro e per li omeni de Marcelixe. La qual limosina obligò el dito faxo la caxa soa che zaxo in contrà del Borgo e le tere soe che zaxo in le contrè del Pré, de Piazolo e Prognolo. E così sta per instrumento fato da Guielmo d'Avanzo da Lavagno noaro e per i s[o rexi] è scrita.

A translation of the document follows:

MCCCCVII, indiction XV, October 5. Faccio, son of the late Francesco da Lavagno, ordered in his will that his wife Lucia, Stefano (son of Andrea), and Gaspare (son of Melchiorre), as his heirs, must make, every year on the feast of St. Peter in February, an offering of four "minali" of grain (approx. four bushels) and four "brenti" of wine (approx. 282 liters) to be distributed to the priests who will come to the feast held at Marcellise. The remaining portion will be given to those people present in the church that day and to the poor of that city. If the heirs refuse to comply with this order, they will be forced to obey it by the Treasurer and men of Marcellise. For this offering Faccio gave as a guarantee his house, located in Borgo, and his lands situated in the districts of Prato, Piazzola and Prognolo. This act has been notarized by Guglielmo d'Avanzo da Lavagno, and this stone was inscribed with the contribution of Faccio's heirs.

CONJECTURAL EMENDATION [1]

by George Kane

Conjectural emendation as an editorial practice has a bad name in English studies. What A. J. Wyatt once called indulgence 'in the luxury of personal emendations' [2] has seemed to imply a kind of capriciously irresponsible selfishness inappropriate to a discipline dedicated to the preservation of a tradition, and for all the time that has passed since he wrote thus in 1894 there is still a feeling that such self-indulgence is, if not 'the greatest', certainly a grave 'disqualification for discharging duly the functions of an editor'. [3] Further, the suspicion of presumptuousness that attaches to all emendation falls most heavily upon the kind called conjectural, which, as I understand the term, is practised when an editor rejects the evidence afforded by his manuscripts and in defiance of this proposes as the lost original a reading for which no manuscript evidence exists. The situation that has generated this attitude (which I do not think I have misrepresented) is of some complexity: while the unsatisfactory character of received texts is generally acknowledged, and the need for good editions is manifest, the fairly extensive, but not very well coordinated discussions of the theory and practice of editing have fallen short of agreement.

---

[1] This essay is based on a paper read to the Oxford Medieval Society on 3 March 1966.
[2] *Beowulf with the Finnsburg Fragment*, ed. A. J. Wyatt, rev. R. W. Chambers (Cambridge, 1948), p. xxvi.
[3] Ibid.

One principal objection to conjectural emendation — it has also been laid against less venturesome kinds of editing — is that it includes an element of uncontrollable subjectivity. The popular conception of that subjectivity is excellently illustrated in Vinaver's introduction to his edition of Malory: he is there writing about his own situation when confronted with the necessity of evaluating conflicting evidence from two sources, the Winchester manuscript, and Caxton's print of a lost manuscript.

> The traditional method consists in selecting from each of the two texts or groups of texts the 'best' readings they can offer so as to produce what is often inappropriately called a 'critical' text... the value of such a text depends on the clear understanding that what is 'best' is not what seems best to the critic, but what is attributable to the author. And it so happens that it is not humanly possible for any critic, however cautious and competent, to maintain this distinction. For the more he is bent on his task, the less he can conceive of himself and the author as two distinct individuals whose ways of thinking and writing are inevitably unlike, who are both liable to err, each in his own unaccountable way, just as they are capable of choosing two equally 'good', but conflicting, forms of expression. There may be various degrees of skill in the handling of the situation, and various degrees of accuracy in the results; but the procedure proves in the end... disastrous;... the fault lies ... with certain habits of mind inseparable from any practical application of the method, habits which broadly speaking amount to the belief that whatever satisfies one's taste and judgement must be 'good,' and that whatever is 'good' belongs to the author.[4]

For anyone who agrees with him Vinaver's objection must apply *a fortiori* to the conjecturing editor, who rejects as 'bad' an actual, received, often unanimously attested reading, and prefers, would set in its place a hypothetical reading, one which he himself has invented. What wild fancies must we expect of him when even editors soberly regarding a choice of manuscript readings are incapable of sustained intellectual discipline?

---

[4] E. Vinaver, *The Works of Sir Thomas Malory* (Oxford, 1948), i, pp. xcii-xciii.

For such anxieties there are undoubtedly grounds in the history of textual criticism. The capricious, or inept or misguided conjectural emendation is one of its recurrent themes. Of Bentley, for instance, 'impatient, ... tyrannical, ... too sure of himself', A. E. Housman wrote

> he corrupts sound verses which he will not wait to understand, alters what offends his taste without staying to ask about the taste of Manilius, plies his desperate hook upon corruptions which do not yield at once to gentler measures, and treats the MSS. much as if they were fellows of Trinity. [5]

Bentley was not, Housman also implies, altogether intellectually honest or wholly secure against self-delusion: 'many a time when he feigned and half fancied that he was correcting the scribe, he knew in his heart... that he was revising the author'. [6] In the century following Bentley's, less brilliant but equally wayward, irrational and arbitrary conjecture appears to have been a common practice of editors of classical texts. [7] Two extreme attitudes can be observed: Bentley's seemingly arrogant *Nobis et ratio et res ipsa centum codicum potiores sunt* [8] and the more romantic one expressed by Dr. Johnson:

> The allurements of emendation are scarcely resistible. Conjecture has all the joy and all the pride of invention, and he that has once started a happy change, is much too delighted to consider what objections may rise against it. [9]

Excessive subjectivity, an identification with the author leading to the assumption that the editor perfectly commanded his style, or a supersession of author by editor, were bound to discredit both conjectural emendation and, by association, to some extent at least the whole practice of editing. Whether this effect was

---

[5] A. E. Housman, *Selected Prose*, ed. J. Carter (Cambridge, 1961), p. 29.
[6] Ibid.
[7] Compare Housman, p. 43.
[8] Quoted by A. Dain, *Les Manuscrits* (Paris, 1949), p. 151.
[9] *Johnson on Shakespeare*, ed. W. Raleigh (London, 1931), p. 60.

altogether just has not seemed to matter; and the brilliance of many conjectures, especially in the texts of the Greek and Roman poets, some so intrinsically excellent that for most readers they own the status of received readings, has not sufficed to check it. The demonstration of the fallibility of editorial judgement had been too extreme.

If therefore a modern editor, especially of a vernacular text, professed to identify corruption when his manuscripts did not necessarily indicate this (that is when the archetypal reading of the manuscripts was not in doubt), and further professed confidence in his ability to restore the actual words of his author, he was behaving at best ill-advisedly, at worst with unbecoming conceit of himself. The current scepticism about conjecture extended, as it may still do, to the whole editorial process, and one form of the flight from judgement has been 'to condemn any critical treatment of manuscript material beyond a mere reproduction of the extant tradition or of one of its representatives'.[10] 'One should' (I quote a student of Bédier reporting the master's view) 'select a manuscript which is of the poet's own dialect, which is relatively old, which does not have many mechanical defects and one should reproduce this text without attempting correction unless there is a proved slip of the pen... versification should not be corrected.'[11] This appeared the judicious, the laudable scholarly course: 'möglichst die lesungen der handschrift zu wahren'.[12] Housman, however, drew attention to another aspect of the conservative editor's mentality: 'an editor who wishes to be praised... must defend the MS. tradition not only where it appears to be right but also where it appears to be wrong';[13] and again, 'assuredly there is no trade on earth, excepting textual criticism, in which the name of prudence would be given to that habit of mind which in ordinary human life is called credulity'.[14] We have, I hope, laid aside the caustic address of

---

[10] Vinaver, op. cit., p. xciii. Compare Housman, pp. 105, 106, and K. Sisam, *Studies in the History of Old English Literature* (Oxford, 1953), p. 30, n.
[11] U. T. Holmes, reviewing E. B. Ham, *Textual Criticism and Jehan le Venelais* in *Speculum*, xxii (1947), 469.
[12] R. P. Wülker, quoted by Sisam, op. et loc. cit.
[13] Housman, p. 105.
[14] Ibid., p. 43.

Housman's generation of editors, but perhaps in textual criticism our world is still as topsy-turvy; at any rate it might seem so when an eminent contemporary editor asserts in all seriousness that 'The line of least resistance in textual studies is to declare a reading corrupt and substitute one's own.'[15]

That statement, however plausible it may *prima facie* seem, does not accurately represent the situation. It must mean, in its context, that emending conjecturally is in general easier than accounting for a received reading. But that proposition is manifestly false because, if conjectural emendation is correctly practised, it must begin with and embrace accounting for the received reading; it is thus, as the more comprehensive operation, obviously a more difficult one than any which it comprises.

Moreover the statement does not reflect general opinion. This, as I see it, has two main attitudes: one that the excesses to which conjectural emendation has been carried have made it disreputable; the other that since it is very often possible to conjecture alternative readings for a crux, none of which can be validated, the more disciplined scholarship is to refrain from the activity.

These attitudes, on the face of it, seem reasonable; moreover they should, one might think, serve to moderate speculation, to control the operation of judgement, to safeguard the desirable principle of restraint. If, however, the arguments behind them are examined they appear with less credit. For instance: conjectural emendation is an activity which has been, and thus can be, badly conducted; because of this possibility it ought to be avoided. Or, conjectural emendation is an activity at which one can make mistakes; it is thus dangerous to an editor's reputation and he should therefore avoid it. Or, conjectural emendation cannot produce results of absolute certainty; it is therefore unprofitable and should be avoided. The first and second of these lines of thinking condemn themselves as mean-spirited; the third loses force from the indisputable consideration that there are very few results of literary scholarship in general for which the claim of absolute certainty can be made. In view of this the presumptive character of the results of textual criticism, and

---

[15] Vinaver, p. xciii.

specifically of conjectural emendation, cannot cogently be invoked as a special, arbitrarily applicable objection to these particular forms of the activity. Such arguments lack force and we dismiss them easily; but there still survives a deep-seated objection to conjectural emendation, arising from a very natural human state of mind, the instinct for security.

That instinct would be best satisfied if the texts of ancient authors were generally sound.[16] Since that is not the case the next best reassurance would be to have available a system of editing which would eliminate or at least reduce the possibility of error in that unfortunately necessary process by removing the element of judgement from the operation or minimizing it; there should be a formula whose answers would replace the irresponsible, subjective decisions of erratic editors. It was to perform this function that the system called recension was devised. The twin considerations that it seldom if ever works (because stemmata turn out to be bifid, thus affording no casting vote, or because the evidence permits no stemma to be constructed), and that some impudent critics have presumed to discredit its logic as well as its practicability, have failed to dismiss the *fata Morgana* of a mechanistic system of editing. That continues both to exert its attraction and to obscure the real nature of the situation.

To this last the great modern theorists of textual criticism (I think particularly of Maas, Pasquali and Greg) have not been blind. They recognized and proclaimed the indispensability of judgement in editing. Above all Maas, and there is irony here, for he is nowadays often invoked as the modern exponent of recensionism, emphasized the editor's obligation to the ultimate exercise of judgement, the conjectural emendation which is my subject: 'Erweist sich die Überlieferung als verdorben, so muss versucht werden, sie durch divinatio zu heilen.'[17] The eclectic treatment of his theories is like that suffered by those of Alphonse

---

[16] Compare Housman, p. 43: 'The average man, if he meddles with criticism at all, is a conservative critic.... He believes that the text of ancient authors is generally sound, not because he has acquainted himself with the elements of the problem, but because he would feel uncomfortable if he did not believe it.'

[17] P. Maas, *Textkritik*, 3., verbesserte und vermehrte Auflage (Leipzig, 1957), p. 10.

Dain, now most often followed in a relatively unimportant objection to unduly minute collation, but in fact a merciless critic of erroneous notions about editing. Dain too pronounces on conjectural emendation, in terms strikingly similar to those first of Maas, then of Housman: 'Si le texte transmis est mauvais, on n'a pas le droit de ne pas essayer de l'amender.... Ce qui est détestable, de toute façon, c'est de garder un texte mauvais par souci de s'écarter le moins possible des leçons du manuscrit.'[18]

These uncompromising statements were made by critics with wide experience, not just of the early literature of one vernacular, but of the long history of textual transmission in two classical languages, men thus well apprised of the hazards and difficulties of conjectural emendation. They might seem to restore the matter to its correct proportions. The 'line of least resistance' is not unbridled emendation (which would in any event be quickly subjected to ridicule) but the attitude of total scepticism about the capabilities of editing which, abrogating decision, shifts responsibility to a manuscript and prints this — on the argument which I have heard 'that one would at least have an authentic medieval form of the poem, as opposed to one incorporating the dubious hypotheses of a modern editor'. A harder course is to accept the principle that 'the duty of an editor is to edit', and to use available manuscript evidence for reconstructing an archetypal text. But the hardest course of all is to recognize the axiomatic corruption of such an archetype, and to face the implications of this condition. Each of these stages must be a more anxious, exacting, and challenging operation; but the second and third cannot fail to protect the study of literature against the postulate implied in the first: that its data are false to an indeterminate but certainly large extent. And they avoid the unhistorical corollary of the doctrine of passive 'editing': that the ancient or the medieval public did not care about the quality of its texts.

If nevertheless what Maas has called the 'reprehensible fear' of admitting that textual criticism is an operation which may not attain completely satisfying results[19] prevails, there is a harder

---

[18] *Les Manuscrits*, p. 159.
[19] *Textkritik*, p. 13.

argument still, which seems to create an intellectual obligation to conjectural emendation. This was first (as far as I know) formulated by Maas: 'In the nature of things it is much more harmful when a corruption remains unidentified than when a sound text is unjustly attacked... the unsignalled corruption vitiates the general stylistic impression.'[20] It has been more explicitly stated by Dr Sisam:

> To support a bad manuscript reading is in no way more meritorious than to support a bad conjecture, and so far from being safer, it is more insidious as a source of error. For, in good practice, a conjecture is printed with some distinguishing mark which attracts doubt; but a bad manuscript reading, if it is defended, looks like solid ground for the defence of other readings. So intensive study with a strong bias towards the manuscript reading blunts the sense of style, and works in a vicious circle of debasement.[21]

Old and Middle English scholars will know how large this circle can be; the lexicography, the grammatical study, the notions about metre, our critical judgements and the literary history of the periods are embraced in it.

This concurrence of Maas and Sisam extends to a further conception of the function of conjecture: for Maas it is an essential part of what he calls *Examinatio*, 'Prüfung' of the quality of the received text;[22] Sisam correspondingly believes that 'there would be a real gain if conjecture, instead of being reserved for the useful but disheartening task of dealing with obvious or desperate faults, were restored to its true functions, which include probing as well as healing.'[23]

---

[20] *Textkritik*, p. 13: 'Natürlich ist es viel schädlicher, wenn eine Verderbnis unerkannt bleibt, als wenn ein heiler Text zu Unrecht angegriffen wird... die nicht bezeichnete Verderbnis schädigt den stilistischen Gesamteindruck.'
[21] *Studies*, p. 39.
[22] *Textkritik*, p. 33: 'Konjektur, 'richtig' oder 'falsch,' [ist] ein wesentlicher Teil der examinatio, d.h. der Prüfung, ob der überlieferte Text der beste ausdenkbare ist oder nicht'; and p. 13: 'jede Konjektur reizt zur Widerlegung, durch die das Verständnis der Stelle jedenfalls gefördert wird.'
[23] *Studies*, p. 44.

These considerations, which from their nature are not lightly to be dismissed, seem to define the true, ancillary function of textual criticism: an activity designed not to afford its practitioners either an outlet for self-expression or a secure and comfortable occupation, but to contribute to the right understanding and evaluation of older literature. They express the means by which that function will be exercised: through restoring, or attempting to restore, or indicating the damage suffered by texts in transmission, not in order to 'improve' these but to recover their historical truth, in itself and as a basis for other knowledge. Thus active editing, whether positive in establishing originality of readings, or negative in merely identifying corruption, or conjectural, in proposing hypothetical original readings which would account for putative corruptions, appears an intellectual responsibility, and one which from its character it would be wrong to abdicate or to restrict because its problems are not often or always conclusively soluble. In these terms conjectural emendation loses any character of unbridled self-indulgence and seems, rather, a valuable activity, hazardous indeed to the reputations of those who undertake it, but if correctly practised more likely to promote knowledge than to mislead.

Supposing the force of such arguments to be accepted it might seem desirable to look again at the theory and practice of conjectural emendation. In such a reconsideration the question is bound to come up how the results of the practice can be validated; to this the answer is that a conjecture can be validated conclusively only by the emergence of new textual evidence which supports it; otherwise it can appear as only more or less probably correct. That is a part of the nature of textual criticism, to which I shall recur. There is a second, related question: how the danger of 'improving the poet's work by brilliant conjecture' is to be avoided. This must be answered in terms of the degree of danger, which will depend on the nature of the text, and the quality of its author. There are, to be sure, some Middle English writers whose works invite improvement; I am not concerned with them. In the case of a major poet the danger must seem small from several considerations: first there is the intrinsic unlikelihood of any editor possessing such a capability; second, there is the extreme probability (demonstrable as such beyond reasonable doubt) that a bad reading in a great poem is scribal, not authorial, which must limit the number of occasions where the danger is real; third, the observation of a rationale in conjecture can restrain the creative impulses of an editor. There remains a further question: is the twentieth-century editor as good a judge of the originality of readings as, say, a Middle English scribe copying a near-contemporary poem? Has he any grounds for challenging a reading which, from its unanimous attestation, was evidently acceptable to many such scribes? At the risk of arrogance my answer must, with respect to a competent editor, be affirmative. He has a purpose, to recover what his author actually wrote; from all indications scribes, if they had any purpose of a comparable order, had a different one in which the concept of originality of readings was not included. And his equipment is, except in some notable cases of isolated detail, superior to that of the scribes: he has the comparative evidence of his collations, which they lacked; with the advantage of print he has a better general and particular knowledge of the text than theirs; and he has access to information about the history of lexis, grammar and dialect which no scribe (at least in medieval England) could have possessed. [24]

Of the above questions the fundamental one is the first. Various opinions about the means of assessing the probable truth of a conjectural emendation are to be found in the literature of textual criticism. For instance Housman specified 'fitness to the context and propriety to the genius of the author' as 'the indispensable things'. [25] Hall in his *Companion to Classical Texts* required that a conjecture must satisfy both the two tests of 'Transcriptional Probability' and 'Intrinsic Probability', that is the conjecture and corruption must be in a paleographically explicable relation, and the conjecture must 'suit the context, the author's style and vocabulary, and any general laws which have been proved to

---

[24] Compare Sisam, *Studies*, pp. 36-7: 'A defender of the manuscript readings... might argue that the scribes were well trained, and that they knew more about Old English usage, thought and tradition than a modern critic can. I doubt if this holds good for the earlier poetry.' Textual criticism is in debt to Dr Sisam for giving this doubt the support of his authority.

[25] Housman, p. 51.

apply to his works'.[26] Maas formulated two criteria, a primary one of the appropriate quality of the style and substance of the conjectural reading, and a secondary one of its likelihood to have given rise to the suspect or impossible received reading.[27] These and similar generalizations, whether satisfactory in themselves or not, might well fail, however, to allay the doubts of the sceptic, for all, ultimately, operate by the subjective judgement which he distrusts.

But if, as seems to be the case, subjective judgement is an invariable element of all editing except the most elementary, and since editing seems an indispensable activity, it is necessary to ask two questions: what justification is there for our sceptic's deep-seated distrust, and how can the dangers of subjectivity be minimized? I find the answer to both questions in the nature of the study of literature. This comprises very few activities where subjectivity in some form or other does not play a major part; we accept its presence in many cases; can we reasonably balk at it in others? Where we take the presence and function of subjectivity for granted we know how to test it. We study not the particular attractiveness of any of its conclusions, but the quality of the processes by which this was attained. We do not discard the practice of literary or interpretative criticism because bad criticism has been written; we scrutinize its assumptions, measure its affective constituents against our own responses, apply the tests of logic to its inferences, repeat its processes to better effect, thus incidentally advancing knowledge. To me it seems that the conclusions of textual criticism, and particularly of conjectural emendation, can be similarly tested, and the subjective element in them thus controlled.

As I understand editing an edited text has no absolute authority: it is as sound or unsound as the case the competent editor can make out for it. An edition constitutes an attempt to account for available phenomena in terms of what is known about

---

[26] F. W. Hall, *A Companion to Classical Texts* (Oxford, 1913), p. 151.
[27] *Textkritik*, pp. 11-12, esp. p. 12. His general discussion implies a third criterion, the consensus of competent judgement, 'die Übereinstimmung aller Urteilsfähigen,' adding that this is 'freilich ein schwer zu umgrenzender Begriff': on p. 13 he writes, of conjectural readings, 'nur die besten werden sich durchsetzen'.

the circumstances which generated them. To that extent it has the character of a scientific activity. It operates by advancing hypotheses to explain data, and tests such hypotheses in terms of their efficiency as explanations. Those which pass the test it accepts as presumptively, not absolutely true; they remain subject to revision or rejection if new data come to light or more efficient hypotheses are devised. Its character implies an editorial obligation to expose its procedures and the precise extent to which their results are speculative for scrutiny.[28] In such a process conjectural emendation can represent itself as not merely legitimate, but even on particular occasions strongly indicated, and it will be directed less by Maas's *Fingerspitzengefühl*, though that must play its part, than by deductive and inductive thought. Thus viewed it resumes the character of a respectable activity, one meriting a better name than *divinatio*. We can, admittedly, seldom if ever estimate the absolute truth of its conclusions, but correspondingly we can never know absolutely of any ancient texts except autographs that their words are the words of the authors. All textual criticism except the most elementary is an assessment of relative probabilities, and the authority of ancient texts must always vary — in the last analysis indeterminably — from line to line. 'Wer sich fürchtet', wrote Maas, 'einen unsicheren Text zu geben [and one might add 'oder zu bearbeiten'], wird besser tun, sich nur mit Autographa zu beschäftigen.'[29]

I suppose that the feature of conjectural emendation logically rather than psychologically hardest to accept is its rejection of unanimous manuscript testimony. In Housman's words

> The MSS. are the material upon which we base our rule, and then, when we have got our rule, we turn round upon the MSS. and say that the rule, based upon them, convicts them of error. We are thus working in a circle, that is a fact which there is no denying.[30]

---

[28] Maas, *Textkritik*, p. 13: 'die Texte als die Grundlage jeder philologischen Forschung sollten so behandelt werden, dass über den Grad der Sicherheit, der ihnen zukommt, möglichste Klarheit herrscht.'
[29] *Textkritik*, p. 13.
[30] Housman, p. 145.

In other words, we reject certain evidence on the grounds of other evidence from the same source; this strikes at the principle of authority. But may it perhaps not be that the force of the principle of authority in textual criticism has been misconceived? Let us look on the preceding situation from another aspect. The editor of a major poet must begin with a presumption of the excellence of his author; he is also governed by an axiom that texts, including archetypal texts, are corrupt. The excellence of his author is a matter of consensus of critical judgement; the axiom is a matter of manifest fact. Further, that excellence has survived notwithstanding the axiomatic deterioration of his texts, and must thus once have been even greater than the received texts now represent it to be. Is it then such bad thinking for his editor, where the text seems inferior in particulars although unanimously attested, to impute the falling off to archetypal scribal corruption? Such an inference, as the logic of literary studies goes, might seem good rather than suspect.

It is, of course, subjective, speculative and hazardous. The subjectivity enters when, in a situation where manuscripts offer no choice of readings, the editor carries out a comparison between the received text and his *idea* of the uncorrupted poem, of how the poet would and would not write. Assessing the quality of the received text he concludes that it exhibits characteristics which, in situations where manuscript evidence was divided, were produced by scribal variation. It is speculative because the editor goes on to propose what the poet actually did write, if he did not write the words unanimously attested by the manuscripts, having regard to his performance elsewhere. It is hazardous, although more to the editor's reputation than the poet's, because of the possibilities of error. The editor may mistake in identifying archetypal corruption, from a misconception of his author's *usus scribendi*, in which I include matters of language and literary form; or from a misunderstanding of his meaning, local and general. And he may conjecture badly, either through failure to identify the causes and processes of corruption which should guide him back to the original reading, or through lack of flair, *Fingerspitzengefühl*, which is an indispensable part of his equipment. But taking full account of this situation I will assert that the editor has not so much a right as an intellectual obligation to attempt the recovery of truth. The risk is to himself; however inept he may be he will not — I invoke Maas and Sisam — injure the poet.

Assuming that an editor who accepts this obligation is competent, are there any means by which he can protect himself against the dangers of his undertaking? The answer may lie with Maas, who describes the theoretical situation in which ideal conditions for conjecture would exist. In this situation evidence would be such as to permit a classification of errors specifically likely in particular periods of history, literary kinds, and types of transcription, either from manuscripts with surviving exemplars or from manuscripts whose exemplar can be reconstructed by recension. By this means the probable incidence of any specific type of error in given circumstances could be established. In addition it would be possible to ascertain the quality of the archetype, and this could happen where such an archetype was reduced to the status of a variant text *(Variantenträger)* or even of a derivative text *(codex descriptus)* through earlier branching of the tradition, or where it appeared as a quotation *(Zitat)*. In such a situation the demonstrable classes of error would also, Maas asserts, be presumable in those areas of the text where no control is available, and no means of checking the archetypal quality exists. In other words a knowledge of the incidence of the typical corruption to which any given work was exposed or susceptible, and the possibility of assessing the quality of its archetypal text, that is the exclusive common ancestor of the surviving copies, would be the ideal determinants first of the need for conjecture and second of its accuracy.[31]

The tone in which Maas describes this situation suggests some doubt on his part about the likelihood of its actually ever occurring. In fact it is instanced in *Piers Plowman*. Each version of this poem survives in many copies, and its archetypal text can generally be recovered without difficulty; thus Maas's ideal classification of typical error is abundantly possible. For long passages two, or even all three versions, correspond: where unrevised B corresponds to A the B archetype has the character of a *codex descriptus*; where B corresponds to unrevised C it appears in C

---

[31] *Textkritik*, pp. 11-12.

as a *Zitat*; where the three versions correspond B has both characters. Each revision was carried out on a copy of the immediately preceding version antecedent to the archetypal copy of that version; thus the quality of the archetypal texts can be assessed by comparing them where they correspond.

The editing of *Piers Plowman* will then afford an ideal occasion for reexamining the relation between the theory of conjectural emendation and its practice. From the reexamination it will appear that the distance between the rationale and its confident application must vary from crux to crux and can be immense. Instances of demonstrable archetypal corruption will range from those where the original can be conjectured with some assurance of acclamation to others where, while the received reading is manifestly corrupt, neither text nor context affords any indication of the words of the lost original. This situation is in the nature of the activity. The logical respectability of conjectural emendation is unassailable: the material question in any given editorial situation must be whether it was worth attempting, and this will be answered in terms of the competence of the particular editor. Criticism of conjectural emendation, as of all active editing, must bear not on the legitimacy of the operation but on the quality of its execution.

THE VALUE OF INTERPRETATION
IN TEXTUAL CRITICISM

by Aurelio Roncaglia

The value of interpretation in textual criticism becomes immediately obvious when we consider which operations of textual criticism can be performed without having recourse to interpretation. At most, only one, which is the preliminary acknowledgement of possible external circumstances which might, in fortunate instances, lead to an initial ordering of the materials of one tradition. Everything else depends strictly on interpretation.

The same stemmatic procedure — indispensable whenever one is faced with a multiplicity of witnesses — being founded on the recognition of errors common to several witnesses, presupposes an interpretative act and, furthermore, must be constantly maintained and regulated by interpretive care.

In order to limit in some way the subject, we might begin by clarifying the distinction between the two convergent processes of INTERPRETATIO and of RECENSIO. Compared with the latter, directed towards the establishment of the text through the utilization of "external evidence," in which the text is preserved, interpretation might be defined as directed towards the establishment of the text by means of referring to the context, on the assumption of the immanent necessity (valued as "internal evidence") of a functional relationship between the rational and irrational elements in both text and context. Along this line I am tempted to propose a parallel between what in the field of textual criticism interpretation represents, compared to stemmatology, and what in the field of linguistics structuralism represents, compared to the reconstructive genealogy.

However, such an analogy appears to be inapplicable as soon as we realize that, while linguistic structuralism operates on a limited number of elements and situations, the interpretation of a text has to deal with a practically unlimited number of elements and a vast variety of situations. The functional relationship between text and context is an "open" one, and its immanent necessity is far from that of a logico-mathematical type which operates within the rules of RECENSIO, whenever one deals with a "closed" tradition. It is because of this that, as Ernesti stated, INTERPRETATIO NON POTEST MATHEMATICE ESSE CERTA. Here we are dealing with facts difficult to categorize or, at least, with facts which cannot be exhausted in a series both finite and homogeneous in its categories; each interpretative problem constitutes a case in itself.

Nonetheless it might be reasonable to ask ourselves if it is not possible and profitable to indicate some principles which might introduce us into unlimited interpretative casuistry, without presuming to provide a method for systematic classification, but giving some concrete points of reference, as stimuli. A theory of interpretation, assuming its feasibility, goes beyond the scope of the present paper which will be limited to providing some very elementary examples. I have chosen at random both simple and exemplary cases from the texts with which I have been working recently; consequently, in this connection I must apologize for having used mostly non-Italian texts.

All these examples pertain to the most proper and exclusive domain of textual criticism, such as punctuation, separation of words, conjectural integration of *lacunae*, and the choice between readings of equal "stemmatic" value; and, of course, they could be naturally grouped according to such extrinsic phenomena. However, because of the scope of this paper I would prefer to present them in accordance with a more intrinsic and dynamic principle, that of the notion and function of the context.

1. What do we mean by "context"? How may we put into practice the dialectic process, in which the context helps recover

the exact reading of the text, confused or lost because of the vicissitudes of the tradition or because of the editor's negligence?

The term "context" must first be interpreted in its most immediate and obvious meaning. Each element of the expressive chain must be evaluated as it functions with the other connecting elements: each word, each sentence integrates itself with the words and sentences which precede and follow it in the fantastic and logical continuity of the discourse. This is so obvious that it seems superfluous to mention. However, there is nothing more daring than to presume that an interpretation based on the immediate context should be, for this reason, immediately understood by the editor and, by the same token, be immune from the risk of being overlooked. No reading is so clear that it is beyond question; similarly, no editor, attentive as he may be, is without his moments of inattention. Incongruities, even those easily recognizable, pass unnoticed to trained critics and are carried on by inertia into the most widely read texts. I offer the following example, taken from a text which is "the text" *par excellence* of our literature, the *Divina Commedia*.

From Moore's edition (Oxford, 1894) to that of Vandelli for the Società Dantesca Italiana (Florence, 1921),[1] and from these to the greater part of those in use today,[2] accompanied or not by a commentary, the passage from *Paradiso* XXI, 43-51, reads as follows:

> 43 E quel che presso più ci si ritenne,
> si fé si chiaro, ch'io dicea pensando:
> "Io veggio ben l'amor che tu m'accenne".
> 46 Ma quella ond'io aspetto il come e il quando
> del dire e del tacer, si sta; ond'io,
> contra il disìo, fo ben ch'io non dimando.
> 49 Per ch'ella, che vedea il tacer mio
> nel veder di colui che tutto vede,
> mi disse: —Solvi il tuo caldo disìo—.

It seems evident that[3] the middle tercet *(Ma quella... non dimando)* continues what Dante "dicea pensando"; therefore, the

---

[1] It is this also in the recent edition: *Le Opere di Dante: testo critico della Società Dantesca Italiana*, 2nd edition (Florence, 1960).

[2] Up to Sapegno's last edition (Milano, 1957).

[3] I say this not only because the subjective present is maintained with

quotation, which began in v. 45 with "io veggio," does not end in that same line (where, on the contrary, a semicolon might suffice instead of a period), but rather in v. 48, after "non dimando." [4] Moreover, among the early commentators, Francesco da Buti observed in his interpretation that: "Our author imagines what he said in his thoughts, besides the spoken words *(io veggo ben... accenne)*, also those which now follow *(Ma quella... dimando)*; and how Beatrice, being aware of his hidden thought, urged him to ask." [5] Among modern editors, [6] if I am correct in my research, only Guerri (Bari, 1933) adopted the punctuation that corresponds to this interpretation, one ignored by most critics. [7]

2. Another example, which concerns the separation of words rather than punctuation, is taken from a lesser known text; the passage in question has been extensively commented on by the noted editor Carl Appel. [8]

In the *canso* PER FAR ESBAUDIR MOS VEZIS by the troubadour Peire Rogier (BdT. 356,6) the rhyme word in v. 39 — *EISSETZ* in MSS ABNR, *EISSEZ* in DK, *EISSIEZ* in J, *ISSETZ* in C — caused perplexity in Appel who, in printing

re no'm qual que ja l'am eis setz

asked himself: "Is my analysis in *illam amem ipse sextus* acceptable?". His major doubts were focused on the admissibility of the form SETZ < SEXTUS, on which he has argued at length.

---

sharp coherence: *aspetto* 46, *sta* 47, *fo, dimando* 48, and *veggio, accenne* 45, as opposed to the objective past: *ritenne* 43, *fé, dicea* 44: *vedea* 49, *disse* 51, but also for the development of the thought.

[4] Momigliano, commenting on vv. 46-48, speaks of a "presente drammatico, affatto eccezionale."(Dramatic present, not exceptional at all.)

[5] Edited by C. Giannini (Pisa, 1962) vol. III, p. 590.

[6] Obviously, the error was caused by the printing of the quotation marks, and no complaint can be lodged against the editors, such as Brunone Bianchi (Florence, 1857) and Giambattista Giuliani (Florence, 1880), who did not use that punctuation.

[7] Mario Fubini, in his *Due studi danteschi* (Florence, 1951), p. 99, has suggested a correction of the current punctuation of the text of the *Divina Commedia* (Par. XXXII, 147-48).

[8] C. Appel. *Das Leben und die Lieder des Trobadors Peire Rogier* (Berlin, 1882).

Yet, in my opinion, what is least acceptable is precisely the meaning. According to his interpretation, the troubadour in love would be declaring that he does not care at all about being the sixth among the lady's lovers! Anyway why sixth? The numerical specification adds a disquieting shade of grotesque pedantry to a very unusual concept in the poetry of the troubadours. One would be tempted to ask: "Who were the other five?". However, within the context, one could look in vain for the slightest indication of a predecessor or companion of Peire. The immediate context, which follows the line in question, develops a completely different theme:

> Doncs amarai
> so qu'ieu non ai?
> Oc, qu'eyssamen n'ay joy e pretz
> e son alegres e joyos,
> quant res no n'es, si cum ver fos.

The poet declares himself ready for an unrequited love, content to keep love alive in his heart, even if it does not reflect reality; and it is a perfectly logical argument (obviously understood according to the "logic" of "courtly" love) and not strange at all. It should be noted that the conjunction DONCS ties these lines to the problematic affirmation, immediately preceding them, and one will spontaneously feel like asking himself if that affirmation of carelessness is not referred just to the unsuccessful possession (SO QU'IEU NON AI), to the lack of conformity between reality and sentiment (QUANT RES NO N'ES).

A careful analysis reveals that the internal consistency involves a semantic equation between "l'am eis setz" and "amarai so qu'ieu non ai." This equation becomes clear when we read EISSETZ as a single word $EISSETZ < EXCEPTUS$ (that is, "excluded from her favors"). The term is well documented as a preposition (cf. SW. II, 338); therefore, it will not be surprising to find it used as a participle-adjective, whenever that function presupposes this use.

3. From the example just cited, it appears evident that the notion of context necessarily implies the structural study of the language in which the text is written. We can not properly

evaluate the functional relationship between text and context unless the reader recreates in himself that familiarity that the author had with his own language, its grammatical structure and its syntactic and lexical possibilities. The greater the familiarity, the smaller the number of mistakes will be which are caused by "ignoratio elenchi" in the area of linguistic possibilities. Here is another example from a troubadour. The recent edition by Aimo Sakari[9] presents and interprets the beginning of a *canso* by Guillem de Saint Leidier (BdT. 234, 16) vv. 1-4, as follows:

> Malvaza m'es la moguda
> d'estiu, don val meins mos chans,
> que gaieza m'a tolguda,
> no fes e trics e soans:

"La fuite de l'été, m'est désagréable et mon chant y perd, car elle m'a enlevé la gaieté — ce que n'a fait ni la tromperie ni le dédain." Such an interpretation is hardly tenable. NO FES could perhaps mean "n'a fait," but the object of this verb, which the editor interpolates in his translation, could not be omitted from the text. In order to maintain Sakari's interpretation, we should read, "[SO] NO FES TRICS E SOANS" or rather, "NO [˙L] FES E TRICS E SOANS." But that is not necessary if we read as we should:

> que gaieza m'a tolguda
> no-fes e trics e soans.

interpreting, "ché slealtà, inganno e spregio m'han tolta gioia." ("since unloyalty, deception and disdain have brought me unhappiness"). Sakari was evidently misguided by his inability to recognize in *no-fes* a substantive formed according to a system of composition rather common among the troubadours from Marcabru on.[10] Sakari was also misled by the singular "m'a tolguda" which he has wrongly interpreted as dependent on "la moguda d'estiu" (1.1), while it has the three substantives of line 4 as subject, they being considered as a logical unit and

---

[9] In the *Mémoires de la Société Néophilologique de Helsinki*, XIX, 1956.
[10] Cf. *Cultura neolatina*, XVII (1957), p. 37, note for l. 22.

therefore constructed in the singular, according to a syntactic form very frequent in the *langue d'oc*.[11]

4. Everyone must have realized, after considering the example just cited, that the notion of language implies, up to a certain extent, that of style. Interpretation should not be determined solely by the sense of the passage or by the rules of grammar. There are principles of style which deserve the same consideration given those of meaning and grammar. They might suggest a correction even in instances where meaning and grammar would seem adequate. They must be carefully judged especially when we are dealing with two readings of equal stemmatic value. Here is an example.

There exist eight manuscripts of the moral *sirventese* BEL M'ES DOUS CHANS PER LA FAYA by Bernard di Venzac (BdT. 323, 3): ADEIKNz and C. For vv. 43-44 the editors — R. Zenker (1900) and A. Del Monte (1955)[12] — follow ADEIKNz, accepting the reading:

> Ges puois de mal no s'esglaia
> qe'l mieills de ben s'a tolgut

(Del Monte translates it, "Non inorridisce poi affatto del male chi s'è tolto il meglio del bene"). They reject the reading of C, "Des piegz de mal no s'esglaya que mielhs de be s'a tolgut." On the contrary, it seems to me that we can obtain a better reading from C, both for internal congruity of style and sense (always considering the variants in the other manuscripts, particularly 43 Despueis EN, 44 Quil DEIK):

> Del piegz de mal no s'esglaya
> qui'l mielhz de be s'a tolgut

("del peggio del male non si spaventa, chi ha respinto da sé il meglio del bene"). The MIELHZ DE BE preserved by the context

---

[11] *Ibid.*, XIII (1953), p. 28f.
[12] R. Zenker, *Die Lieder Peires von Auvergne* (Erlangen, 1900), pp. 144 ff; A. Del Monte, "Tre liriche trovatoriche," *Studi in onore di S. Santangelo* (Catania, 1955) I, pp. 26 ff.

is reliable support for restoring PIEGZ DE MAL in the text, as given by C. The antithesis thus regained is very close to the troubadoric taste and particularly to Bernart de Venzac's refined style, for it allows us to attribute PIEGZ to an innovation of the scribe of C, even taking into account his impartial and clever interventions. It is worth noting that, among all the MSS, C is the only one to preserve the correct attribution of the composition.

5. Finally, we must consider the context not only for what it says, but also for what it does not say. The silence of the literary context might serve as negative evidence when compared with certain readings and interpretations and lead us to search for a different reading and interpretation within the linguistic context, that is, within the possibilities offered by the author's language. We might find an appropriate example for it in the *AUTO DA INDIA* by Gil Vicente.

The scene opens with the protagonist lamenting, not because her husband must leave with the fleet of Tristano da Cunha, but because the departure is not going to take place: because "DIZEM QUE NÃO VAI JA." The maid asks, "QUEM DIZ ESSE DESCONCERTO?," and her mistress answers (vv. 17-19, as the verses are usually read): [13]

> Disserão-m'o por mui certo
> que he certo que fica ca.
> Ó Concelos me faz isto.

In the Italian translation by Enzio Di Poppa Vulture: [14]

> Me lo diedero per certo
> ch'egli non se ne va più.
> E chi fa questo è il Concello;

And in the more literal one by Giuseppe Carlo Rossi, [15] "Me l'hanno data per cosa che non ammette dubbi che è sicuro ch'egli resta qui. Fa ciò il Concellos!". Who is this Concellos "Guasta

---

[13] See Gil Vicente, *Obras completas* with preface and notes by prof. Marques Braga (Lisbon, 1942-44), vol. V, p. 90.

[14] Gil Vicente, *Teatro* (Florence, 1953-54), vol. II, p. 437.

[15] G. C. Rossi, *Teatro portoghese e brasiliano* (Milan, 1956), p. 55.

mestieri"? "Evidently," Rossi explains, "it is the name of the man who has given the news about the suspended departure." "Probably," Enzio Di Poppa specifies, "he was a shipowner from Lisbon." This traditional explanation, repeated from commentator to commentator, was validated by the authority of Donna Carolina Michaëlis de Vasconcellos, who proposes the following identification: [16] "CONCELLOS: no AUTO DA INDIA, a protagonista, mulher de um homem que embarca para a India na armada de Tristão da Cunha (1509), queixa-se por um sujeito dêsse nome impedir a saída da frota. Provávelmente nome familiar, abreviado, de Jorge de Vascogonçelos (ou Vasconcellos) fidalgo que, de 1501 até falecer em 1525, foi armador e provedor dos armazens e armadas da cidade de Lisboa. Nas Côrtes de Júpiter êsse mesmo — jà velhote — aparece alfenando os cabelhos (grisalhos?) no corteio da Infante D. Beatriz. Como versificador, relacionado e aparentado com outros cortesãos trovadores como J. Rodrigues de Sá e Meneses, êle figura no Cancioneiro Geral, ora com o nome por extenso, ora com o nome abreviado." Thus, here is a character certainly well known by Gil Vicente and easily identifiable by the audience of the time, who would not be forced, as the modern reader, to look at the explanatory footnote. All the same, I wonder whether that strangeness which we feel today would disappear, if we could effectively grant ourselves the conditions and the knowledge of any of Gil Vicente's contemporaries. In any case, would not the allusion remain abrupt and isolated, gratuitous as it were? What function would the sudden evocation of a real character who is not mentioned again have within the dramatic economy of the text? Would there not be a discrepancy between those generic plurals DIZEM, DISSERÃO and this precise and imperious name? And would not the expression ME FAZ ISTO remain too concise and vague? Vague almost to the point of ambiguity: is Concelos the one who brought the news (as it seems evident to Rossi) or the one who has prevented the fleet's departure (as stated by Michaëlis de Vasconcellos)? Furthermore, is it certain that that

---

[16] In the Indice de nomes próprios, included in the fourth of her Notas vicentinas (Coimbra, 1922), p. 271; reprinted in Ocidente (Lisbon, 1954), p. 394.

name "familiar, abreviado" would have suggested immediately the identification? Michaëlis de Vasconcellos observes that, in the *Cancioneiro Geral*, the shipowner-poet is referred to as "ora com o nome por extenso, ora com o nome abreviado"; however we remark that the extended form is *Jorge de Vascogonçelos*, and the shortened one is *Jorge de Vasconçelos*, [17] never simply *Concelos, o Concelos*. Would it have sufficed to have said this?

These doubts have led me to check the passage with the basic source for our knowledge of Vicente's text: the *Copilaçam* of 1562 edited by Luis Vicente, Gil's son. [18] There on p. CXCV r., line 19 reads as follows:

O concelos mefaz isto.

Even though the absence of the capital letter is not by itself decisive, it has suggested to me, together with the realization that the edition of 1562 does not usually separate one word from the other, a division of the words and an interpretation different from the current ones. By interpreting

O! Con celos me faz isto!

as "Oh, che rabbia mi fa ciò," we have, instead of a strange and gratuitous intrusion of a historical character, an exclamation so consistent with the context and so natural as to appear certain. CELO (= zelo < Latin ZELUS [19]) is a rather common word in archaic Portuguese, together with the obviously indigenous CIO and its derivative CIUME, and Gil Vicente, "employs it several times ... in the plural and in the singular" indulging in word games, as noted by P. Teyssier. [20]

6. The example just cited could serve as a warning that mistakes in the division of words may creep in and remain

---

[17] *Cancioneiro Geral* ed., A. J. Gonçálvez Guimarãis (Coimbra, 1910-1917), vol. IV, pp. 199 and 321; pp. 206, 217 and 313.

[18] Easily accessible in the "reimpressão facsimilada" edited by the Biblioteca Nacional (Lisbon, 1928).

[19] For the history of the word in the Romance languages, see M. Grzywacz, *Eifersucht in den romanischen Sprachen* (Bochum, 1937).

[20] P. Teyssier, *La langue de Gil Vicente* (Paris, 1959), p. 413.

unnoticed even where they would least be expected: in dramatic texts, the life of which periodically disengages itself from the conditions of a visual and individual reading in order to transfer itself into the concrete form of the theatrical recitation in front of an audience: in a form, that is, in which the continuum of the discourse would tend to reassert itself at once, independently of the written word.

The same example might also serve to remind us that, beyond the literary and linguistic context, there exists an extra-literary one of historical and practical nature. Carolina Michaëlis was referring to such a context in the case of Gil Vicente, and although her appeal to historical fact in that case did not provide the correct interpretation, this does not invalidate the usefulness and necessity of such recourse in many other instances. [21] On this occasion I will limit myself to examples which do not go beyond the notion of linguistic and literary context. What are its limits? Certainly neither those of a single passage nor those of a single work. Technically, context is defined by the whole literary and linguistic tradition in which the text is a part; the sources and the stylistic models constitute context, as does the traditional dialectic argumentation, as I believe the following example will demonstrate.

The tercet which accompanies the apparition of the celestial Venus in Boccaccio's *Ameto*, starts as follows according to the text presently accepted (which is that by N. Bruscoli, [22] because of the lack of a truly critical edition):

---

[21] I could provide some examples which I had the opportunity to consider elsewhere; however I do not want to repeat here some interpretative solutions already in the public domain. In the case of Marcabru, whom I have interpreted in *Actes et Mémoires du Ier Congrès international de Langue et Littérature du Midi de la France* (Avignon, 1957), p. 54f, the clarifying context is constituted by the Pythagorean anecdote concerning the modal ethos, present in the medieval scholastic culture and certainly well known to the troubador; in the case of LORINO, which I have illustrated in *Lingua nostra*, XIV (1953), p. 42, the "negative" context is constituted by common experience, namely that a horse, after a long gallop, must not be left in the fresh air, AL REZZO, risking pneumonia.

[22] Bari, 1940. This portion of the text is reproduced without corrections, by C. Salinari in vol. VIII, dedicated to Boccaccio, in the Ricciardi series, "La letteratura italiana: storia e testi."

> I' son luce del cielo unica e trina,
> principio e fine di ciascuna cosa,
> de' qual me'n fu né fia nulla vicina.

But how does the third line tie in with the two preceding ones. It seems hardly acceptable that DE' QUAL might equal "delle quali," "tra le quali" referred *ad sensum* to all created things. I wonder whether I should rather read it D'EQUAL, putting a colon rather than a comma at the end of line 2. To support such a reading, I might compare it with v. 55 of Petrarch's famous canzone *Vergine bella*:

> cui né prima fu simil, né seconda,

which, in turn, elaborates on what he already said about Laura in the sonnet *Del cibo*, vv. 5-6:

> chi né prima, né simil, né seconda
> ebbe al suo tempo;

referring particularly to its Latin derivation and, in general, to the literary tradition that we could define as "the topos of incomparability": from Horace, *Carm.* I, 12, vv. 17-18

> Unde nil maius generatur ipso
> nec viget quidquam simile aut secundum,

and from Martial, XII 8, 2

> Cui par est nihil et nihil secundum,

and also from writers such as Pliny the Elder, *Nat. Hist.* 32, praef. 1: "Nec par aut simile potest inveniri."

7. In the sense just suggested, context might be determined not only by the preceding literary tradition but also by that following the text. The following case might serve as example.

A syllable is evidently missing in the first line of the composition in which William IX of Aquitaine elaborates on the metaphor, already known to Lucilius and Artemidorus, of the two horses who are two ladies (BdT. 183, 3):

Companho, faray un vers covinen.

Jeanroy [23] proposed to emend:

Companho, faray un vers [des] covinen;

on the other hand Crescini [24] reads:

Companho, faray un vers [tot] covinen.

These are only conjectures, which could be easily replaced by others, such as [be] COVINEN, [molt] COVINEN, etc., without being able to bring about any decisive element in favor of either one or the other. The context, in its strict sense, does not help us to solve the choice (at the most, it might confirm that COVINEN is here an adjective, because the word recurs again in rhyme in the same composition (v. 20) as a noun). However, that less immediate and wider literary context which is constituted by the subsequent troubadoric tradition might help us. In fact, in a composition by Bernart de Venzac, [25] we find a line practically identical (except for the absence of the initial vocative Companho). The obvious assumption is that Bernart de Venzac is imitating William IX; all the more since we have in the same composition, and even in the same stanza, other expressions which recall similar ones by the Duke of Aquitaine. [26] Therefore, it is logical to restore [qu'er] COVINEN also in William. Neither does the absence of the -s constitute an obstacle, since William overlooks it also in line 13 of the same composition: LAUNS FO DELS

---

[23] A. Jeanroy, Les Chansons de Guillaume IX, 2nd ed. (Paris, 1927), p. 31.

[24] V. Crescini, Manuale per l'avviamento agli studi provenzali, 3rd ed. (Milan, 1962), p. 163.

[25] PUS VEY LO TEMPS FER FREVOLUC (BdT. 71, 3), ed. Carl Appel, Provenzalische Inedita (Leipzig, 1890), p. 50, v. 5:
    faray un vers qu'er covinens

[26] Cf. in the preceding line AURAS and VENS coupled together, as already in William IX, PUS VEZEN DE NOVELH FLORIR (BdT. 183, 1, v. 4); and in other preceding lines the series FER ... SALVATGA ... ESTRANHA, which recurs in the same strophe about the two horses, vv. 14-15 FER'ESTRANHEZA ... FERS E SALVATGES; and already in the first line the opening formula PUS VEY, in William PUS VEZEM.

MONTANHIERS LO PLUS CORREN. Thus, in case the immediate context is insufficient to indicate the preferable integration, the remote context, constituted by a whole literary tradition, may help to regain the proper reading, or at least the most historically justifiable one (it is clear that the infraction of the usual rules of agreement is legalized by the immediate context, instead of constituting an objection). The historical interpretation, considered as an appeal to the remote context, brings us to identify a material witness to be added to the other available ones in a higher stemmatic position: here INTERPRETATIO reaches RECENSIO and integrates it.

8. Even if we rely on the literary tradition, we must not only consider the sense, but also the style. As the notion of context is enlarged so is the possibility of incorporating other corrections, thus increasing the possibility of rationalizing readings or emendations. Here is another example of it.

The third line in the "chanson de toile" of *Bele Aye,* preserved in the *Roman de Guillaume de Dole,* vv. 1183-1192, is irregular:

a un fil i fet coustures beles.

Evidently something is missing in the first hemistich (the verses are "epic" decasyllables *a minori*). In order to correct this irregularity Bartsch [27] introduced the verb *file* after the substantive *fil,* separating the proposition into two independent clauses:

a un fil [file]: i fet coustures beles.

This addition, based on obvious considerations of diplomatic probability (possibility of omission because of haplography, given the repetition of the same syllable *fil*), does not seem probable once we look at the meaning. From the immediate context, it is obvious that the girl is sewing or, more precisely, embroidering *(coustures beles).* It is sufficient to imagine the scene in order to realize that it is not possible to perform simultaneously the operations of spinning and embroidering. Furthermore, it does

---

[27] K. Bartsch, *Altfranzösische Romanzen und Pastourellen* (Leipzig, 1870), n° XII, p. 17.

not seem likely that the poet has concentrated and juxtaposed in one representation two different moments of the operation. This has probably led Servois,[28] Lejeune,[29] and finally Saba[30] to attempt another solution, at first much simpler and uncompromising, by integrating an ET conjunction at the beginning of the line:

[et] a un fil i fet coustures beles.

In this way the meaning of the sentence is not altered, and we can easily imagine that in initial position an ET (especially if represented in the original by the usual abbreviation 7) might have been skipped by the copyist. However, not even this solution can be considered thoroughly satisfactory. In fact, there is not one single word, however meaningless it might be, that lacks stylistic value, and the initial conjunction would alter the paratatic rhythm which generally characterizes the style of the "chansons de toile."

Furthermore, it is possible to suggest a third solution, based on stylistic considerations, by situating the text in its "stylistic context" which, in general terms, is constituted by the traditional style of the "genre." In fact, we do find the girl who sews or embroiders A UN FIL D'OR in other "chansons de toile":

> Fille et la mere se sieent a l'orfroi,
> a un fil d'or i font orieuls crois...
>
> Bele Yolanz en chambre koie
> sor ses genouz pailes desploie,
> cost un fil d'or, l'autre de soie...

Even in the *Yvain*[31] the three hundred *puceles* workers of the *Chastel de Pesme Avanture*

---

[28] Jean Renart, *Le Roman de la Rose ou de Guillaume de Dole*, ed. G. Servois (Paris, 1893), p. 36.
[29] Jean Renart, *Le Roman de la Rose ou de Guillaume de Dole*, ed R. Lejeune (Paris, 1936), p. 28.
[30] G. Saba, *Le "chansons de toile" o "chansons d'histoire"* (Modena, 1955), n° II, p. 54.
[31] Edited by W. Foerster, 4th ed. (Halle, 1912), vv. 5195-96.

qui diverses oeuvres fesoient,
de fil d'or et de soie ovroient.

Thus, we are dealing with a traditional formula which corresponds to a traditional and characteristic type of embroidering, and the assumption would be that the same formula ought to be read also in our passage:

a un fil [d'or] i fet coustures beles

This should appear obvious to anyone who remembers the fixed formulas which medieval poets used in the composition of "chansons de geste" and of "chansons de toile."

The paratactic construction is therefore preserved and the meaning has been improved. It would be superfluous to say that the girl sews A UN FIL. With what else could she have sewn? On the other hand, if we had specified that the girl was sewing "double thread," we would have had only a technical specification without any literary function. However, to say that the girl embroiders A UN FIL D'OR, elevates her work and contributes to create that feudal-aristocratic setting, that "epic" solemnity, in which lives the sentimental fantasy of the "chanson de toile." Thus, it is more important to find an addition that satisfies the meaning and the style rather than to look for a rational motivation to justify the omission. Carelessness is not always supported by a logical reason, while the composition is. Moreover, considerations of internal coherence, pertinent to the logical and stylistic interpretation, must have precedence over those of diplomatic probability in textual criticism.

9. In conclusion, the notion of "context" includes not only what we have called "immediate context," but also the whole literary and linguistic tradition to which the text historically belongs. I would also like to add an observation about the linguistic tradition. In addition to the documented language we must think of undocumented possibilities structurally admissible within the given system. In this way interpretation helps both the linguist and the textual critic, by integrating the resources of both. One instance occurs in those corrections brought about through HAPAX (i.e. an infrequent form), a case less exceptional

than we might think.[32] The following is a particularly interesting example of it. The hypothesis of a HAPAX, morphological rather than lexical, represents only the first stage of a critical process, the latter being able to confirm the hypothesis by eliminating the initial character of singularity to the attested form:

> Cortesamen vuoill comensar
> un vers, si es qui l'escout'ar

("Courtoisement je veux commencer un vers, s'il est quelq'un pour l'écouter maintenant"); thus there begins, according to Dejeanne's reading, the composition that Marcabru sent "a'N Jaufré Rudel outra mar" in defense of his own conception of *cortesia* as *mezura* (BdT. 293, 15).[33] The ESCOUT' AR has bothered me since the first reading and not so much because of the use of the truncated form AR at the end of the line and sentence (certainly an unusual but not exceptional case[34]) but rather for the apparent superfluity of the adverbial emphasis. We understand that Marcabru probably felt the need for an introduction which was both skeptical and hopeful in singing about "cortesia" ("se pure c'è, e speriamo che ci sia, qualcuno disposto ad ascoltarmi"), but we do not quite understand the stress put on the reference to the immediate present (a present which seems to be identified with the very act of singing, or more precisely with the exordium itself) when the poet announces:

> Lo vers e'l so vuoill enviar
> a'N Jaufré Rudel outra mar,
> e vuoill que l'aujon li Frances
> per lur coratges alegrar.

The need for a rhyme is not a sufficient reason for a troubadour such as Marcabru. Hence, one question came to my mind: should

---

[32] Cf. the cases of MATINIA, MES, CHAIRIC, S'ARDI in Marcabru's double "romanza" of the "stornello messaggero," in the *Actes et Mémoires du Ier Congrès International de Langue et Littérature du Midi de la France* (Avignon, 1957), pp. 47-55.
[33] J.-M.-L. Dejeanne, *Poésies complètes du troubadour Marcabru* (Toulouse, 1909), p. 61.
[34] Cf. Guillaume Anelier de Toulouse, *Histoire de la guerre de Navarre*, ed. F. Michel (Paris, 1856), v. 417: "Barons, tornem gaut'ar."

I not read ESCOUTAR? Should I not recognize in the subordinate of a hypothetical sentence in an archaic and Gascon troubadour a form of that future subjunctive (which results from the already old confusion between perfect and future tense [85]) that the Provençal grammars do not mention [36] but which has been preserved in the limited Ibero-Romance area leaving some relics also in Old Italian? [37]

I believe I can now confirm this hypothesis and remove Marcabru's example from its isolation through a second example, found in a subordinate clause of a hypothetical sentence from another Gascon troubadour. I found it in the *sirventese* (*Be'm plai us usatges que cor* by Arnaut de Comminges — BdT. 28, 1, vv. 5-6 —):

> Be'm plai us usatges que cor
> e qu'is vai er mest nos meten,
> e'm plai que dure longamen:
> que cel que forssara'l menor.
> c'autre sia que lui forsar.

Here too, the editors [38] print FORS'AR; and again more evident here than with Marcabru the AR is superfluous and detrimental to a precise interpretation. As is generally known, Gascony has always been a very conservative region. [39] A type of conditional derived from the simple Latin future is still preserved in the Bearnese area and in the region of Barèges. [40] The identification of a relic of future subjunctive in medieval Gascon authors is therefore a possibility structurally admissible and feasible.

---

[35] Cf. Aulo Gellio XVIII 2, 14.
[36] Not even A. J. Henrichsen's recent and accurate *Les phrases hypothétiques en ancien occitan* (Bergen, 1955).
[37] Cf. C. De Lollis, "Di alcune forme verbali nell'italiano antico" in *Bausteine...Mussafia* (Halle, 1905), pp. 1-8; G. Rohlfs, *Historische Grammatik der italienischen Sprache* (Bern, 1949-54), vol. II, § 592, p. 386.
[38] A. Kolsen, *Dichtungen der Trobadors* (Halle, 1916-19), n. 49, p. 217; A. Jeanroy, *Jongleurs et troubadours gascons* (Paris, 1923), p. 75.
[39] Cf. the recent article by K. Baldinger, "La position du Gascon entre la Galloromania et l'Ibéroromania" in *Revue de linguistique romane*, XXII (1958), pp. 241-289.
[40] Cf. G. Rohlfs, *Le Gascon* (Halle, 1935), § 449, pp. 146-47.

ON THE TEXT OF THE *TRISTRAN* OF BÉROUL

by T. B. W. Reid

The evolution of the story of Tristran and Yseut has formed one of Professor Vinaver's most constant preoccupations during more than forty years of scholarly activity. Near the head of the literary tradition of that story stands the romance of Béroul; preserved in a single manuscript of exasperating defectiveness, it raises in an acute form the general problem of the editing of medieval texts, a problem to which Professor Vinaver has devoted an important discussion of principles.[1] The first modern edition of the romance, that of Ernest Muret (*S.A.T.F.*, 1903), was an outstanding example of the application to a difficult text of well-informed scholarship and literary imagination, resulting in a very freely emended version. The subsequent change in the general climate of editorial opinion, associated particularly with the work of Vinaver's revered master Joseph Bédier, impelled Muret in later editions (*C.F.M.A.*, 1913; 2nd ed., 1922; 3rd ed., 1928) to restore a number of the readings of the manuscript; the edition of A. Ewert (Oxford 1939) is still more conservative; and 'L. M. Defourques', in revising Muret's text (*C.F.M.A.*, 4th ed., 1947), has often followed Ewert and has rejected many of the emendations that Muret had retained in 1928. There remain, however, substantial differences between the texts of Ewert and of Defourques, and neither is universally accepted as 'canonical'; it may therefore be worth while, at the risk of labouring the obvious, to consider with reference to Béroul some of the questions confronting the

---

[1] For Prof. Vinaver's essay, see above pp. 139-66.

editor of an Old French poem of which only one manuscript survives.

I

It is now very generally agreed that the guiding principle of such an editor should be to interfere with the text of the manuscript 'as little as possible'; but this formula is not in practice very helpful, since it is extremely difficult to define what is meant in this context by 'possible'.[2] It would be quite logical to demand that the editor should simply print as his text a transcription of the manuscript, on the grounds that whatever was written down by a medieval scribe may well have been possible in his time, and that a modern critic cannot without arrogance presume to teach the scribe his business: all editorial interpretation would find its place elsewhere, in footnotes or commentaries. Almost always, however, the editor in fact considers it his duty to incorporate at least part of his interpretation in his text: he adds diacritics, distinguishes *i* from *j* and *u* from *v*, alters word-divisions and introduces capital letters and punctuation. In so doing he is intervening forcibly between the reader and the manuscript; and the only justification for this intervention is the assumption that he fully understands the meaning of the text, and can perceive the grammatical and stylistic intentions of the scribe (and usually by implication of the author) even where no direct evidence of them is provided by the signs that actually stand in the copy.

On such matters as punctuation, word-division, etc., however, critics may well disagree. Let us consider, for example, certain passages in Béroul:[3]

```
1105   A vos ne mesferoit il mie
       Mais vos barons en vos ballie
1107   Sil les trovout nes vilonast
       Encor en ert ta terre en gast
```

---

[2] Cf. F. Whitehead, 'The Textual Criticism of the *Chanson de Roland:* An Historical Review,' *Studies in Medieval French presented to Alfred Ewert* (Oxford, 1961), pp. 76-89; see especially p. 86.

[3] The passages discussed are printed without emendation and without punctuation or diacritics, but otherwise according to modern conventions and with abbreviations resolved.

(we need not here consider whether the editors are right in putting a full stop after *mie* and replacing the second *vos* in l. 1106 by *sa*). Muret corrects *nes* 1107 to *ne*, 'if he found them or ill-treated them'; Ewert and Defourques restore *nes*, apparently understood as *ne* (< *nec*) + *les* (which Defourques admits is an unusual enclisis); all editors put a comma after *vilonast* and appear to take ll. 1106-7 as the protasis and l. 1108 as the apodosis of a hypothetical sentence. Even apart from the problem of *nes*, however, this does not provide a very convincing construction. An alternative interpretation, taking *nes* in its normal sense of *ne* (< *non*) + *les*, would be to put a question-mark after *vilonast*: 'But your barons, if he found them in his power, would he not ill-treat them? Your land will yet be ravaged as a result.' Such rhetorical questions occur commonly in the poem.

> 4414 Devant le jor prist a toner
> A fermete fu de chalor.

All editors put a comma after *a fermeté* and understand this as a locution meaning 'assurément, sans doute'; Tobler-Lommatzsch (III, 1751) also translates 'sicherlich', but only with a query and without citing any other example. We should perhaps read rather 'A fermeté fu de chalor' in the sense of 'It was [by way of] a guarantee of [subsequent] heat'; for the sense cf., a little later, 'Li soleuz fu chauz sor la prime, Choiete fu et nielle et frime' 4119-20; for *fermeté* 'guarantee' cf. Godefroy III, 762, and for the attributive use of *a* cf. ll. 2243, 4184 and Tobler-Lommatzsch I, 6, ll. 22-6, also administrative formulas such as 'a plus grant seürté', 'a plus grant fermeté et segurté des devant dites chouses' (Godefroy VII, 409; X, 671).

The case is a little different in two other passages:

> 146 Pense il que nen ait pechie
> Certes oil ni faudra mie
> 148 Por Deu le fiz sainte Marie
> Dame ore li dites errant
> 150 Quil face faire un feu ardant

and:

>   303 Bien les veise entrebaisier
>   Ges ai oi si gramoier
>   305 Or sai je bien nen ont corage.

Here Ewert punctuates with a full stop after *Marie* 148 (so also Muret) and after *gramoier* 304, presumably because in each case the following line begins with a large initial. As he himself says, however, these initials 'do not correspond to divisions in the narrative';[4] the presence of an initial in the manuscript is no evidence that a sentence is intended to end with the preceding line, and all editors in fact put a comma before the large initial at l. 3123. The passages quoted should therefore be punctuated according to the sense of the words and without regard to the initials; ll. 147-9 should run 'Certes oïl, n'i faudra mie. Por Deu, le fiz sainte Marie, Dame, ore li dites errant...' (so in Defourques' edition; for *por Deu* followed by an imperative cf. ll. 198-200, 797-8, etc.), and ll. 303-5 should run 'Bien les veïse entrebaisier; Ges ai oï si gramoier, Or sai je bien n'en ont corage' (as in Muret's and Defourques' editions; l. 305 constitutes a consecutive clause depending on *si* 304).

Again, the word-divisions of the manuscript are often arbitrary (in ll. 3362 and 3368, for instance, the scribe writes *life lon, acuer lion*, which all editors interpret as *li felon, a Cuerlion*). If elsewhere we find

>   2243 Et sil estoit a son plesir
>   Vos a prendre et moi de gerpir,

this does not oblige an editor to print 'Vos a prendre et moi de gerpir', with a change of preposition before the second of two parallel infinitives of which there is no other instance in the text; we should read with Muret's S.A.T.F. edition 'et moi degerpir' (for non-repetition of the governing preposition before a second infinitive cf. 'por armes prendre Et a moi lor servise rendre' 2175-6, 'Que me sueffres a esligier Et en ta cort moi deraisnier' 2855-6). The scribe also writes

---

[4] *Ed. cit.*, p. x. Even C. A. Robson, who attaches some importance to their incidence (*Studies ... presented to A. Ewert*, pp. 58, 64), admits that many are not where he would expect them to be ('the manuscript evidence is disappointing,' p. 66).

4219   Dex fait chascune si fiere en jure
       Tant en a fait apres droiture

(we are not here concerned with the correction, made by all editors, of *chascune* to *chascuns*). The end of l. 4219 is obscure; Muret (who emends to *a jure*) and Defourques, followed by Tobler-Lommatzsch, take *jure* as the noun 'oath' (as in l. 3244); Ewert prints *en jure* but does not gloss it. We should surely read 'si fiere enjure!', understood as 'so cruel a wrong!'; for the noun *enjure, injure* cf. Tobler-Lommatzsch IV, 1395; for the sense of *fiere* cf. ll. 1186, 3160; the exclamatory construction without verb is probably paralleled by 'Si grant desroi, tel felonie!' 559, where the comma placed by all editors after l. 558 should be replaced by a full stop.[5]

Finally, there is the question of possible lacunas in the manuscript text. The presence of a line without a rhyming partner is usually adequate evidence that one line has been omitted by a copyist; but where there is no gap in the series of rhymes, an editor's insertion of points of suspension, implying the omission of at least two lines, depends on his judgement of what 'makes sense'. Muret thought there were some 25 such lacunas in Béroul; Ewert and Defourques reduce the number to ten (of which only eight are common to both lists). Even this is probably excessive; there is no need, for instance, to follow all the editors in assuming a lacuna between ll. 2836 and 2837. The passage runs in the manuscript

       2832   Li miens amis que Dex tenort
              Ne tennuit pas la herbergier
       2834   Sovent verrez mon mesagier
              Manderai toi de ci mon estre
       2836   Par mon vaslet et a ton mestre
              Non fera il ma chiere amie.

Here the 'Non fera il' of l. 2837 is Tristran's reply, in the normal Old French form,[6] to Yseut's request 'Ne t'ennuit pas la her-

---

[5] In l. 4220 *en* refers to *enjure*; *faire droiture de* appears to be used in the sense of *faire droit de* 3435, 'dispose of, justify oneself against (a charge).'
[6] Cf. l. 567 and *Studies... presented to M. K. Pope*, p. 309.

bergier!' 2833: 'Let it not incommode you to take lodging there!' ... 'Nor will it, dear love!' It is true that three lines intervene between the request and the reply; but the content of l. 2833 would remain all the more clearly in the hearer's mind because it had already been expressed earlier in Yseut's speech, 'Por moi sejorner ne t'ennuit!' 2819. Other doubtful lacunas are those indicated by the editors at ll. 1055-6 and 3170-1 (see below pp. 264 and 259).

II

In cases such as those which have just been cited, the editor, by the mere fact of printing the words of the manuscript in accordance with the normal conventions of modern punctuation, finds himself obliged to pronounce a series of somewhat subjective judgements on the interpretation of the text. But an editor normally does much more than this. He also decides that certain words or letters occurring in the manuscript are erroneous, either in the sense that the scribe has written down something that he did not intend to write or in the sense that he has intentionally written down something that could not have belonged to the original. The editor's grounds for this decision are, broadly speaking, grammatical, metrical or contextual: he judges, from his accumulated knowledge of the literature of the period, that these readings are not in accordance with the grammatical or metrical usage to be attributed to the author, or that they do not 'make sense' in the context as he understands it. In theory, the editor might in the presentation of his text confine himself to this negative role: he might reproduce the manuscript with the portions he considered unacceptable either omitted and relegated to the 'rejected readings', or printed in their place but with some typographical indication of their suspect status;[7] any positive suggestions about what might have stood in the original would be made in the notes. In practice, however, even the most conservative editor goes a good deal farther. In some of the cases where he judges the manuscript reading to be impossible, he is

---

[7] Cf. Whitehead, art. cit., p. 87.

prepared to say what the scribe ought to have written, and to introduce into his edited text words or letters that are not in the manuscript.

The editor may claim that he has corrected only 'obvious' errors; and in some cases all critics are in agreement both about the existence of the error and about its elimination. Where, for example, the Béroul manuscript reads

>239 Je ne pensai faire tel sainte
>   Ne foir men a tel poverte,

it would be generally conceded that *sainte* must be an error for *perte*. The fact remains, however, that every alteration of the manuscript text depends on a judgement which is in some degree subjective; and a reading that one critic condemns as an obvious error may seem to another to make sense as it stands and to need no correction. The scribe of Béroul writes

>2321 De lui proier point ne se saint
>   Quil les acort au roi se plaint
>2323 Qar ja corage de folie
>   Nen avirai ja jor de ma vie.

In addition to corrections and punctuation with which we are not here concerned (*faint* for *saint* 2321, *je* for *ja* 2324, colon after *plaint*, guillemets or quotation marks before *Qar*), all editors correct *se* 2322 to *si* and read 'De lui proier point ne se faint Qu'il les acort au roi, si plaint: "Qar ja corage..."'. The editors do not gloss *plaint*; if it is to be taken in its normal sense of 'complains', it is inappropriate in the context, and the following speech begins very oddly with *Qar*. It is possible, on the other hand, to retain the *se* of the manuscript in l. 2322 and to read 'De lui proier point ne se faint; Qu'il les acort au roi se plaint: "Qar ja corage..."'. On this interpretation l. 2322 is an independent sentence in which *Qu'il les acort au roi* is the complement of *se plaint*, and *Qar* has its normal causal sense. The meaning and construction thus attributed to *soi plaindre*, 'implore (that...)', is an unusual one, but it is exactly paralleled by that of the compound *soi conplaindre* in 'Molt se conplaint com angoisos, Sire, que l'acordasse a vos' 433-4, where Muret in his *S.A.T.F.*

edition glosses 'supplier avec plainte' and Tobler-Lommatzsch 'fleht'. For the order of the clauses in l. 2322 cf. 'Qu'il ne plorast ne s'en tenist' 262; for *proier* 2321 with a direct object of the person and without a *que*-clause cf. l. 543 and *Cligés* 994, 997, etc.

III

The danger of introducing an arbitrary alteration of a possibly correct reading, like that of imposing an arbitrary punctuation on the text, is therefore a very real one. The warnings of the more conservative critics are indeed salutary; but the editorial principles suggested as a safeguard are not always acceptable. Vinaver, for instance, stigmatizing the procedure of some editors as 'disguised collaboration with the author', insists that the reading of the manuscript must be preserved 'as long as it is *possible* that it comes from the original' (*art. cit.*, p. 158). His anxiety to provide an objective criterion of 'possibility', however, leads him to formulate a definition which is open to serious criticism: ' "impossible" readings', he says, 'are those which can be shown to result from scribal errors; such readings it is our duty to correct'.

The scribal errors in question are those types of mechanical error which arise from the sequence of processes necessarily involved in the action of copying; they are very acutely analysed in the earlier part of the article (pp. 141 ff.): misunderstanding of the model, conscious but mistaken correction, homoeoteleuton, duplication, contamination, arrhythmia (dittography and telescoping or haplography) and their combinations. Since these errors are purely scribal, they concern only the relation between the extant copy and its immediate model;[8] they do not involve the original as such except in the rare cases where the author is judged to have made a 'scribal' error in writing down what he has just composed. Vinaver's application of the results of his analysis to the correction of scribal error may be illustrated by quoting one of his Old French examples (pp. 147 f.). A passage in the Oxford *Folie Tristan* runs in the manuscript

---

[8] Vinaver suggests that it may sometimes be possible to reconstruct also the reading of the model of the model; but the only examples he gives are in fact based upon a comparison of two texts.

99 Tiltagel esteit un chastel
    Ki mout par ert e fort e bel
101 Ne cremout asalt ne engin ki vaille.

Vinaver deduces that in the scribe's model the first verb in l. 101 took the form *cremt*, but that at the moment of writing the *m* the scribe's eye wandered to the line above and seized on the *m* of *mout*, with the result that he set down *cremout* by contamination.

This may indeed have been what actually happened as the scribe copied the line. Vinaver concludes, however, 'It will be observed that we have in this instance corrected a corrupt line in the *Folie Tristan* by a mere reproduction of the mechanism of copying, without the aids of versification and grammar, but that our emendation has produced a reading which is both linguistically and metrically sound.' Here he is surely confusing two processes which are logically quite distinct, the detection of scribal error and its correction. The fact that the letter-sequence *mout* occurs in the manuscript in two successive lines is not in itself any ground for suspecting a scribal error. What arouses the critic's suspicion is in the first instance the length of the line: on the basis of his knowledge of Old French verse he judges that, in spite of the evidence of the manuscript, the author would not have written a line which (even assuming the second *ne* to be elided) contains nine counted syllables instead of eight. The critic then tries to locate the error within the line. At this stage he might conjecture, for example, that *asalt* was an error for a monosyllabic noun, perhaps *ost* (palaeographically the two words are not very dissimilar, and both can mean 'attacking army'). He further observes, however, that *cremout* is abnormal both morphologically [9] and syntactically, [10] and he judges that the author would probably not have used

---

[9] It shows the Western first-conjugation imperfect ending *-out* attached to the stem of a verb of another conjugation. Such hybrid forms are sometimes found in Anglo-Norman, cf. P. Fouché, *Le Verbe français* (Paris, 1931), p. 237.
[10] It is a past tense form but has a dependent clause with the verb in the present subjunctive. This construction, however, is by no means unknown, cf. in Béroul 'N'i ot baron tant fort ne fier Qui ost le roi mot araisnier' 863-4, 'Ainz ne fu rois qui n'ait regart' 1928.

it in this context. The critic thus identifies the form *cremout* as the element in the line most likely to be different from what the author wrote. It is only after this conclusion has been reached that the presence of the word *mout* in the previous line may become relevant; only then can the hypothesis be formulated that at some stage in the transmission the first verb-form in l. 101 was written *cremt*,[11] and that a copyist (not necessarily the scribe of the extant manuscript) transformed this, by contamination with *mout,* into *cremout.* The fact that this hypothesis is based on a known form of mechanical scribal error may then be considered to confirm the diagnosis that the form *cremout* was the erroneous element in the line as found in the manuscript; but the mere presence of conditions permitting contamination is not itself evidence that *cremout* was an impossible reading.[12] It must be noted that whereas at the second stage, that of correction, the critic is mainly concerned with the activities of a copyist, at the first stage, that of detection, what he is attempting to reconstruct is the probable practice of the author, not that of the copyist of the scribe's model; there is no positive reason to suppose that the latter (or indeed any other copyist in the transmission) was less ignorant, less negligent or less prone to improve on his model than the scribe of the extant manuscript; it is in fact only by intervening on behalf of the author that we can presume to correct the work of the scribe.

No degree of familiarity with the patterns of mechanical scribal error, then, can help an editor to identify 'impossible' readings in his manuscript. Evidence against a reading can only take the form of a statement that it is inconsistent with what a given critic considers to be the linguistic or metrical usage of the author's time and place, or the contextual requirements of the work itself (rebutting evidence in its favour will consist in the citation of analogous passages). Once the editor has decided that the weight of the evidence is definitely against the genuineness of a manuscript reading, he has to consider whether the correct

---

[11] The normal form of 3 sing. present indicative is *crient;* but *cremt* would be a possible spelling in Anglo-Norman, cf. in *Horn,* ed. M. K. Pope (Oxford, 1955), 1 sing. *crem* 314, etc., 3 sing. *criemt* 1038 (so written in the base MS.).

[12] Cf. Whitehead, *art. cit.,* p. 85, n. 2.

reading can be established with enough probability (for certainty is rarely attainable) to justify introducing it into the text. Here the known possibilities of mechanical error can sometimes be decisive. In Béroul, for example, homoeoteleuton accounts for

    1807 Sa chemise out vestue,

where, since the line is two syllables short, the rhyme-word is *nue* and the reference is to Yseut, the model evidently read 'Sa chemise out Yseut vestue'; dittography for the line quoted by Vinaver,

    957 Tos a genoz sont en ligliglise,

where error is indicated by the length of the line and is situated in the termination by the fact that there is no known Old French word *ligliglise* or *igliglise* ('en l'iglise' is no doubt what the scribe intended to write, though not necessarily what stood in his model or in the original: while Vinaver and Ewert are prepared to accept this reading, in spite of the identical rhyme with 'defors l'iglise' 958, Muret and Defourques believe that the author wrote 'chiet en la glise'). Most frequent in Béroul are errors belonging to Vinaver's first category, those where the scribe has mistaken one letter for another similar letter, e.g. *f* for *s* or vice versa. There can be little doubt, for example, that in such lines as

    1039 Plore Tristran molt sait grant duel

or

    1318 Et je ne vuel ma soi mentir

the editors are justified in correcting *sait* and *soi* to *fait* and *foi* (cf. also l. 2321, quoted above, p. 251). There are good grounds for seeing further instances of the same error in two passages where Ewert retains the manuscript reading:

    1325 Ce que dirai cert de segroi
            Dont je sui vers le roi par soi

and

    3313 Dist Perinis dame par soi
            Bien li dirai si le secroi.

Though *par soi* can in Old French mean 'by oneself, alone', and *soi* can in certain contexts mean 'him' rather than 'oneself', there is no evidence of the existence of any construction approaching either *dire a aucun par soi* in the sense of 'tell someone in private', or *estre par soi vers aucun d'aucune chose* in any sense. On the other hand, *par foi* as an asseverative formula is very common (cf. ll. 163, 172, 178, 614, etc.), and the locution *estre par foi a* (or *od*) *aucun (d'aucune chose)* is well attested in the sense of 'be bound in duty to someone (in respect of something)', cf. Tobler-Lommatzsch III, 1966, also 'Si'n es vers moi par seirement', *Eneas* 3848; we should therefore follow Muret and Defourques in correcting *soi* to *foi* in these passages.

IV

Among the readings which in any manuscript text are judged to be corrupt, only a small proportion can usually be shown to arise from a mechanical scribal error resulting from the process of copying as such. There is, however, another and often larger class of errors which can also in many cases be corrected with some confidence: these are the errors which can be ascribed to the habitual but idiosyncratic practices of a particular scribe.[13] Their recognition depends (as does, in the last analysis, much text-critical work of all kinds) on a process of reasoning which is in a sense circular or at best spiral. On the basis of his knowledge of the language and literature of the period and his impression of the content and form of the poem as a whole, the critic formulates the hypothesis that a given erroneous reading of the manuscript corresponds to a different reading which he might have expected to find in the original; if it turns out that the application of the same principle of correspondence to other suspect passages produces further altered readings which in the critic's judgement can plausibly be attributed to the original, it may be legitimate to deduce the existence of a scribal idiosyncrasy and to correct the text accordingly.

---

[13] They are mentioned in passing by Vinaver, but lie outside the scope of his enquiry (p. 142).

Most of the idiosyncratic errors of the scribe of the Béroul manuscript have in fact been identified by Ewert, who has set them out in detail [14] and corrected them in his edition. It seems possible, however, to postulate one or two more.

There is fairly clear evidence that the scribe was in the habit of reading a whole couplet of his model at a time and obtaining a general impression of its content and form before beginning to copy it down; his recollection of what he had read was sometimes inaccurate but might nevertheless impose itself in spite of his subsequent piecemeal reference to the model as he wrote. This is no doubt why he has so often set down the same ending in both lines of a couplet. It is true that the original is generally thought to have included a certain number of identical rhymes, perhaps a rather higher proportion than is usual in Old French romance; and all editors, even Muret in his first and most radically emended version, retain such rhymes as *par foi: en bone foi* 1381-2, *enbuschiez s'est: au Pas est* 3613-4, and similarly in ll. 1849-50; 1871-2, 2651-2, 3963-4, 4363-4, 4397-8. All editors, however, agree that one of the identical endings is grammatically or contextually unacceptable in ll. 417-18, 973-4, 1391-2, 1553-4, 1693-4, 3461-2, 3999-4000, 4085-6; and another dozen such rhymes are rejected by at least one of the editors. Such duplicated line-endings may therefore be reasonably regarded as evidence of scribal error, though they do not of course provide any indication of the correct reading. This is true also of another reflection of the same habit of the scribe's, the fact that in two passages he has written three lines on the same rhyme, with repetition of one of the rhyme-words. [15] It should be observed, first of all, that at ll. 1631-2 he wrote

> 1631 Et sil enmi lande lataint
> Com il savient en i prent maint
> Et sil enmi lande lataint.

---

[14] 'On the Text of Béroul's *Tristran*,' *Studies... presented to M. K Pope*, pp. 89-98.

[15] Muret was inclined to see in the supernumerary lines 'des variantes de rédaction, accueillies par un scribe peu attentif' (*C.F.M.A.* ed., p. viii); but this explanation, retained by Defourques, is surely very improbable. It would imply that the scribe of the extant copy had access either to the author's original draft or to an exact copy of it.

In this instance he has expuncted the third line; but on another occasion, after the line 'Quar Governal, ce m'est avis', he writes without correction

> 1833 Sen ert alez o le destrier
> Aval el bois au forestier
> En ot mene le bon destrier.

Here he has extended his couplet to three lines by writing in both first and third place what is in substance the same line, with the same rhyme-word. The error is similar but rather more complex in

> 697 En son cuer dist quil parleret
> A la roine parleroit
> Al ajorner se il pooit.

Here again the scribe has extended the couplet to three lines by duplicating one of the rhyme-words and, with some distortion, one of the line-openings (*al ajorner* was suggested in form by the written appearance of *a la roine*, in substance probably by the notion 'ainz l'ajorner' which had just been expressed in 'ainz que la nuit ait fin' 692). In neither of these cases is it possible to be certain what stood in the scribe's model, and the editors' decision is somewhat arbitrary. For ll. 1833-4 they all print 'S'en ert alez o le destrier Aval el bois au forestier', though the model, and the original, might equally well have run 'Aval el bois au forestier En ot mené le bon destrier'; for ll. 697-8 they print 'En son cuer dist qu'il parleroit A la roïne, s'il pooit', but comparison with ll. 1631-2 and 1833-4 suggests that an at least equally probable source of the manuscript reading would be 'En son cuer dist que s'il pooit A la roïne parleroit'.

Now, a third type of error resulting from the scribe's practice of memorizing a couplet at a time — but here one which indicates its own correction — is the interversion of the lines. Such interversion has been recognized by all editors in ll. 857-8, 1879-80 and 3365-6, and by Ewert also in ll. 1505-6, 3029-30 and 4285-6. There are, however, other passages where the same error seems to have been made. In ll. 3168-71 the manuscript reads

3168 Li cuer el ventre li froidis
      Devant le roi choi enverse
3170 Pasme soi sa color a perse
      Qentre ses braz len a levee.

All editors assume that at least one couplet has dropped out after l. 3170; but it is perhaps more probable that there is no lacuna, that ll. 3169-70 have been interverted by the scribe and that we should read 'Pasme soi, sa color a perse; Devant le roi choï enverse, Q'entre ses braz l'en a levee'. Again, a passage in the appeal addressed by Perinis to Arthur on behalf of Yseut runs in the manuscript

3440 Cent i aiez de vos amis
      Vostre cort soit atant loial
3442 Vostre mesnie natural
      Dedevant vos iert alegiee.

Here l. 3442 is meaningless in its context; l. 3443 is clearly intended as a consecutive clause depending on l. 3441 (it is so explained in Defourques' note, although the punctuation of his text, as of those of Muret and Ewert, is inconsistent with this interpretation); we should no doubt read 'Cent i aiez de vos amis, Vostre mesnie natural; Vostre cort set a tant [16] loial, Dedevant vos iert alegiee'. Other couplets which may well have been interverted by the scribe include ll. 67-8, 2611-12 and 4309-10; and Muret may have been right in seeing interversion also in ll. 1379-80, 2825-6 and 3115-16.

The three groups of errors which have just been mentioned indicate incidentally how conscious the scribe was of the rhyming character of his text. [17] There is also other evidence of the same

---

[16] There is no authority for taking *atant* (so printed by all recent editors) as an alternative form of *tant;* we must certainly read with Muret's S.A.T.F. ed. *a tant* (for the construction *savoir* + object + adjectival predicative complement introduced by *a* see Tobler-Lommatzsch I, 17, ll, 41-4, also *Yvain* 1789).

[17] It is true that he has sometimes, through distraction or misunderstanding, replaced a line-ending by a word which does not rhyme at all, as in ll. 239, 867, 1171, 1535, 1698, 2253, 2683, 2799, 3583, 4107, 4171 (it will be noted that these errors are nearly all in the first line of the couplet).

preoccupation, as, for example, in his occasional attempts to carry on a rhyme beyond the couplet to which it belongs: thus he writes

> 2505 Dex dist Ogrins graces te rent
> Tristran sachiez asez briment
> 2507 Orez noveles du romenz
> Tristran decent met jus son ent,

where *romenz* and *ent* are clearly corrupt, and are contextually emended by all editors to *ro*[*i*] *Marc* and *arc*.[18] It therefore seems probable that a word may sometimes have been miswritten in the interior of a line under the influence of the rhyme-words of the couplet in which it occurs: so, for instance, *soi* in

> 819 Por ce ne se vout vers le roi
> Mesfaire soi por nul desroi˜

(it is unlikely that the original included a double expression of the reflexive notion; the editors correct *ne se vout vers* to *ne vout envers* or *ne vout il vers*, but it is the *se* accompanying the finite verb and not the *soi* with the infinitive that is in accordance with normal Old French syntax); the second *entre* in

> 1987 Lespee nue an la loge entre
> Le forestier entre soventre
> 1989 Grant erre apres le roi acort

(it is fairly clear from the context that the forester does not actually enter the bower); *fort* in

> 2365 Vos en iriez a sa cort
> Ni avroit fort sage ne lort
> 2367 Sil veut dire que...

(*fort* does not give an acceptable sense either as an adjective, 'anyone, strong, wise or foolish', or as a noun, 'any strong man, wise or foolish'). In such cases the rhyme accounts for the error;

---

[18] Cf. also l. 4065, where *si les pernons* appears to have been substituted for *alons les prendre* because the preceding rhyme-words were *connoison*[*s*]: *bricons* 4063-4.

the correction usually remains uncertain, though it is probable that l. 1988 should run 'Le forestier en vet soventre'.[19]

The scribe was also in general highly conscious of the metre of the octosyllabic line (only a very small proportion of the lines as he has written them are metrically incorrect, and many of these show other signs of negligence). When an error in one part of the line results in the loss of a syllable, he has sometimes restored the measure by introducing an extra syllable elsewhere. Thus in

> 3483 Et dit Evains li filz Dinan
> Asez connois Dinoalan,

trisyllabic *Urïen* (well attested as the name of Yvain's father) has been erroneously replaced by disyllabic *Dinan* (the name of the fief of Dinas, but here evidently suggested by *Dinoalan* 3484), and the missing syllable has then been supplied by the insertion of an unnecessary initial *Et* (for the normal formula cf. 'Dist Perinis: "Ja en iron"' 3382 and ll. 3313, 3495, etc.). Similarly in

> 3294 Di li que il set bien marches

it is probable that the erroneous omission of *un* before *marches* has been compensated by the substitution of *que il* for *qu'il*. This metrical preoccupation can even lead the scribe to give the feminine form to a masculine adjective or participle. In the passage

> 2697 Ainz berseret a veneor
> Nert gardee a tel honor
> 2699 Con cist sera beaus douz amis

it is evident that l. 2698 is corrupt. All recent editors take the final letter of *gardee* as representing the conjunction *et*; but this is never elsewhere in the text written *e* in the interior of the

---

[19] Cf. l. 3152, where the manuscript reads 'Nus ne sut ne ne voit soventre,' or perhaps better 'Nus nel sieut ne n'en voit soventre' (the scribe often omits the titulus and preconsonantal *l*, and confuses *u* and *n*; for *sieut* 'follows,' cf. l. 1962, for *voit* 'goes' cf. ll. 1271, 1511, etc.). Cf. 'Eurialus s'en vet soantre,' *Eneas* 5127; 'Si compaignon en vont soentre,' *Partonopeus* 3449.

line,[20] while *ainz* in the sense of *onc* 'ever' is elsewhere, as is normal in Old French, used exclusively with the preterite.[21] It therefore appears probable that the scribe's model read 'Ne fu garde a tel honor'; he erroneously replaced *fu* by *ert*[22] and then restored the measure by simply giving the past participle the feminine form *gardeë*. Something very similar has happened in

> 4317 Tries la clanbre est grant la doiz
> Et bien espesse li jagloiz

(where it is generally agreed that *clanbre* is an error for *chanbre*). All editors translate *jagloiz* by 'glaïeul', 'sword-grass', evidently taking this form as the nominative singular of the plant-name from Latin *gladiolum* which in Old French is normally *glajuel* or *jagluel*.[23] Grammar, rhyme and sense, however, are all at variance with this interpretation: *jagloiz* must be an error for *jagloloiz*, nominative singular of *jagloloi, glajoloi* 'iris-bed, plantation of sword-lilies or sweet sedge', a derivative in *-oi* from *-etum* which is well attested in Old French.[24] The scribe has transformed *jagloloiz* by haplology, into *jagloiz*,[25] and has restored the measure by arbitrarily giving the feminine form to the adjective *espés*.

Among the scribe's other idiosyncratic errors are those arising from his failure to understand the syntax of his model.[26] In particular he has often altered, omitted or inserted conjunctions, relatives and certain adverbs; but as these errors have in most

---

[20] Initial *E* appears in l. 3185 only (Ewert, *ed. cit.*, pp. xii f.).

[21] Cf. ll. 498-9, 561, 582, 1161, 1167, etc. (in all some 20 examples).

[22] No doubt intended as a future, probably under the influence of the futures in ll. 2699-702; he has also written *ce mert avis* 2700, corrected by all editors to *ce m'est avis*.

[23] Cf. Muret, *C.F.M.A.* ed., p. x; Defourques, p. ix.

[24] Cf. Tobler-Lommatzsch IV, 352 and *Twelve Fabliaux*, ed. T. B. W Reid (Manchester, 1958), p. 117.

[25] Another example of this shortened form is cited by Godefroy IV, 627 from the version of *Partonopeus* in MS. B. N. fr. 19152, 'Si a dur lit sanz nul jagloi'; but here it appears to be an error for the *argroi* (i.e. *agroi* 'equipment') of the Crapelet ed., l. 658 (cited by Godefroy I, 169).

[26] Cf. Ewert, *art. cit.*, pp. 95, 97.

cases been corrected by one or more of the editors,[27] they need not be considered here.

V

Not only, then, can there be differences of opinion about the acceptability of a manuscript reading: even in those cases where it is generally recognized that the text is corrupt, and where the corruption can be accounted for by one of the known types of mechanical or idiosyncratic scribal error, critics do not always agree about its correction. Agreement is even less to be expected where the source of the error remains obscure, as is often the case in Béroul. Besides the passages already referred to, where the corrections made by the two most recent editors diverge,[28] there are a number of others in which it is possible to argue for corrections different from any of those of the editors. A few examples may be given.

(1)
41 Sire molt dist voir Salemon
      Qui de forches traient larron
43 Ja pus nel amera nul jor.

The plural verb *traient* is inconsistent with the singular object pronoun contained in *nel*. The editors correct *nel* to *nes;* but since absolute *qui* 'he who', 'whoever' is normally treated as a singular (none of the 400-odd proverbs in Morawski's collection beginning with *qui* has a plural verb), it is evidently *nel* that is correct and *traient* that is corrupt. In explanation of ll. 42-3 Muret and Defourques *(Index des noms propres,* s.d. *Salemon)* refer to a passage in *De Marco e de Salemons,* 'Qui en sa meson Atret lou larron Domage i reçoit'; but this proverb (analogues of which are listed by Morawski, nos. 39, 977, 1180, 1526) has really nothing in common with the one cited here except the word *larron*. The essential element in Béroul's proverb is the ingratitude of the thief

---
[27] Thus (to cite one type among many) the scribe's *Que* initial of the line is rejected by all editors in ll. 231, 2449, 4003, by Muret in ll. 1382, 1384, 4401, by Ewert in l. 2021.
[28] See ll. 382, 819, 916, 922, 957, 1030, etc.

rescued from the gallows; it actually corresponds to Morawski's no. 1048, 'Lerres n'amera ja celui qui le respite des fourches', for which he cites from an Anglo-Norman manuscript the variant 'ne amera qui lui reynt de f.'[29] The emendation required is therefore the replacement of *traient* by *raient* (third person singular present indicative of *raiembre* 'redeem').

(2)
1055 Par Deu fait el se je mes jor
     Qant li felon losengeor
1057 Qui garder durent mon ami
     Lont deperdu la Deu merci
1059 Ne me devroit lon mes proisier.

Although for the author *jor* and *losengeor* form a rhyme (cf. *jor: enor* 25-6, etc.), all editors assume that there is a lacuna between ll. 1055 and 1056. There is, however, no reason to doubt that the clause beginning in l. 1055 is the protasis to the apodosis expressed in l. 1059, and if there were an additional couplet between ll. 1055 and 1056 the sentence would be unusually long and clumsy. It is therefore more probable that the manuscript text is complete, but that *mes jor* in 1045 is corrupt. It may well be an error for *m'esplor* (cf. the references to Yseut's tears in ll. 903, 1046). An example of the reflexive verb *esplorer* 'burst into tears' is cited from *Doon de Mayence* by Godefroy and Tobler-Lommatzsch; for the rhyme cf. *pecheor: plor* 911-12; for the hypothetical construction with present indicative in the protasis and conditional in the apodosis cf. ll. 176-7, 190-2, 227-9, 2714-5, etc.

(3)
1648 Longuement par Morrois fuirent
     Chascun deus soffre paine elgal
1650 Qar lun por lautre ne sent mal
     Grant poor a Yseut la gente
1652 Tristran por lie ne se repente
     Et a Tristran repoise fort

---

[29] Cf. also 'Raembez de forches larron Quant il a fait sa mesprison, Ja mes ne vos amera,' *D'un preudome qui rescolt son conpere de noier* 69 ff. (*Twelve Fabliaux*, p. 4).

1654   Que Yseut a por lui descort
       Quil repente de la folie.

This important passage has been discussed in detail (down to l. 1654) by Vinaver.[30] He shows that Ewert and Defourques are right in retaining *ne sent* 1650 (Muret had emended to *resent*): *soffre paine* refers to the endurance of physical hardships and privations, *ne sent mal* to the lovers' unawareness of these miseries, a contrast similarly expressed in ll. 1364-6 and 1784-5.[31]

Further problems, however, remain. The first is presented by the conjunction *Qar* in l. 1650: Vinaver argues convincingly that it cannot here have its usual sense, that of a causal co-ordinating conjunction 'for', and he hesitates between two other interpretations, coordinating *car* 'therefore', 'then' and subordinating *car* in the sense of *que* consecutive, 'so that', 'with the result that'. The first of these uses, however, is cited only from *Alexis* 613 and *Adam* 124 and 171, in contexts different from that of our passage, while the second is rather late and predominantly Eastern.[32] Since the scribe has so often altered conjunctions (cf. above p. 262), it is perhaps more likely that *qar* is here simply an error, probably for *mais* (cf. l. 1785).

A second problem is that of the logical relation between ll. 1649-50 and the lines which follow. Vinaver is no doubt right in maintaining that there is no causal or explanatory relation, but rather a contrast which does not happen to be specifically marked by any particle: the same contrast is implied in 'Aspre vie meinent et dure; Tant s'entraiment de bone amor, L'un por l'autre ne sent dolor' 1364-6, where l. 1365 lacks the explicit *Mais* of the parallel passage 'Fu ainz maiss gent tant eüst paine? Mais l'un por

---

[30] 'Pour le commentaire du vers 1650 du *Tristan* de Beroul,' *Studies... presented to A. Ewert*, pp. 90-5.

[31] For the sense of *sentir* cf. also 'La plaie saigne; ne la sent, Qar trop a son delit entent' 733-4, and 'Yseut s'esjot, or ne sent mal' 1274, where *ne sent mal* expresses Yseut's indifference to the physical pain caused by her bonds, ll. 1051-4. Vinaver takes 'l'un por l'autre ne sent mal' 1650 (and the similar statements in ll. 1366, 1785) as meaning 'they do not feel their privations because they share them' (p. 92); but it is difficult to see how *por* can have anything but the causal sense which he rejects, 'each is indifferent to these privations because of the presence of the other.'

[32] Cf. Tobler-Lommatzsch II, 41, ll. 17-31.

l'autre ne le sent' 1784-5. The colon placed by Muret after l. 1650, and retained by Ewert and Defourques, should therefore be replaced by a full stop, and the immediately following lines taken to mean '[Yet] Yseut is afraid that Tristran will repent for her sake; and Tristran, for his part, is deeply grieved that Yseut is at odds [with the King] because of him...'

This, however, leaves out of account l. 1655, which is not discussed by Vinaver. All editors consider that the manuscript text is erroneous here: Muret assumes a lacuna between ll. 1654 and 1655. Ewert and Defourques emend *Quil* to *Qu'el*. The editors do not explain how they understand l. 1655; and whether the subject is *el* or *il*, there does not seem to be any normal syntactical function in which such a *que*-clause, with subjunctive verb, could be attached to what precedes. It may be suggested that ll. 1653-5 would make sense with four small emendations (instead of the one proposed by Ewert and Defourques), reading 'Et Tristran repoise si fort Que Yseut a por lui descort Qu'il se repent de la folie'. The general construction of the passage would then be the same as in 'Qar j'ai tel duel c'onques le roi Out mal pensé de vos vers moi Qu'il n'i a el fors que je muere' 109-11; for the use of *Tristran* as a dative without preposition cf. 'Toz fait joie' 1548, 'Qui la roïne ont quis meslee' 3498, 'Li rois offre les garnemenz Perinis...', 3528-9, also with strong pronoun objects 'Que lui ne poist' 1117, 'lui n'en poise' 2404; the verb *repentir* is normally reflexive in Old French, cf. ll. 307, 1378, 1652, 2160, 2299, 2326.[33] It would be quite in accordance with the scribe's known proclivities that he should have dropped out the *si* in l. 1653 (especially after *-se*) and the *se* in l. 1655 and should then have restored the measure (cf. above p. 261 f.) by introducing respectively the preposition *a* and the form *repente* for *repent*.

This reconstruction of the text would of course destroy any presumed parallelism between the description of Yseut's feelings and that of Tristran's. But in spite of the *re-* of *repoise* 1653, there is no such parallelism in the version of the manuscript. Vinaver speaks of 'la *poor* d'Iseut et l'anxiété de Tristan' (p. 94):

---

[33] It appears, very exceptionally, as an intransitive in l. 1390; the use of the infinitive without a reflexive pronoun, as in l. 2271 and (substantivally) in l. 1394, is not of course evidence of intransitivity.

we are indeed told that Yseut is afraid, but not that Tristran experiences any similar anxiety. The two sentences, so far from being the expression of corresponding and reciprocal fears on the part of the two lovers, are both concerned exclusively with Tristran's reactions: Yseut is afraid that Tristran will repent for her sake, and in fact he, on his side, is so distressed by her situation that he does repent. This interpretation is not, however, in any way inconsistent with the general tenor of the Morrois episode, or indeed with the theme of the poem as a whole: while the two lovers undergo the same hardships and are equally indifferent to them, while Yseut's physical sufferings are the greater, it is Tristran's thoughts and feelings that are stressed, for he is the true protagonist of the romance.

(4)
2447   Mon cheval gardera mon mestre
        Mellor ne vit ne lais ne prestre
2449   Qanuit apres solel couchier
        Quant li tens prist a espoisier
2451   Tristran sen torne avoc son mestre.

The scribe, momentarily mistaking l. 2449 for part of Tristran's speech (and no doubt influenced also by the *Qant* of l. 2450), has erroneously written *Qanuit*. All editors correct to *Anuit;* but this adverb in the text, as normally in Old French, means 'last night' or 'tonight' and is used only in reference to the situation of a speaker (cf. *anuit* 3958, *enuit* 2281, 2647, 4294). What is required here is surely *La nuit* 'that night', from the point of view of the narrator (cf. ll. 679, 701, 2651, 4089).

(5)
3454   Ja ne voist il sanz paradis
        Se li rois veut quil larara
3456   Et qui par droit nel aidera.

In l. 3455 all editors correct, no doubt rightly, to *qui la n'ira* (the *l'a* for *la* in Muret's later editions and in that of Defourques is merely a misprint). In l. 3454 they print *s'anz*, understanding 'May he who does not go there (i.e. to Yseut's *deresne*) ... never go into Paradise'. This, however, requires *anz (enz)* to be taken as a preposition, a usage of which there is no other instance in the text; it also postulates a most exceptional position of the reflexive pronoun (the normal word-order would be neither *Ja ne voist il se* as in the manuscript, nor *Ja ne voist se il*, described as 'la construction normale' in Defourques' note, but *Ja ne se voist il*); moreover, pronominal *aler* is hardly ever found without the adverb *en*. The line must therefore be corrupt. Muret in his S.A.T.F. edition corrected it to 'Ja ne voist il en paradis'; but though this is grammatically irreproachable, it could hardly have given rise to the manuscript reading. It may be suggested that the original ran 'Ja ne voie il saint paradis'. For the use of the verb *veoir* in a similar formula cf. 'Ja ne voie Deu en la face, Qui trovera le nain en place, Qui nu ferra d'un glaive el cors!' 841-3 (see also ll. 58-9); for *saint paradis* cf. *Rol.* 1522. The scribe might well have confused the verb-forms *voi(e)* and *voist*, since he has dropped a final *-st* in *tenti[st]* 1530 (:*s'esbaudist*) and *fu[st]* 1726 (also, according to Muret, in *porpensa[st]* 647 and *fu[st]* 4112); and he has elsewhere written *-an-* for *-ain-* (*nan* 1311 for *nain*, *sanz* 2346 for *s'ainz*, etc.).

(6)
3663 Pensent vaslet et escuier
      Quil se hast de nus alegier
3665 Et des tres tendre lor seignors.

The manuscript text of l. 3664 is clearly corrupt. All editors adopt the emendation of G. Paris 'Qu'il se hastent de soi logier'; but the construction thus attributed to the verb *penser* is abnormal, and the notion that the squires think first of finding a lodging for themselves is hardly plausible enough to justify the introduction of the verb *logier*. It seems more probable that the infinitive *alegier* in the sense of 'lighten', 'relieve (of a burden)' [84] goes back to the original, and that ll. 3663-4 should be corrected to read 'Passent vaslet et escuier Qui se hastent d'eus alegier...', referring to their loads of material for the tents and pavilions of their masters. The scribe has elsewhere misread forms of the verb *passer* (cf. *parler* for *passer* 3694, *port* for *past* 3975) and confused *qui* and *qu'il* (*qu'il* is corrected to *qui* by all editors

---

[84] Cf. Tobler-Lommatzsch I, 278-9.

in l. 3683, by Muret and Defourques in l. 3526; conversely *qui* stands for *quil* = *qui le* in l. 4149).

(7)
3971 De vos sorchauz sil les veut vendre
     Puet il cinc soz desterlins prendre
3973 Et del aumuce mon seignor
     Achat bien lit si soit pastor
3975 Ou un asne qui port le tai.

Muret and Ewert attach l. 3973 to what follows (semicolon or full stop after *prendre*), Defourques rather less plausibly to what precedes (comma after *prendre*, full stop after *seignor*); all editors correct *port* to *past*. It is difficult to believe that the scribe's version of l. 3974 is what the author wrote; and Muret emended it, correcting *si soit pastor* first to *ci soit entor*, later to *et covertor*. In assuming that it was the second hemistich that was corrupt, he was no doubt influenced by the declensional irregularity of *pastor* as a nominative singular; but though there is no other instance in the text of a similar usage with a noun in *-or*, there are many irregularities among other imparisyllabic types (those attested by rhyme include nominative singular *home* 188, 4205, *garçons* 3888, accusative singular *sire* 4212, *ber* 1178). As far as the sense is concerned, the second hemistich of l. 3974 is quite in harmony with l. 3975, and it is more probably the first that is corrupt: *lit* is very unexpected in the context, and there is no obvious justification for *bien*. It may be suggested that in the original the line ran 'Achat berbiz, si soit pastor'.

VI

It may well be that few of the new corrections or interpretations proposed above will be accepted by all editors and critics of Béroul. If any of them are admitted to be reasonably probable, however, they will serve to illustrate the difficulties inherent in current editorial practice. When an editor says that he has reproduced his manuscript with the minimum of change, he means that among the numerous readings he considers to be manifestly corrupt, he has eliminated some because their correction seems to him fairly certain, but has retained others because their correction seems to him uncertain (passages which he considers only probably corrupt are, of course, also retained). But the dividing lines between manifest and probable corruptions, and between certain and uncertain corrections, are to a considerable extent subjective, as is evidenced by the divergences between different editions of the same text. There is therefore every justification for Vinaver's endeavour to establish objective criteria of scribal error. The principles he proposes, however, can serve only to aid in the correction (not the detection) of a limited number of mechanical errors; and even if some idiosyncratic errors are similarly corrected, it is probable that the majority of the corrupt readings in the manuscript will remain standing. It may be questioned whether it is either logical or profitable to confine correction to such a small proportion of the errors in the manuscript in the hope of attaining a measure of objectivity, especially when the introduction of punctuation simultaneously opens another door to subjectivity. It is no doubt true that an edition thus conceived presents a text less remote from the original than that of the manuscript; but it is also true that what it presents is not, and does not profess to be, either the poem as it was written down by the scribe (or, for that matter, by the copyist of the scribe's model) or the poem as the editor thinks it was composed by the author.

Should not an edition provide something more positive than this? The reader is surely entitled to know exactly what stands in the manuscript, and this he can learn only from a complete transcription retaining the scribe's word-divisions, use of u and v, s and f, etc., and either his actual abbreviations or a clear indication (e.g. italics) where an abbreviation has been resolved. On the other hand, the reader is also entitled to know exactly what a competent editor, after careful investigation and reflection, thinks the author probably wrote; and this too should be given in full in the form of a continuous text. [35] The only really satis-

---

[35] With the omission of any corrupt passages for which the editor feels unable to suggest a probable correction.

factory form of edition is therefore one that gives these two versions side by side in parallel columns or on facing pages.[36] Thus presented, the editor's reconstruction of the original can be seen in its proper perspective, as the fruit, not of a presumptuous disguised collaboration with the author, but of a tentative and undisguised collaboration with the scribe.[37]

---

[36] This presentation may not be considered economically justifiable where the manuscript text is reasonably correct; in such cases the traditional arrangement might suffice, provided that the footnotes gave not only the rejected readings but also full information about scribal forms.

[37] For a further elaboration of the points discussed in this essay, see T. B. W. Reid, *The "Tristran" of Béroul: A Textual Commentary* (Oxford: Blackwell, 1972).

THE NATURE OF AN EDITION

by Christopher Kleinhenz

The preceding essays in this collection have been concerned with the material compilation and external embellishments of Medieval manuscripts and with various critical approaches to these codices. We have examined the many theoretical and practical problems encountered in the preparation of a critical edition and have observed some of the means available to the editor for their resolution. However, before proceeding to the final step in this process, that of presenting the text on the printed page, it would perhaps be advisable to review briefly the several types of editions and to define in simple terms their distinct nature.

As noted in the Introduction, the intent (generally utopian) of any edition is to recreate or reconstruct the work of the author from existing evidence. The nature of the edition ultimately determines the variety and the amount of information that is necessary for a complete understanding of the text in its generalities and its particulars. It could be argued, at times quite convincingly, that the FACSIMILE edition would be the best possible way of allowing the text to speak for itself. Indeed, a photographic reproduction of the original manuscript(s) would be most suitable for a text fraught with ambiguities. However, while this would afford maximum latitude in interpretation, it would at the same time restrict the reading public to those knowledgeable in Medieval paleography and a host of related skills.

One step removed from the manuscript and its mechanical reproduction, the DIPLOMATIC edition represents accurately in print the text of the codex. Since the success of this variety is directly proportional to the paleographical competence of the editor, the diplomatic edition merits either praise for its perfection or ignominy for its failures. This type is especially commendable when it preserves an exact transcription of a manuscript that has subsequently been lost, damaged, or destroyed; it is condemnable when it contains faulty readings or when it interprets, even in the smallest possible way (for example, in the expansion of abbreviations, the supplying of punctuation or other diacritical marks, or the grouping of letters into words).

The goal of the editing process is the establishment of the CRITICAL TEXT. This interpretative text, founded on sound critical procedures, will form the basis for the three remaining varieties of edition, which I prefer to term GENERAL, CRITICAL, and VARIORUM. Each may be distinguished from the others primarily by the extent of the critical apparatus *(apparatus criticus)* and by the type of general and specific information accompanying the text.

The VARIORUM edition *(cum notis variorum)* is the largest and most complete volume, containing virtually everything pertaining to the life of the work. In addition to the presentation of the critical text with complete apparatus (as in the critical edition, see below), there are notes that, as the term variorum implies, incorporate commentary taken from numerous sources (scholarly books, essays in journals, and so on). Other important features are the elucidation of passages by the citation of similar phrases from other authors, the reproduction, completely or in part, of the text(s) that influenced the work, and the evaluation of its place in and its impact upon the literary tradition. Perhaps the most outstanding representative of this category is the Shakespeare variorum, edited by Horace Howard Furness, which, besides the above-mentioned "extras," provides information regarding the staging, costumes and actors, the success of the performance, the influence on subsequent literature, and other similarly related topics. In short, the reader has at his disposal in such a volume an extraordinary amount of material, more than enough for an adequate comprehension of the work.

At the other extreme is the GENERAL edition, which usually includes no discussion of textual problems, for it has been prepared for those whose interests lie outside the realm of *Textkritik* or *Textgeschichte*. Intended either for the general public or for a definite audience within this larger group, the text is accompanied only by notes of a factual or interpretative nature. Many works in this category (anthologies, popular editions of the classics) could properly be called scholastic editions, which would indicate their intended use in the classroom. In this case, the nature of the audience dictates the format and the choice of accompanying material. Suppose for a moment that we were editing Dante's *De Monarchia* for use in literature classes; it would necessarily be accompanied by a far different set of notes than the same text would, if it were being prepared for the student of history or political science. On the one hand, the student and critic of literature would hope to find some discussion of the imagery, the use of Biblical allusions, and the position of the work in the author's artistic development. On the other hand, the political scientist and historian would expect comparisons with contemporary treatises on the same topic (Boniface VIII's bull *Unam Sanctam*, and the slightly later *Defensor Pacis* of Marsilius of Padua), together with references to Aristotle and St. Thomas Aquinas, so as to elucidate the genesis of Dante's political thought. To be sure, notes of both kinds are not mutually exclusive; indeed, the ideal general edition would provide a harmonious blending of the two and thus cater to the interests of both audiences.

In some cases, textual and philological matters, which are usually omitted in the general edition, manage to insinuate themselves in the abundant interpretative commentary. Sometimes this shift of attention, while insufficient for reclassification, makes the nature of these works tend toward that of the critical edition. Good examples of this sort may be found in the volumes of the Droz "Textes Littéraires Français" and in the Ricciardi collection of Italian literature.

Passing then to the third and final incorporation of the critical text, we recognize in the CRITICAL edition the best possible compromise between too little and too much. For, being accompanied by the information necessary to view the work in its proper perspective, the text is allowed to speak for itself and can be presumed to fulfill the original intention of the author, who certainly expected his reader to deal with the text on its own terms in its own context. Besides its principal obligation of providing a sound text established in accordance with approved procedures, the critical edition must include an introduction, in which information is provided on the author's life, works, and language (his own, in case the holograph [autograph manuscript] exists, or that of the base manuscript). Moreover, depending on the circumstances, there should be sections devoted to the discussion of the manuscripts and their stemmatic relationship, to previous scholarship (editions and commentaries), problems of authenticity and chronology of works, the general method of the edition (the criteria followed in the transcription, typographical conventions used, and so on), and the abbreviations of manuscripts (Paris, Bibliothèque Nationale MS 844 = *M*) and editions (Arnaut Daniel, *Canzoni*, ed. G. Toja [Firenze, 1960] = *Toja*). Ideally, notes should be located on the same page as the text and, in most cases, should be divided between textual matters (manuscript variants or, in the case of *codex unicus*, emended readings) and interpretative concerns (editorial variants, metrical explanation, linguistic analysis, philological exegesis, historical data, and esthetic commentary). In those cases where the language of the text is extremely difficult or ambiguous (as is generally true with the Provençal troubadours), a literal translation would be in order. Concluding the volume should be a comprehensive glossary, together with any appropriate indices (proper and place names, first-lines of poetry, and so on) or appendices (literary material or archival documents relating to the text in question, extended critical commentary on the text, annotated bibliography).

The ideal presentational format for any given text ultimately depends on the preference of the editor and on the intrinsic nature of the text itself — poetry or prose, with special consideration given to their sub-classifications (lyric, romance, novella, etc.), as well as to chronicles, archival documents, letters, and so on. Nevertheless, it is essential to adhere to one fundamental principle: all material necessary for the elucidation of the text must be presented in the clearest possible manner. As a part of the practical preparation, the editor should examine carefully several editions of texts similar to that on which he intends to work, for only in this manner can he observe the various ways, successful or not, in which others have presented their text.

Outstanding examples of the critical edition may be found in the volumes published by the Société des Anciens Textes Français, as well as in the following series: Les Classiques français du moyen age (Champion); Collezione di opere inedite o rare (Commissione per i Testi di Lingua); French Classics (Manchester University Press); and Blackwell's French Texts.

In order to illustrate some of the characteristics of the so-called "ideal" format for the presentation of a text, I have included on the following pages my own edition of a sonnet by Paolo Lanfranchi da Pistoia, a minor thirteenth-century Italian poet. Because of the inclusion of information regarding manuscripts, editions, metrics and language, the format for an edition of lyric poetry differs from that of most other texts, where such material would be more appropriately presented in an introductory section. However, the form for the variants and the general content of the notes would be the same for any text. The following critical edition is divided into five parts: 1) all necessary textual information; 2) the text itself; 3) variant readings in the manuscripts and related peculiarities; 4) special sections devoted to particular topics; and 5) notes of an interpretative nature.

The following abbreviations have been used in the edition:

Manuscripts

    Es   α N 6 4; It. 1154 (formerly X B 10). Modena, Biblioteca Estense.

    Q   Barb. Lat. 3953 (formerly XLV, 47). Vatican City, Biblioteca Apostolica Vaticana.

Editions

    Baudi   Carlo Baudi di Vesme, ed., "Poesie provenzali ed italiane di Paolo Lanfranchi da Pistoia," *Rivista sarda*, I (1875), pp. 391-404.

    Lega   Gino Lega, ed., *Il Canzoniere Vaticano Barberino Latino 3953 (già Barb, XLV, 47)*, Bologna, 1905.

    Zac   Guido Zaccagnini, ed., *I Rimatori pistoiesi dei secoli XIII e XIV*, Pistoia, 1907.

    Zac[1]   Guido Zaccagnini and Amos Parducci, eds., *Rimatori siculo-toscani del Dugento, serie prima: pistoiesi, lucchesi, pisani*, Bari, 1915.

Secondary Material

Rohlfs   Gerhard Rohlfs, *Historische Grammatik der italienischen Sprache und ihrer Mundarten. I. Lautlehre*, Bern, 1949.

I

DE LA ROTA SON POSTI EXEMPLI ASAI

Manuscripts: Es 13 (Sonectus); Q 142 (Paulo lafranchi da pistoia).
Editions: Baudi, 397 (composite of Es and Q); Lega, 153 (diplomatic transcription of Q); Zac, 72 (composite of Es and Q); Zac[1], 28 (after Q).
Base and Orthography: Q.

De la rota son posti exempli asai,
che çira e volze e no dimora en loco,
e mete en bono stato quel ch'à poco,
4 al poderosso dà tormenti e guai.
Or, ché no 'l pensi? Po' che tu l[o] sai
che picola favilla fa gran foco,
no t'alegrare tropo nì dar çoco,
8 ché no se' certo come finerai.
Si alcun è che vezi in malo stato,
en quel medesmo tu pòi avenire,
11 ch' a te né [a] lui Dïo no à çurato.
Azo veduto per li tempi [un] sire,
che la Ventura l'à sì governato
14 che plu che vita desira morire.

VARIANTS: 1. *Veduto ho dela r. li e. a.* Es. 2. *che uolta e gira* Es; *çira e* Q (*e* added above line in a different hand). 3. *quelo* Q (*o* expuncted); *quello che dapocho* Es. 4. *tormento assai* Es. 5. *Or dūque ch non p. tu ch sai* Es; *no tel p. po che tul* Q (*tul* written in different hand over effacement). 6. *che* lacking Q; *gran*] *grande* Q. 7. *De nō te ralegrar ne far gran ioco* Es; *dar*] *dare* Q (*e* expuncted). 8. *se'*] *si* Es. 9. *Guarda se tu uidi alcuno ī mal s.* Es. 10. *ch̄ tu m. inquello p.* Es. 11. *E sai ben ch d. nō la iurato* Es; *la ç.* Q (*l* expuncted). 12. *Chio o v. si p lo tempo ire* Es. 13. *la fortuna a lomo si g.* Es. 14. *desia de m.* Es.

NOTES:

Meter. Sonnet: ABBA ABBA CDC DCD.

Language. It should be noted that the language of MS Q reveals the heavy Venetian coloration of the scribe (from Treviso) and of the compiler and *corrector,* the well-known poet Niccolò del Rosso. Of special interest is the use of ç and z to represent palatal g in initial and medial position respectively (cf. Rohlfs, *Grammatik,* §§ 156, 218).

Subject Matter. The sonnet treats the familiar theme of the vicissitudes of Fortune. For the popularity of this topic in Medieval literature, see Howard Rollin Patch, *The Goddess Fortuna in Mediaeval Literature* (Cambridge, 1927). This and Lanfranchi's other sonnet on the wheel of Fortune (*Quatro homin sum dipincti ne la rota*) reveal a remarkable originality in their blending of *topoi:* the lament of an individual laid low by Fortune; the consolation of another in similar circumstances; and the didactic presentation of the nature of the goddess.

2. Zac follows Es.
4. Baudi interprets *da* as preposition.
5. Baudi and Zac follow Es. Zac construes the second quatrain as a single question. Zac^1 follows Q, but, together with Baudi, considers vv. 5-6 as a single question. The emendation *tu l[o] sai* is for the meter (the *l[o]* is pleonastic and anticipates v. 6).
6. Cf. James 3:5 "Ecce quantus ignis quam magnam siluam incendit!," and Dante, *Paradiso* I, 34: "Poca favilla gran fiamma seconda."
7. Zac follows Es. Zac^1 claims to adhere to Q, but present *dar gran gioco,* which makes the verse one syllable too long. *Dar çoco:* "darsi gioia" ("to give joy to oneself"), synonymous with *t'alegrare.*
9. Zac^1 retains the *tu* of Es: *che tu veggi.*
11. The emendation is necessitated by the meter and the parallelism of the construction: *a te né [a] lui.* Baudi, Zac, and Zac^1 follow Es in the retention of *l (nō la iurato),* which is expuncted in Q.
12. The emendation clarifies the sense of the verse (and appropriately fills the space left blank between *tempi* and *sire* on the folio in Q).

BIBLIOGRAPHY FOR FURTHER READINGS IN TEXTUAL CRITICISM

Andrieu, Jean. "Pour l'explication psychologique des fautes de copiste." *Revue des études latines*, XXVIII (1950), pp. 279-292.
———. "Principes et recherches en critique textuelle." *Mémorial des études latines... offert à... Jean Marouzeau*. Paris, 1943, pp. 458-474.
Avalle, d'Arco Silvio. *La Letteratura medievale in lingua d'oc nella sua tradizione manoscritta*. Torino, 1961.
———. *Principi di critica testuale*. Vulgares Eloquentes, 7. Padova, 1972.
Barbi, Michele. *La Nuova filologia e l'edizione dei nostri scrittori da Dante al Manzoni* Firenze, 1938.
Bédier, Joseph. *La Tradition manuscrite du "Lai de l'Ombre." Réflexions sur l'art d'éditer les anciens textes*. Paris, 1929.
Bieler, Ludwig. "The Grammarian's Craft: A Professional Talk." *[Classical] Folia*, X (1958), pp. 3-42.
Brambilla Ageno, Franca. *L'Edizione critica dei testi volgari*. 2 vols. Parma, 1967.
Cantarella, R. *Introduzione allo studio della filologia classica*. Napoli, 1938.
Castellani, Arrigo, *Bédier avait-il raison? La Méthode de Lachmann dans les éditions de texte du moyen age*. Fribourg, 1957.
Chaytor, Henry John. *From Script to Print. An Introduction to Medieval Vernacular Literature*. Cambridge, 1950.
Chiari, Alberto. "L'Edizione critica." *Tecnica e teoria letteraria*. Problemi ed Orientamenti Critici di Lingua e di Letteratura Italiana. 2nd ed. Milano, 1951, pp. 231-295.
Collomp, Paul. *La Critique des textes*. Paris, 1931.
Contini, Gianfranco. "Rapporti fra la filologia (come critica testuale) e la linguistica romanza." *Actes du XIIème Congrès International de Linguistique et Philologie Romanes*. Bucharest, 1970. I, pp. 47-65.
Dain, Alphonse. *Les Manuscripts*. Paris, 1949 [2nd ed., 1964].
Dearing, Vinton A. "Abaco-Textual Criticism." *The Papers of the Bibliographical Society of America*, LXII (1968), pp. 547-578.
———. *A Manual of Textual Analysis*. Berkeley and Los Angeles, 1959.
———. "Some Notes on Genealogical Methods in Textual Criticism." *Novum Testamentum*, IX (1967), pp. 278-297.
———. "Some Routines for Textual Criticism." *Transactions of the Bibliographical Society*. "The Library" (London), 5th series, XXI (1966), pp. 309-317.

Dekkers, Dom Eligius, O.S.B. "La Tradition des textes et les problèmes de l'édition diplomatique." *Traditio,* X (1954), pp. 549-555.
Dondaine, Antoine. "Un Cas majeur d'utilisation d'un argument paleographique en critique textuelle (Vat. lat. 781)." *Scriptorium,* XXI (1967), pp. 261-276.
Faral, Edmond. "A propos de l'édition des textes anciens: le cas du manuscrit unique." *Recueil des travaux offert à M. Clovis Brunel.* Paris, 1955. I, pp. 409-421.
Fourquet, Jean. "Fautes communes ou innovations communes?" *Romania,* LXX (1948-49), pp. 85-95.
———. *Le Paradoxe de Bédier.* Paris, 1946.
Froger, Dom Jacques. "La Collation des manuscrits à la machine électronique." *Bulletin d'information de l'Institut de Recherches et d'Histoire des Textes,* XIII (1964-65), pp. 135-171.
———. *La Critique des textes et son automatisation.* Paris, 1968.
———. "La Critique textuelle et la méthode des groupes fautifs." *Cahiers de lexicologie,* III (1962), pp. 207-224.
———. "The Electronic Machine at the Service of Humanistic Studies." *Diogenes,* LII (1965), pp. 104-112.
Funaioli, Gino. "Lineamenti d'una storia della filologia attraverso i secoli." *Studi di letteratura antica.* Bologna, 1946. I, pp. 185-356.
Geschichte der Textüberlieferung der antiken und mittelalterlichen Literatur. 2 vols. Zurich, 1961 and 1964.
Gilbert, Penny. "Automatic Collation: A Technique for Medieval Texts." *Computers and the Humanities,* VII (1973), pp. 139-147.
Greg, Sir W. W. *The Calculus of Variants: An Essay on Textual Criticism.* Oxford, 1927.
———. "Recent Theories of Textual Criticism." *Modern Philology,* XXVIII (1930-31), pp. 401-404.
Grigsby, John L. "A Defense and Four Illustrations of Textual Criticism." *Romance Philology,* XX (1967), pp. 500-520.
Hall, F. W. *A Companion to Classical Texts.* Oxford, 1913.
Ham, Edward B. "Textual Criticism and Common Sense." *Romance Philology,* XII (1959), pp. 198-215.
Hill, Archibald A. "Some Postulates for Distributional Study of Texts." *Studies in Bibliography,* III (1950-51), pp. 63-95.
Housman, Alfred Edward. "The Application of Thought to Textual Criticism." *Selected Prose.* Ed. John Carter. Cambridge, 1961, pp. 131-150.
Irigoin, Jean. "Stemmas bifides et états du manuscrits." *Revue de philologie,* 3rd series, XXVIII (1954), pp. 211-217.
Jannaco, C. *Appunti di filologia italiana.* Firenze, 1945.
Kane, George. "Classification of the Manuscripts." *Will's Vision of Piers Plowman and Do-Well.* London, 1960. Especially pp. 53-64.
Kennedy, Elspeth. "The Scribe as Editor." *Mélanges de langue et de littérature du moyen age et de la renaissance offerts à Jean Frappier.* Genève, 1970. I, pp. 523-531.
Legge, M. Dominica. "Recent Methods of Textual Criticism." *Arthuriana,* II (1930), pp. 48-55.
Maas, Paul. "Textkritik." *Einleitung in die Altertumswissenschaft.* I, part VII. Eds. A. Gercke and E. Norden. Leipzig, 1927 [2nd ed., 1949; 3rd., 1957]. Tr. Barbara Flower. *Textual Criticism.* Oxford, 1958.

Marichal, R. "La Critique des textes." *L'Histoire et ses méthodes*. Paris, 1961, pp. 1247-1366.
Martens, Günter, and Hans Zeller, eds. *Texte und Varianten. Probleme ihrer Edition und Interpretation*. Munich, 1971.
Masai, François, "Principes et conventions de l'édition diplomatique." *Scriptorium*, IV (1950), pp. 177-193.
Mazzoni, G. *Avviamento allo studio critico delle lettere italiane*. Firenze, 1951.
Normas de transcripción y edición de textos y documentos. Consejo Superior de Investigaciones Científicas. Escuela de Estudios Medievales. Madrid, 1944.
Palermo, Joseph. "Les limites du roman de *Cassidorus*: l'apport des manuscrits de Bruxelles." *Romance Philology*, XIV (1960-61), pp. 22-27.
Pasquali, Giorgio. *Filologia e storia*, Firenze, 1964.
———. *Storia della tradizione e critica del testo*. Firenze, 1934 [2nd. ed., 1952].
Quentin, Dom Henri. *Essais de critique textuelle*. Paris, 1926.
Reynolds, Leighton D., and Nigel G. Wilson. *Scribes and Scholars: A Guide to the Transmission of Greek and Latin Literature*. Oxford, 1968.
Roques, Mario. "Établissement de règles pratiques pour l'édition des anciens textes français et provencaux." *Romania*, LII (1926), pp. 243-249.
Santangelo, S. "La Critica dei testi." *Saggi critici*. Modena, 1959, pp. 157-161.
Shepard, William P. "Recent Theories of Textual Criticism." *Modern Philology*, XXVIII (1930-31), pp. 129-141.
Soranzo, Giovanni. *Avviamento agli studi storici*. Milano, 1950.
Spongano, Raffaele, ed. *Studi e problemi di critica testuale*. Bologna, 1961.
Stählin, O. *Editionstechnik*. 2nd ed. Leipzig, 1914.
Timpanaro, Sebastiano. *La Genesi del metodo del Lachmann*. Firenze, 1963.
Varvaro, Alberto. "Critica dei testi classica e romanza. Problemi comuni ed esperienze diverse." *Rendiconti dell'Accademia di Archeologia, Lettere e Belle Arti di Napoli*, XLV (1970), pp. 73-117.
Walberg, Emmanuel. "Prinzipien und Methoden für die Herausgabe alter Texte nach verschiedenen Handschriften." *Zeitschrift für romanische Philologie*, LI (1931), pp. 665-678.
West, Martin L. *Textual Criticism and Editorial Technique Applicable to Greek and Latin Texts*. Stuttgart, 1973.
Whitehead, Frederick. "The Textual Criticism of the *Chanson de Roland*: An Historical Review." *Studies in Medieval French Presented to Alfred Ewert*. Oxford, 1961, pp. 76-89.
Willis, James. *Latin Textual Criticism*. Urbana, 1972.
Zarri, Gian Piero. "L'Automazione delle procedure di critica testuale, problemi e prospettive." *Lingua e stile*, VI (1971), pp. 397-415.
———. "Linguistica algoritmica e meccanizzazione della *collatio codicum*." *Lingua e stile*, III (1968), pp. 21-40.
———. "Il Metodo per la recensio di Dom H. Quentin esaminato criticamente mediante la sua traduzione in un algoritmo per elaboratore elettronico." *Lingua e stile*, IV (1968), pp. 161-182.
———. *Primi risultati nell'applicazione dei calcolatori ai problemi di critica testuale (costruzione degli stemmata codicum)*. Marseille, 1971.

Zarri, Gian Piero and Enrico Maretti. "L'Arte dell'edizione critica è da meccanizzare?" *Actes du XIIème Congrès International de Linguitsique et Philologie Romanes.* Bucharest, 1970.

——, and Enrico Maretti. "Su un'applicazione dei calcolatori relativa alla *collatio codicum:* un ausilio moderno per l'edizione critica dei testi." Istituto Lombardo, *Rendiconti: Classe di lettere e scienze morali e storiche,* C (1966), pp. 321-332.

GLOSSARY

apparatus criticus: the ensemble of notes, variants, and introductory material necessary for the presentation and interpretation of the text

archetype: the common source of all extant MSS and, for all practical purposes, to be identified with the original version of the work

autograph: a MS written in the author's own hand

codex: a manuscript book, which is composed of folios in gatherings of varying number

codex unicus: the sole surviving MS of any given text

collation: the process in which one MS is chosen as the base text and the readings of all other extant MSS are compared with it, so as to determine the critical text of a work

conjunctive errors (variants): defective readings which reveal that two or more MSS either were copied one from the other or derive from a common source

constitutio textus: the attempt to establish the critical text of an author's work through the related processes of recensio, examinatio, emendatio, and interpretatio (see below)

contamination: the presence in a MS of readings that reveal influence from more than one source ("horizontal transmission"), as often occurs when a scribe combines several exemplars to make his copy

deteriores: refers to inferior MSS which are generally late in the tradition and more likely to reveal defects in the transmission

difficilior lectio probior (or *potior*): when presented with two readings, one easier to understand (facilior lectio) and one more difficult (difficilior lectio), the editor generally accepts the latter to be the more reliable or "original," on the assumption that the scribe would tend to alter (interpolation) or simplify (trivialization) the text he was copying in the easiest possible manner

dittography: the writing of a word or a group of letters twice, instead of once

divinatio: the correction of a defective MS reading by conjecture

editio princeps: the first printed edition of a work, usually reserved for the Renaissance editions of Greek and Latin texts

eliminatio codicum descriptorum: the process of discarding those MSS (the codices descripti) which upon examination prove to be copies of or to derive from earlier codices and thus can contribute no new or valuable evidence toward the establishment of the text

emendatio: the editorial phase in which the text, found to be corrupt in the examinatio stage, is emended, if possible, through application of numerous techniques (selectio, divinatio, interpretatio, etc.)

examinatio: the examination of the primitive text established in the recensio process to determine its authenticity

exemplar: the MS from which a certain scribe makes a copy

folio: a single MS leaf, generally numbered in the top right-hand corner of the recto and ruled. The folio is commonly considered to be the entire sheet, folded in the middle so as to form what would be two separate leaves (four pages). Folios are then bound together in gatherings, which, collected, form the codex. The number of folios in a gathering determines the name: quaternus = four sheets = eight leaves = sixteen pages; quinternio = five sheets = ten leaves = twenty pages; and so on

haplography: the writing of a word or group of letters once, which should be written twice

homoeoteleuton: "likeness in the ending," refers to the process in textual criticism by which corrupt passages are emended by resorting to the conjectural theory that the scribe, in his transcription, could have passed from the ending of one word to that of another having the same letters and thereby committed an error. Cf. homoearchon: "likeness in the beginning" and homoeomeson: "likeness in the middle" *hyparchetype:* the common source of a group of MSS within the tradition of a work, but not to be confused with the archetype (see above)

interpretatio: the elucidation of the text through word division, capitalization, punctuation, etc., and the resolution of certain textual problems on the basis of internal evidence

lacuna: a break or gap in the MS, which may be attributed either to a lapse on the part of the scribe or to physical mutilation or deterioration of the MS itself

palimpsests: "scraped again," a MS (generally parchment) that has been used more than once, the earlier writing having been erased

recensio: the first phase in the making of a critical edition, in which all MS evidence for a text is carefully assembled, evaluated, and finally used as the basis for the reconstruction of the archetype

recentiores: a term by which "more recent" MSS are designated

recentiores, non deteriores: that is, the more recent MSS are not necessarily inferior, for they might be the copies of older, more authoritative exemplars

recto: the front side, usually numbered, of a MS folio (leaf)

selectio: the process of choosing between two variants of relatively equal stemmatic value

separative errors (variants): defective readings which reveal that one MS is not copied from another

stemma(ta) codicum: the "family tree" of MSS, which demonstrates their relationships one to the other

usus scribendi: the rationale for emendatio or selectio in those cases where it is possible to determine or choose the reading that best conforms to the "style of writing" of the author

variant: an alternative reading carried by another MS

verso: the reverse side of the recto (see above)

vulgate: a popular, widely-accepted text to which attest numerous MSS and/or editions

NORTH CAROLINA STUDIES IN THE ROMANCE LANGUAGES AND LITERATURES

I.S.B.N. Prefix 0-88438

Recent Titles

FROM VULGAR LATIN TO OLD PROVENÇAL, by Frede Jensen. 1972. (No. 120). -920-0.

GOLDEN AGE DRAMA IN SPAIN: GENERAL CONSIDERATION AND UNUSUAL FEATURES, by Sturgis E. Leavitt. 1972. (No. 121). -921-9.

THE LEGEND OF THE "SIETE INFANTES DE LARA" (*Refundición toledana de la crónica de 1344* versión), study and edition by Thomas A. Lathrop. 1972. (No. 122). -922-7.

STRUCTURE AND IDEOLOGY IN BOIARDO'S "ORLANDO INNAMORATO," by Andrea di Tommaso. 1972. (No. 123). -923-5.

STUDIES IN HONOR OF ALFRED G. ENGSTROM, edited by Robert T. Cargo and Emmanuel J. Mickel, Jr. 1972. (No. 124). -924-3.

A CRITICAL EDITION WITH INTRODUCTION AND NOTES OF GIL VICENTE'S "FLORESTA DE ENGANOS," by Constantine Christopher Stathatos. 1972. (No. 125). -925-1.

LI ROMANS DE WITASSE LE MOINE. *Roman du treizième siècle.* Édité d'après le manuscrit, fonds français 1553, de la Bibliothèque Nationale, Paris, par Denis Joseph Conlon. 1972. (No. 126). -926-X.

EL CRONISTA PEDRO DE ESCAVIAS. *Una vida del Siglo XV*, por Juan Bautista Avalle-Arce. 1972. (No. 127). -927-8.

AN EDITION OF THE FIRST ITALIAN TRANSLATION OF THE "CELESTINA," by Kathleen V. Kish. 1973. (No. 128). -928-6.

MOLIÈRE MOCKED. THREE CONTEMPORARY HOSTILE COMEDIES: *Zélinde, Le portrait du peintre, Élomire Hypocondre*, by Frederick Wright Vogler. 1973. (No. 129). -929-4.

C.-A. SAINTE-BEUVE. *Chateaubriand et son groupe littéraire sous l'empire.* Index alphabétique et analytique établi par Lorin A. Uffenbeck. 1973. (No. 130). -930-8.

THE ORIGINS OF THE BAROQUE CONCEPT OF "PEREGRINATIO," by Juergen Hahn. 1973. (No. 131). -931-6.

THE "AUTO SACRAMENTAL" AND THE PARABLE IN SPANISH GOLDEN AGE LITERATURE, by Donald Thaddeus Dietz. 1973. (No. 132). -932-4.

FRANCISCO DE OSUNA AND THE SPIRIT OF THE LETTER, by Laura Calvert. 1973. (No. 133). -933-2.

ITINERARIO DI AMORE: DIALETTICA DI AMORE E MORTE NELLA VITA NUOVA, by Margherita de Bonfils Templer. 1973. (No. 134). -934-0.

L'IMAGINATION POETIQUE CHEZ DU BARTAS: ELEMENTS DE SENSIBILITE BAROQUE DANS LA "CREATION DU MONDE," by Bruno Braunrot. 1973. (No. 135). -934-0.

ARTUS DESIRE: PRIEST AND PAMPHLETEER OF THE SIXTEENTH CENTURY, by Frank S. Giese. 1973. (No. 136). -936-7.

JARDIN DE NOBLES DONZELLAS, FRAY MARTIN DE CORDOBA, by Harriet Goldberg. 1974. (No. 137). -937-5.

Symposia

LOS NARRADORES HISPANOAMERICANOS DE HOY, edited by Juan Bautista Avalle-Arce. 1973. (No. 1). -951-0.

When ordering please cite the *ISBN Prefix* plus the last four digits for each title.

Send orders to:

University of North Carolina Press
Chapel Hill
North Carolina 27514
U. S. A.

The Department of Romance Studies Digital Arts and Collaboration Lab at the University of North Carolina at Chapel Hill is proud to support the digitization of the North Carolina Studies in the Romance Languages and Literatures series.

www.ingramcontent.com/pod-product-compliance
Lightning Source LLC
Chambersburg PA
CBHW030608230426
43661CB00053B/1895